The Four Seasons Of Manuela A Biography The Love Story Of Manuela Saenz And Simon Bolivar

Victor W. Von Hagen

Books by Victor W. von Hagen

OFF WITH THEIR HEADS

ECUADOR THE UNKNOWN

QUETZAL QUEST

TREASURE OF TORTOISE ISLANDS

JUNGLE IN THE CLOUDS

HERMAN MELVILLE'S ENCANTADAS

THE TSÁCHELA INDIANS OF WESTERN ECUADOR

MISKITO BOY

THE ETHNOLOGY OF THE JICAQUE INDIANS OF HONDURAS

THE AZTEC AND MAYA PAPERMAKERS

SOUTH AMERICA CALLED THEM

SOUTH AMERICAN ZOO

MAYA EXPLORER: THE LIFE OF JOHN LLOYD STEPHENS

THE GREEN WORLD OF THE NATURALISTS

ECUADOR AND THE GALÁPAGOS ISLANDS: A HISTORY

FREDERICK CATHERWOOD, ARCH[T]

THE FOUR SEASONS OF MANUELA

*THE FOUR SEASONS
OF MANUELA*
A Biography

Calgary, noviembre de 2013

Para: mi amigo Fabio

De: tu amigo Lucho

La historia de Simón Bolívar
se puede seguir de diferentes
maneras. A través de Manuelita,
la "libertadora del libertador",
como él mismo decía, escrita
por V. W. Von Hagen, es una de
ellas; pero existen otras que,
ojalá, las podamos conocer.
Con todo mi aprecio, tu
amigo, Luis Lasso.

THE FOUR SEASONS
OF MANUELA

A Biography

The Love Story of Manuela Sáenz and Simón Bolívar

by

VICTOR W. von HAGEN

IN COLLABORATION WITH CHRISTINE VON HAGEN

Duell, Sloan and Pearce · *New York*
Little, Brown and Company · *Boston*

DUELL, SLOAN AND PEARCE—LITTLE, BROWN
BOOKS ARE PUBLISHED BY
LITTLE, BROWN AND COMPANY
IN ASSOCIATION WITH
DUELL, SLOAN & PEARCE, INC

Published simultaneously
in Canada by McClelland and Stewart Limited

PRINTED IN THE UNITED STATES OF AMERICA

For
S I L V I A

CONTENTS

Autumn

The Years 1827–1830
PART THREE. Bogotá

Winter

The Years 1830–1856
PART FOUR. Paita

MANUELA SÁENZ

1797–1856

Spring
The Year 1822

PART ONE
Quito

1

A WOMAN OF QUITO

By june of 1822 the battle for Quito was over.

The main body of the defeated Spaniards had been captured, the fugitives flushed out from their hiding places in the frigid uplands of the Andes, and all the prisoners mustered for the march to the sea. For days the long lines of hated royalists, contemptuously called *godos*, still dressed in their blue and gold uniforms, straggled coastward under guard, an amorphous body of men, humiliated and defeated, moving their feet over the cold earth, down through valleys still fresh with the violence of war.

The land was beautiful. An immense sun flooded the bare mountains and gave the gray-brown, treeless hills a chromatic luster. Yet its rays could not heat the pallid atmosphere, or warm the miserable soldiers, and nightfall brought winds and cold. As the prisoners struggled downward, the unburied dead lay where they fell, their emaciated bodies an offering to the condors which followed the snaking columns of men.

Guards flying the red, gold and blue gonfalons of the Republic of Gran Colombia rode beside the prisoners, urging them on with the points of their partisans. They were uniformed in ill-fitting homespuns, green piped with red, and they rode their horses barefooted, bracing their feet in shoe-shaped brass stirrups, their bare heels were festooned with huge-roweled spurs, like the gaffs of a fighting cock. The faces of the troops were Indians' faces, round and copper-colored, with straggling beards and slanting Mongolic eyes, for such was the racial heritage of the fighters who had defeated the battle-proud legions of imperial Spain on the dizzy slopes of the Andes above Quito.

As the shuffling columns passed along the road, Indians muffled in woolen ponchos ran from their houses to look in silence at the long lines of the *godos*, the "Goths." For these were the enemy who for the last fifteen years had turned their ancient land into a battle-field, who had impressed them like pack animals into the army, and had used them as one more weapon against the rising forces of independence. But the battle-weary prisoners were oblivious to the stares of the Indians. They were beyond the reach of hatred.

In a narrow mountain pass, where centuries of trudging feet had worn a deep wedge into the earth, the column of prisoners suddenly bumped to a halt. From its head came the short rasp of command, and they were ordered to flatten themselves against the walls of the pass. A caravan, going toward Quito, was working itself up in the opposite direction. It was a squadron accompanying some person of importance, for its officer taking the salute of the barefooted lancers was well groomed and handsome in his green uniform and high black patent-leather Wellington boots. And the mounted troops of the squadron were soldierly in appearance, booted and spurred. Behind the troopers came the cargo mules weighed down with ill-balanced trunks — women's traveling trunks, tied with raw leather thongs, and behind the trunks two female slaves. They were both mounted. The first, a fine-featured light-skinned Negro, very ill at ease, rode sidesaddle. Her head was turbaned, golden earrings fell from her pierced ears, yet she wore a soldier's green uniform, covered by a thick Indian poncho. She made no answer to the shouts of the soldiers as she rode by, brushing against them with her out-turned legs. Not so the other who followed astride; she flung back their ribaldries, even turning in the saddle to continue the banter.

This Jonotás, Spanished from "Jonathan," was immensely ugly. Her black face was pitted with pox scars and her frizzled hair was trimmed down until it looked like an ink-black doormat flung across the top of her head. But her face had an extremely mobile expression, and there was a libidinous look in her eyes; she wore her soldier's uniform deeply open at the neck, so deep in fact that one could see the dark shadows of her breasts.

There was a sudden movement up the line, a craning of necks and a pressing outward, as man after man the soldiers flattened themselves against the sides of the declivity. Prancing up the narrow half-path toward them came a spirited black horse, its strong neck arched against the tug of reins and bit, its ironshod hoofs dancing a delicate way among the ruts and boulders of the trail. The one who controlled this high-strung mount, by skillful pressure of hand and knee, was clearly a masterly equestrian; prisoners and guards alike were amazed to see that the rider was a white woman.

This was doubtless the person of importance the squadron was escorting. Her face, her bearing and her appointments alike showed it, everything about her suggested pride and elegance. She rode her horse *en amazone*. Her small feet, shod in patent-leather boots, rested lightly in the stirrups, and the golden rowels at her heels tinkled at her mount's movements like little bells. Her bottle-green riding habit, pseudomilitary in cut and decked on the shoulders with gold-tasseled epaulets, revealed an arresting combination of slenderness and sinuous grace. The pink stock at her throat emphasized her oval face, her clear alabaster skin; and the dark hair, braided in heavy coils, showed from beneath her gold-trimmed officer's kepi. There was a faint suspicion of down which accentuated the curve of her full lips, laughing lips which gave her face a wildwood voluptuousness. And her nose, delicate and slightly aquiline, showed the arrogant heritage of aristocratic Spain. But her eyes were dark, challenging and mischievous, and she swept the green-clad republican soldiers with a searching boldness as if she half expected to find an old acquaintance among them. There was something quite untrammeled about her, almost wayward; yet the hands with well-groomed and pretty nails that lightly held the reins bore the tapered fingers of the born lady. They were hands also capable of action. Two enormous brass Turkish pistols, cocked and ready for use, lay there holstered by her knees. The name engraved on their brass mountings was easy to read: *Manuela Sáenz.*

It had been seven years since she had left this Ecuador, this land of her birth, seven eventful years since she was expelled from the Convent of Santa Catalina in Quito and escorted forcibly, under the glances of uncompromising monks, over this same road to the tropic seaport of Guayaquil. There she had been shipped off, in a rebellious mood, to her father in Panama. And now this land, once the Kingdom of Quito, was one of the free states of the Republic of Gran Colombia. Still the form of the government had not changed the essence of the country. The sky still had the color of lapis lazuli, a blue which no artist could capture in the limitations of his palette, and the long line of snow-capped volcanoes, many of them three miles high, were still as she remembered them, giants thrusting their dazzling white glaciers into the Ecuadorian sky. Indian huts, drab and windowless mud houses, spotted the land; the timeless Indians still worked in their fields, cultivating the purple-flowered potato which gave a note of color to the gray of these high plateaus.

Yet for all their appearance of bucolic peace it was dangerous to ride over these mountains in the best of times. Now, with the echoes of war over the land, and a desperate scattered enemy still hiding out from the triumphant patriots, it was, it seemed, an act of folly for a well-bred lady to make the trip from the coast to the mountain-bound city of Quito. So must have thought the patriot soldiers, covertly eying this attractive girl who rode her black horse like a hussar. But when she stopped to question one of the officers about the details of the battle, one of their unspoken questions was answered. She was a woman of Quito. No one could ever mistake that lisp in her Spanish that marks the speech of the equator. And her questions were incisive; the manner of their asking showed that she knew much about the techniques and terminologies of war.

The battle, she learned, had been fought on May 24. And it

had been, in these wars that had raged back and forth across South
America for thirteen years, a battle of decision. The entire Spanish
army, with its officers and equipment, had fallen to the patriot
forces. Now the whole of Ecuador would be incorporated into
the newly formed Republic of Gran Colombia.

It was, in fact, the next to the last step in a giant pincers movement, continental in scale, which was designed to compress the
armies of imperial Spain into a single concentrated region, where a
final victory would assure the liberation of the continent. For years
the ill-armed, ill-trained Americans had fought a terrible war, a
war without rules, against the veterans of Spain. Finally General
Simón Bolívar had cleared Venezuela of the foe, moved into
Colombia, defeated the *godos* there, and driven their remnants
along the backbone of the Andes, southward into Ecuador.

Meanwhile, four thousand miles to the south, and co-ordinated
only by some unseen spirit of triumph, General José de San Martín
had assembled an army in Argentina, had crossed the Andes —
an expedition that dwarfed Napoleon's crossing of the Alps —
and had fallen on the unsuspecting royalists in Chile. The pincers
were at work; Lima fell; the enemy was being compressed into
Peru. To clear Ecuador and further reduce the Spanish power of
movement, a polyglot patriot army was hastily flung together and
marched against fighting opposition up the slopes of the Andes
toward Quito. There the bulk of the royal armies waited in arrogant confidence. General Sucre, the young field commander of
the allied patriot forces, had thought out the strategy. First, he
deployed his forces as if for a frontal attack on Quito, then he
shifted the bulk of his troops under cover of an icy night and
climbed the Pichincha volcano that hung its bulk a mile over the
city. The Spanish commander wakened on the morning of May 24
to see the patriot army looking down his throat. He ordered his
troops to climb that sixteen-thousand-foot mountain and give
battle in and about its serrated rim. Below, people crowded the
roofs, climbing the belfries of the churches to get a glimpse of the
melee that raged above the clouds. But they could see little, and

knew nothing of their fate until the blue and gold figures of the royalists were seen running down the sides of the mountain. Then they knew that the patriot army had won.

All this to the woman of Quito was a triumph. For in the days and months of her twenty-four years she could hardly remember a moment in which there had not been war — wars caused by the fierce desire of her people to be free. She had virtually sucked in these feelings with her mother's milk; she had lived the revolution, witnessed the long course of its barbarity and its idealism, and had taken an active part in it. One of the officers gave her all the details of the battle, naming those of her friends who had been in the final action — there was Larrea, Montúfar, Chiriboga, Ascasubi, D'Elhuyar . . .

Fausto D'Elhuyar . . . now that was a name of all names to evoke a whole train of bittersweet memories.

As Manuela's squadron emerged from the pass and gained the King's Highway, lined with spined agave plants, she remembered. She could recall Fausto very well, very well indeed. How elegant he had seemed in his royal uniform, white piped with gold, and his skintight pants braided with arabesques that moulded his legs like those of a dancer. It had all happened suddenly. And like a summer storm it was over. Fausto had a reputation; he was adept at singeing women. Duennas at formal dances had reason to be agitated when he moved among their little pigeons, eying first this morsel and then that. He was an officer in the King's Guards, one of the privileged. His father was a famous scientist, who had discovered tungsten and published a series of obscure books which were important to the Crown. And, even though his brother was then fighting with the insurgent General Bolívar on the llanos of Venezuela, Fausto kept his position.

Manuela Sáenz was then seventeen. Since her mother's death, the Convent of Santa Catalina had been her home. It was, in old Quito, a famous institution. Its convent walls then meant nothing, or next to nothing. Discipline was loose. Some married women sought sanctuary there to escape the assiduities of their mates, while others were imprisoned, so to speak, by command of the Bishop on application by their husbands, for being too often in other people's beds. Nuns left the walls to spend festive days at home. And it was whispered that the freshly minted children who had free run of the convent had been stamped out by the padres.

Manuela had been placed in Santa Catalina for her education, for it was a school of sorts too; and there she had her learning, such as it was, in more ways than one. The insecurity of her life had made her rebellious, and she was already a formidable person. "I hate my enemies," she would say, "and I love my friends." No compromise here, no dissimulation, no moderation. It was certain that men looked hungrily at her, and that she tilted with many. Yet she routed them all — all, that is, until Fausto appeared. So one night Manuela slipped out of the convent to join him They wandered into the Quito hills together, and under the spell of that Faustian magic Manuela was easily seduced.

When she returned, the abbess of the convent would have none of her. Since she had outraged the decencies of society, she was expelled from Santa Catalina, for she had complicated a situation already difficult. All over Quito, when the scandal came out, people could be heard saying, "That is just what one would expect from a bastard."

The marks of battle, fresh and raw, increased as the squadron neared Quito. Houses were gutted, and fields deserted. More and more frequently they came across condors feeding on the bodies of dead horses — great carrion birds that unfurled the white muffs at their throats and beat at the air with giant wings as Manuela's escort rode by. The bones of the unburied dead lay about too, and broken weapons which the people had no time yet to gather. The land was scarred by war, and yet it was a land Manuela remembered.

She paid little attention to the stiff depersonalized figures hanging from the branches of *molé* trees, for death had been a part of her childhood, and she had seen much the same things a decade ago when the forces of revolution had sent her father in flight from Quito. During these uneasy years she was tortured by her illegitimacy. When she first learned of it, and had been called "bastard" by other children, she was frightened and incredulous. From the days of her first understanding she had known something was wrong, the whispering of her Indian nurse had hinted at it. Later she discovered what it was. Joaquina Aispuru, with whom she lived, was in fact her mother; but her father was married to someone else, and her mother was not married at all. Not to "belong" was in itself bad enough, but worse still were the ideological conflicts of her parents. Her mother was native-born, her father a Spanish *godo*, a finished gentleman whose fidelity to the King of Spain nothing could impugn. There was never a point of rest in her young life. Everything was in conflict. For years even the date and place of her birth were a mystery, and when asked she would answer in studied ambiguity: "My country is all of the Americas, I was born under the equatorial line."

Perhaps the moment of her conception had something to do with it, and perhaps her character was implicit in her genesis. It was a point to think about. For does one partake of one's momentary environment during conception and acquire, as if by osmosis, something out of the pulse of the time and place? Manuela was conceived during that horrible earthquake year of 1797, when a cataclysmic tremor brought down half of Quito.

The earth had opened and spewed out its inner wrath. All along the backbone of the Andes, where an avenue of volcanoes acted as safety valves, the land shook and trembled. For a thousand miles cities felt the shock; but charming little church-filled Quito, lying two miles high on the equator, felt it the worst. The Renaissance tower of the Church of the Fathers of Mercy swayed, then fell into the street, burying hundreds of terrified people in its rubble. Houses collapsed; churches disintegrated, killing thousands who had taken refuge under their great gold-encrusted naves. When the last shock was over, the priests organized a procession, and Indians carrying the Virgin of Earthquakes crawled painfully over the rubble-strewn streets, chanting a litany especially written for moments of this kind. For weeks the countryside was filled with people wandering from ruin to ruin, stunned by the shock. It was a day to remember, that day of destruction in 1797.

Time healed Quito's wounds The dead were buried, the buildings restored, the gaping fissures filled with rubble by legions of Indian workmen. The Viceroy of Peru sent his engineers, and the King of Spain — even though harassed by wars on his frontiers — sent a large gift of money to that "noble and loyal city of Quito " But the wounds of the soul, the cicatrized conscience of the people of Quito, the priests never allowed to heal. It was the endless subject of endless sermons. The earthquake of 1797 had been sent by God to punish them, for Quito had the reputation of being the most licentious city in the whole Viceroyalty. The gaming, the whoring that went on in the houses of the people of quality were known far and wide. A report on these conditions, the *Secret Notices of America,* was so devastatingly accurate that the King's ministers felt it necessary to suppress it.

This moralizing over the earthquake of 1797 fell hard on many a Quito lady, but hardest of all on Joaquina Aispuru. She was now in a condition which made it impossible for her to attend church, for even her hooped skirts failed to hide her pregnancy. To any casual passer-by, let alone the members of the household, it was obvious that Joaquina was with child. And it was to be a bastard.

Joaquina Aispuru was the youngest daughter of Mateo José de Aispuru, a Basque of noble birth who came to America to revive his fortunes. He had married Gregoria Sierra, sired four children, and acquired a large estate in the environs of Quito. By 1797 he was fortunately dead, or the disgrace of his youngest daughter would have killed him. Joaquina lived through the nightmare of her pregnancy, and in due time gave birth to a daughter. On the night of St. Thomas Day, in the semi-darkness of the quarter-moon, a little girl child, wrapped in a fine, delicately fringed shawl, was brought to the rector of a church in one of the outlying parishes of Quito, and there baptized . . . "the 29th of December 1797 solemnly baptized Manuela . . . born two days previously, a spurious child whose parents are not named. . . ."

Parents not named . . . Yet certainly half of Quito's thirty thousand inhabitants could have filled in the blanks of this Manuela's baptismal certificate. Her father was a Spanish nobleman, Don Simón Sáenz y Vergera, Member of the Town Council, Captain of the King's Militia, and Collector of the Decimal Tithes of the Kingdom of Quito. One would not ordinarily have suspected Don Simón. He was a well-known figure in Quito with no reputation for wenching. He went about impeccably dressed in a plumcolored surtout and satin knee breeches; his three-cornered hat rested at the correct angle on neatly powdered hair. He was a man of probity, punctilious in dealing with the King's affairs, a sharp uncompromising businessman. He was married to a noble and wealthy woman, and was the father of four children — one of whom, a son, had been born just a few days before this little byblow.

Simón Sáenz had been born in Spain in the middle of the eighteenth century — in Burgos (said his credentials) in the Villa de Villasur de Herrera, and of a family of distinction. Arriving in Panama during the North American Revolution, he made his way to the Kingdom of Quito, and met and married the moneyed widow Juana María del Campo. He began importing Spanish goods for resale, his business flourished, and the emoluments of his royal offices increased his fortune. He sired his family, and channeled his driving energy into making money and amassing titles of distinction. But card playing, such as the recently introduced French game of *trente-et-un*, and the seducing of young girls did not seem to lie in the category of his interests. So how in God's name, the gossips echoed, had he gotten to eighteen-year-old Joaquina Aispuru?

The birth of Manuela set off its own little war of clacking tongues. Quito often heard more of the battle between the fam-

ilies of this charming little bastard than it did of the revolution
fermenting within the houses of the city.

Everything, as she rode along the King's Highway, seemed to
remind Manuela of her living past; the land, the fields, the houses,
each one evoked some poignant memory. Yet much had changed
in her in the seven years since she had left Ecuador. As her horse
fell into an easy canter behind the squadron of lancers, thoughts
of the troubled past arose to disturb the well-established present.
At the age of seventeen in 1815 she had been an unwanted child-
woman expelled from a convent, her father an exile, her mother's
family hostile, her prospects dim. Now, seven years later, she was
the wife of a wealthy English resident of Lima, mistress of a house
within the walls of the city and another in the fashionable environs; she had been decorated with the coveted Order of the Sun;
she was a charming, self-possessed woman of twenty-four, everywhere respected and everywhere envied.

The highway as they neared Quito was crowded with soldiers.
The Andean savannahs gave way to mountains again, and on all
sides the land rose in untiring sweeps to that rock-hard world
which surrounded Quito. In the distance were the volcanoes that
encircled the city. Beyond it (for in June in the Andes the visibil-
ity is infinite) snow-tipped mountains gave the landscape a feeling of immensity and serenity. Soldiers were in the fields training
in close-order drill; soldiers sat in the doorways of the little grass-
thatched roadside houses cleaning their muskets; soldiers hung
about canteens from which the odor of *chicha,* the native fermented corn-beer, drifted across the landscape; hussars rode by
with a rattle of sabers; soldiers were everywhere As the squadron
approached the built-up edge of the city, beyond the stone bridges
that spanned small rivers, there was an intense activity outside
of the houses. By order of the Commandant — and they had seen
these broadsides pasted up along the highway — all houses were
to be freshly painted for the celebration of the Day of Liberation.
The one-storied houses of adobe were having their sides tinted in

riotous colors, pinks, blues, greens, carmines, by chattering legions
of poncho-clad Indians. All along the road there was an under-
current of excitement. Yet when the squadron approached and the
people saw the well-dressed officers, the strangely-attired Negro
slaves, the number of mules engulfed by trunks and boxes, and
finally the elegant young woman, riding astride, the buzzing activity stopped; the workmen gathered in groups to gape and specu-
late on the identity of the party.

At a rise in the road, the white city could be seen lying in the
valley of Añaquito. Mountains towered over the city, and its out-
skirts extended into the foothills, streets could be seen wandering
up the sharp, steep Andes. It was a delightful colonial city — "the
finest in all South America," the great traveler Alexander von
Humboldt had said of it — before the earthquake of 1797. It was
formed around three principal plazas, from which ran the streets,
straight and narrow, dividing the city into ordered sections like
the squares on a chessboard. In the exact center of Quito was its
principal plaza, laid with flagstones and ornamented with a huge
stone fountain, where animals slaked their thirst and from which
Indians drew water in huge sienna-colored vases for their mas-
ters' households The Cathedral, squat and low — the least impressive of Quito's magnificent churches — stood at one side of
the plaza, and directly across from it was the Archbishop's Palace,
as cold and as remote as God. On another side was the Cabildo,
built in 1534, which housed the city offices — an immense building
under whose portico numerous public scriveners sat at little tables
and, wrapped in ponchos to keep out the insistent cold, wrote
their clients' letters. On the plaza's fourth side stood the palace
of the government, the administrative center of the area which
included the ancient cities of the Presidency of Quito. Above the
city's one-storied dwellings, their doorways sculptured in many
a proud coat of arms, towered the churches of Quito, wonderfully
contrived churches with elaborately carved façades.

The people of Quito were the strangest conglomeration of
castes and social patterns that ever formed a community. Before

the revolution its population exceeded thirty thousand souls. Of these, six thousand were pure-blooded Spaniards, many of them title-proud counts and marquises of so ancient a lineage that they would begin their prayers "Mother of God, our cousin . . ." Those of mixed blood, the *cholos*, numbered more than one third of the people; they were the barbers, the storekeepers, the factors, the artisans, the major-domos, the scriveners. And, since they were a pincushion of resentment, the *cholos* were the active revolutionists. The Indians, the bulk of the population, who dressed in white knee-length cotton drawers and woolen ponchos, were the laborers, the dray animals, the farmers. There was finally, like a factor completing the sum, a scattering of Negroes — all slaves.

This was Quito.

At the gates of the city, the squadron passed a crude gibbet from which dangled a corpse. Its head, tilted to the right, seemed to contemplate the sign stuck to its coat, on which was printed the single word *godo*. Further along they passed iron cages, hanging from the high rafters over the highway; from behind their bars mummified human heads still smiled horribly on the passers-by. To Manuela Sáenz they were relics of the terrifying past; for they were the heads of the patriots who had led the abortive revolt of 1809. In the melee her father had fled, losing his fortune in his headlong escape; and her half sister, a bellicose *goda*, had slipped into an officer's uniform and led a company of royalists back into the city. The Crown had won out that time, and the streets had gagged on the blood of massacred patriots. Manuela had been only twelve, but she remembered vividly the gibbet standing in the plaza, and conspirators of the lesser sort hanged in monotonous succession. Those of higher rank were torn to pieces, their legs and arms being tied to horses which were driven off toward the four points of the compass. For the members of the revolutionary Council was reserved a more suitable demise: cut down from the hangman's noose while still alive, they were decapitated and their heads put into iron cages for display about the city. Then their hearts were ripped from their bodies and tossed into a boiling cauldron in the center of the plaza. By the Viceroy's orders these ceremonies had been witnessed by all the families of the condemned. Manuela especially remembered Carlos Montúfar, son of the Marquis de Selva Alegre, and last of the Council to meet his death. He was made to witness the execution of all the others, his ears were filled with their shrieks and moans; his eyes saw every detail of the torture and bloodletting before his turn came. He had stood there pale as marble, unflinching and unmoved, even when Manuela had eluded the guards and placed in his manacled hands a single half-withered flower

It seemed hardly possible, after all these years of hatred, of war, of torture, that Quito was at last free. And now — she had heard it from a group of soldiers down the road — General Bolívar was expected any day to enter Quito in triumph, to proclaim its liberties, and to incorporate the country formally into the Republic of Gran Colombia. She had only to look about her to see the decorations being raised, the houses being repainted, the tailors sitting at work in the sun-splashed doorways sewing on new uniforms for the officers, to sense the enthusiasm that had taken hold of the city at the prospect of the coming of their hero. Something of the same excitement tingled within herself, for there was no other name in the land that aroused so strong an emotion as that of Bolívar. Victor in a score of hard-fought battles, liberator of Venezuela and Colombia as well as of Ecuador, he was to her, as to thousands of others, the very symbol of the struggle for independence.

Just inside the city's gate, a road block had been set up — a huge pole barring the highway, marked in the red, blue and gold colors of the Republic of Gran Colombia. Soldiers with fixed bayonets stood at one side, and an officer leaning on a cavalryman's saber waited the approach of the little squadron. Extreme caution was being used to examine the papers of all who sought to enter, for it was only two weeks since the battle for Quito, and desperate Spanish soldiers were still hiding in the city and the hills. At the officer's command, Manuela handed him the passport which had thus far cleared her journey. He read in part:

> Lieutenant Colonel Francisco Freicano, Captain of the Port of Lima, certifies the sailing of the English Brig *Deadema,* on the 25th of May, 1822, destination Ecuador. Captain Harper Roche, Master; supercargo James Thorne and his wife, Manuela Sáenz, with her two slaves.

Manuela Sáenz! There were few here who did not know that name. She was remembered all over Quito. The document was passed from hand to hand; officers and soldiers alike looked up at her with astonishment. She had scandalized the city by her very birth, no less than by the escapades of her adolescence; and the quarrels of her divided family had been common talk for fifteen years Other officials came to examine the document, to stare at the familiar name and at the poised young lady, who from the height of her black horse looked down at them with mischief and cool appraisal in her dark eyes. The barrier was raised, and Manuela continued her journey into the heart of town, but the news of her arrival traveled ahead of her. Those who knew the intimate details of her lively past repeated them to all who would listen; those who did not, found the sober truth no impediment to the flight of lurid imagination. Even the expected arrival of Simón Bolívar was at the moment less exciting than this new sensation. For Bolívar, though no doubt a great man, was after all an outlander; but "La Sáenz" was one of their own, and a delightful spice of scandal hung about her name. From door to door, from street to street, the word spread; within the hour all Quito had heard the startling news.

Manuela Sáenz had come home.

2

THE COMING
OF THE DEMIGOD

A SINGLE ROCKET trailing a comet-tail of flame shot into the sky, and thousands of eyes watched it burst into blue and red stars high in the Quito sky. Then the sky became alive with bursting rockets. High on the Panecillo, the sugar-loaf hill that dominated the center of the city, cannon went into action and the thunder of the salute rolled down upon the massed people. Then the bells — all the church bells of the city began clanging at once. The Indian bell-ringers were swinging on the ropes in high glee, oblivious to the chaos of sound above their heads. The crowds, struggling for a place of vantage, were slowly pushed back by the soldiers from the narrow cobbled street, to clear it for the entrance of Bolívar.

All of Quito had turned out for the great event. Here a marquis in old-fashioned court dress, with blue velvet waistcoat massively embroidered in silver, and a three-cornered hat, rubbed shoulders with Indians in woolen ponchos and braided pigtails. A young lady in white muslin, her hair caught up in a Grecian knot, defied the sharp tang in the air to reveal the charms of the Regency style and tripped over the flagstones in her ballet slippers, trying to avoid the soldiers. Barbers, nuns, tradesmen, children were everywhere in the mounting confusion, pushing their way to their appointed places. All along the King's Highway thick-lettered broadsides on the walls proclaimed the day: June 16, 1822. But there

was scarcely a need for it; everyone knew that today Simón Bolívar would make his entrance into the city.

He was coming, and after days of preparation, Quito was ready
for him. The republican troops, victors of the Battle of Quito, had
been furnished with new green uniforms; they had drilled,
marched and wheeled until every soldier knew each military
movement with almost Prussian precision. Arches of triumph at
intervals spanned the highway, and the house fronts were gay
with native laurel and palm fronds from the tropical coast. Along
the route were clusters of little Indian girls dressed as multicolored
angels, waiting impatiently with furled gauze wings; they were to
shower the hero with rose petals. A band of brass instruments,
which no one but huge-lunged Indians could blow in Quito's rare-
fied atmosphere, marched down the street; after it came other
Indians whose arms were locked about a veritable arsenal of fireworks. The enthusiasm was contagious. From every church flew
the republican flag, and the balconied houses that faced the line
of march were emblazoned with bunting of red, blue and gold.
Stalls had sprung up about the Plaza de San Francisco, and there
hucksters in blue homespuns sold corncakes, sausages, saveloys
and cakes, four-pound loaves of bread, wines and fermented corn
chicha. Other sidewalk merchants offered patriotic songs which
had been printed on Quito's one printing press; there were tricolor cockades to put in hats and ribands designed to hang from
the pigtails of Indians; there were all sorts of cheap gewgaws for
the festive occasion.

A hatless rider came careening down the street scattering the
people who had pushed out onto the cobblestones, shouting at
the top of his voice that the Liberator was at the edge of the city.
There was a final rush to places of advantage, a good-natured
scurrying and pushing like a crowd scene in an *opéra bouffe.* The
little Indian angels opened their bright wings to the Andean
breeze and were jostled into their places, while the nuns who
shepherded them shook their wimpled heads as if to say, "It is a
miracle, a miracle."

And it was. By the year 1819 Spain had crushed all organized patriot resistance in the north, and the insurgents had been reduced to small guerrilla bands, poorly armed and half starved. Suddenly General Simón Bolívar broke out of the plains of Venezuela where he had been contained, outflanked the *godos* and marched over the Andes. On the morning of August 9, 1819, he met and destroyed the armies of the Spaniards sent out to capture him at Boyacá. The last Viceroy of New Granada, Juan Sámano, disguised in green cloth cape and a hat of red rubber, abandoned his palace in Bogotá and set off down the river to exile. Within the next two years Bolívar had reconquered Venezuela, cleared Colombia of the enemy, and begun skirmishes on the periphery of Quito that led to its eventual liberation. Now the genius of this victory — Bolívar — was upon them.

The elite of Quito crowded the balconies. For this was not alone a people's victory, but a movement for independence initiated by many of the titled grandees of the city. The Marquis de Selva Alegre, who had given his fortune and the life of his son to the cause, appeared with the prerogatives of his rank in embroidered coat, knee breeches, full-bottomed periwig and ancient tricornered hat of a style which had disappeared a decade ago; he looked down upon the milling crowd with quizzing glances. Most of the other noblemen, despite their republican sentiments, were similarly dressed in the style of the old regime. But the young men had long discarded these reminders of the past and appeared as Regency gentlemen, with dress coat fitting closely to the body, and collar as stiff as the hames of a horse and high enough to reach the ears. The old dowagers still clung to the styles of the 1790's, with the contouche overdress, and all were openly aghast at the new modes from Paris. The young women appearing on the balconies wore light dresses with graceful flowing skirts, the waistline high under the breasts, the neckline square and low, edged with black ribbon or handmade lace.

To the common folk in the street, these aristocratic gatherings were a major part of the show; and none more so than the group

on the balcony of Juan de Larrea's mansion. This was the finest
house in Quito, two stories high, with grilled windows and elaborately carved wooden railings. A dozen ladies and gentlemen of
prominence occupied the balcony; but the one who caught all
eyes was the fascinating being leaning on the arm of Don Juan.
She was dressed in white, a color made fashionable by Gérard's
painting of Psyche — a white lawn trimmed with silver, and cut
low in accordance with the most daring modern fashion. Across
her shoulders she wore a red and white *moiré* sash and under her
left breast was a small golden medal which the better-informed
recognized as the Order of the Sun. Many in the street knew her
by sight; others could identify her by her rich husky voice with
its overtones of raillery and challenge. She in white was Manuela
Sáenz.

In the fevered preparation for the reception of Bolívar, society
had been able to learn only a little of her life since she had left
Quito, but that little was tantalizing. She was married, they knew,
to an Englishman named James Thorne, and she lived with him
in Lima. But no one knew more than that, nor could they guess
why she had chanced the long, hazardous trip to Quito at this
time. Yet the sparkling golden sun medal told much more than
mere gossip. It was the highest decoration that revolutionary Peru
could bestow, and whoever wore it must certainly have served the
insurgent cause with distinction.

Manuela had, in fact, arrived in Lima in 1817; and the year
following her marriage had been the gayest in her turbulent life.
As the wife of a rising merchant she was presented to the Viceroy,
attended the official functions, and became a familiar figure in the
high society of the city. She was even singled out for special favors
by the aging Micaela Villegas, the famous courtesan "La Perri-
choli," whose guest Manuela often was in her box at the Old Comedy Theater.

When James Thorne was away on one of his ships, Manuela
became involved in activities of a very different sort. She moved
in patriotic circles among those who were conspiring against the

Crown. Peru was then on a war footing. The royalists, stung by the defeats in Chile, had at last recognized the dynamic insistence of the revolution, and they were bringing down war stores from Panama. General San Martín with his victorious insurgents was moving up to the frontiers of Peru, and in Lima itself the friends of freedom were plotting to undermine the Viceroy. In the baroque salon of one of her countrywomen, Manuela took fervent part in these conspiracies. It was a dangerous game, and the fact that her husband was English would not have saved her had she been discovered. Still she had run the risks. In her *saya* and *manto*, habiliments loved by the women of Lima, she could move about under effective disguise, for the elastic gown enveloped the body, and the silk veil covering the head allowed only one mobile eye to look out upon the world. In such a garb (it was considered a horrible breach of manners to pull back a woman's veil) women might enter the rooms of their lovers and cuckold their husbands in the light of day without fear of discovery. The *saya* and *manto* clung, displaying with every short step the delicious movements of the body; the costume was one of the miracles of nature; it filled men's minds with amazement. And to Manuela it was a wonderful disguise, for under her dress she could transport seditious proclamations from secret printing presses to those who would paste them all over the walls of Lima in the dark of night.

It was intrigue especially suited to Manuela's talents, and it brought her a certain anonymous fame when the Viceroy declared, "I have been brought by the Public Prosecutor a pile of proclamations introduced into this capital by an unknown woman."

But Manuela's double life as society matron and revolutionary plotter could not remain undiscovered forever; and in time James Thorne found it out. And James Thorne did not like it As a foreigner, he was supposed to be above the battle. Besides, he was a businessman and did not approve of revolution; it disturbed business, it multiplied the problems with officials. He was moreover a Catholic traditionalist, and already this revolution was taking an anticlerical turn, it had a distinct antireligious odor. He not only refused Manuela's suggestion to help the patriot cause with money; he ordered her to desist. And that meant trouble, the first real rift in their marriage. For no one ever really ordered Manuela to do anything She acted exactly as she pleased.

So she continued to work for the revolution, and in 1820 she gained a notable victory. Her half brother José María Sáenz was a captain in the Numancia Regiment of the royalist army Manuela was able to persuade him, and through him his fellow officers, to swing their forces to the patriot side. This defection from the Crown caused the breakdown of the capital's entire defenses, and Lima fell into chaos. People poured into the city from outside to take refuge behind its great walls, and the five gates were heavily guarded for fear of direct assault by the *montoneras*, the fierce mounted partisans of General San Martín. On July 21, 1821, patriot armies moved up to the gates of the city and it fell without a shot. They entered Lima in a snowfall of confetti and rose petals, in the face of many a duke and count and marquis who only a fortnight before had sworn undying fealty to the King of Spain; they too put bicolored cockades in their hats and joined the people in delirious celebration.

It had been, Manuela thought, something like what was happening now in Quito; but here there were among the nobility few dissenters to the new Republic. In the distance she could make out a mass of cavalrymen approaching the city to a crescendo of cheers. Below her the Lord Mayor, holding his silk hat in his free hand, quickly mounted his horse and galloped off with two officers to welcome the entourage. Now there was more confusion at the Larrea doorway as the servants, rolling wine casks before them, tried to force a passage through the crowd. For tonight, in this very mansion, there would be a grand victory ball in honor of Bolívar. But the press of people was too great for the servants; they had to call on the aid of the soldiers. There was a great pushing and shoving before the task was done, to the accompaniment of ribald comment and advice from the onlookers. Some of the younger gentry joined in the chaffering, among them the sharp-tongued Manuela.

That was just what you should expect of "La Sáenz," the eyes of the ancient dames on the balconies seemed to say; and they looked long and disapprovingly at her with their quizzing glances. She had kept Quito in turmoil for all the years of her youth, she had been a hellion. She had a positive genius for finding a human weakness and mocking it. She showed neither humility nor maidenly modesty. She was aggressive, self-confident and volatile — in turn gay, sensitive, quick-tempered and courageous. Of course they understood the reason; she had been unwanted, unloved, a bastard without a position in society — naturally she was as she was. And now this . . . she was back in Quito again, made welcome in the Larrea house, and flaunting a patriotic decoration from Peru.

Yet in fact the Order of the Sun was more than a mere decoration, it was the badge of a new republican nobility. On the 23rd of January of that very year Manuela Sáenz de Thorne had joined an impressive group of one hundred twelve women, outstanding patriots of Lima, who were to receive this honor. They had paraded through the streets to the former palace of the Viceroy, where impressive ceremonies took place. Manuela stood among the great ladies of Lima, many of whom bore ancient titles of nobility — the Countess de la Vega, the Marchioness of Torre Tagle, the Countess of San Isidro — and there she was decorated with the most coveted order in the New World. It seemed hardly possible that within the seven years since she had left Quito in disgrace she had . . .

"Bolívar! Bolívar! Bolívar!" The voices of the city seemed to well up in a single word. As if in answer to the call, the parade of approaching officers stopped, and a squadron of lancers rode out to draw up in single file on either side of the road. Then, from the midst of the brilliantly uniformed figures, a single horseman emerged and came forward — alone. It was Bolívar.

He was mounted on Pastor, his favorite white horse, which he held on a snaffle and gently pricked with his spurs. The animal danced and cavorted, its ironshod hoofs striking a shower of sparks from the cobblestones, its neck curving in a high swan-like arch — a fitting mount for a demigod. And a demigod the people expected, for so great was Bolívar's renown, so heroic his life, so wonderful his achievements in war and peace, that even at the early age of thirty-nine he had been deified in the popular imagination. His physique was not godlike — he was a short man, with delicate hands and small feet that a woman could well envy — but one could see that his body was mobile, meant for action; and as he bowed to the tumult of cheers with proud grace, yet with humility, his figure seemed to grow, and one became unaware that he was not tall.

Bolívar was scarcely a handsome man; his complexion was darkly tanned, his face narrow and his expression somber, his strong mouth and beautiful teeth hidden under a bristling guard's mustache But his deep-set black eyes were lively and penetrating, and his quick smile was utterly charming. In contrast to his staff officers, whose uniforms blazed with enough medals and gold lace to please the barbaric tastes of an Inca, the Liberator wore a plain high-collared tunic with a single medal, and tight trousers of white doeskin. Now, in the saddle before this great and admiring throng, his very bearing showed the gallantry, the gay impetuosity, the courtliness and the courage that were his — qualities that could be summed up in one Spanish word: *hombria*, manhood. Manhood indeed, or perhaps an excess of virility; for here was a man to whom the favors of women were as necessary as meat and drink. This too was a man who loved glory; and even now, as he rode along taking the cheers of the people, one could see that he was ecstatic with the public acclaim.

For those who saw this Bolívar, it was difficult to believe that behind the public figure lay a different and deeper personality. Everything profound loves the mask. And behind this mask was the genius of the South Americas — the soaring imagination, the sense of organization, the strategy in planning campaigns, the knowledge of men, the ability to attract loyal followers — which had given actuality to the dream of independence. Bolívar's protean mind seized upon everything; he arranged battles, diplomacy, education, he designed medals and uniforms; he planned his public appearances as a choreographer would a ballet. There never was a wasted movement in Bolívar; he used strategy alike in war and diplomacy and love His speech reflected his mind — sensuous, sometimes ornate and elaborate, or again simple with a simplicity a bit studied and sometimes overdone. And behind all these contradictions was an immensely powerful will, for Bolívar had battled men, mountains and even the elements to arrive at his present glory.

As he rode on toward the plaza, bowing this way and that — leaning down here to accept a flower from a child, there to grasp the hand of a wounded soldier — there was scarcely a man of those cheering thousands who did not know the events of his life, scarcely a woman who had not heard the intimate details of his prodigious love affairs. Simón Bolívar had been born in Venezuela in 1783, the descendant of an ancient family of great wealth and nobility — he was a marquis in his own right. Though he had been reared in the sprawling hacienda of San Mateo, where tough and wild cowboys herded immense herds of cattle, his education was adequate for the place and time. Geography and literature he had from Andrés Bello, an incipient revolutionist; the elements of arithmetic he learned from a Capuchin monk who had the reputation of being a savant. More important was Simón Rodríguez, master of French and English, an ill-balanced, charming mental vagabond and complete libertine — and scholar, even though he filled his charge with the sentimental romanticism of Rousseau. It was this unfrocked priest who gave Bolívar his love of nature and life, and developed the purple gaud in his writing.

At the impressionable age of seventeen, already adept in love, Bolívar visited Paris with the Marquis de Uztáris, then went to Spain to finish his education at the Royal Military Academy And even though he spoke the soft lisping patois of Venezuela and his complexion was *café au lait*, he instantly charmed the court of Madrid. Soon after his arrival — at least so the gossips said — he had replaced Godoy, the "Prince of Peace," as Queen Luisa's lover. Even at this age Bolívar was reputed as one who made love with the trembling passions of a man beset.

His marriage in 1802 to María Teresa, the daughter of the Marquis de Toro, was an idyll of tragedy; for almost as soon as they returned from Spain to Venezuela, she died of yellow fever. Left young, and rootless, and prodigiously rich, Bolívar again went back to Europe. He moved through Spain and Italy, then, attracted by the rising star of Napoleon, he settled down in Paris to witness the birth of empire and to live the sybaritic life of a man of fashion.

Yet he had his serious moments. Bolívar was much affected by Napoleon, whose military and diplomatic successes were worthy of profound study, and whose extreme simplicity of dress the Liberator was to emulate. The Corsican's influence went deep; as a Frenchman who knew him well later said, "The Emperor was Bolívar's ideal."

And then there was Humboldt. The great scientist, then approaching the height of his powers, had just returned from five years of travel in South America, and was in Paris seeing his publications through the press. The two men met at the salon of Fanny du Villars — to whom Bolívar was linked by ties more intimate than mere acquaintanceship. Their talk turned to the Bolívar hacienda, which Humboldt had visited in Simón's absence, and then later to the political position of Spanish America.

At length Bolívar remarked, "In truth what a brilliant fate, that of the New World — if only its people were freed of their yoke."

And Humboldt had responded, "I believe that your country is ready for its independence But I cannot yet see the man who is to achieve it, to lead it."

It was the sentence which set off the second American revolution.

Everyone knew the course of Bolívar's life after that episode. It

was war, war, war; he lost his fortune, watched Venezuela dissolve
in chaos, escaped to Jamaica and came back to fight again. At
length, with an army resembling the ragamuffins of François Vil-
lon, he outmaneuvered Spain's most famous general, marched a
thousand miles through the Andes, and routed the Spanish at
Boyacá in Colombia. Then, on December 17, 1819, he formed
the union of Gran Colombia, a union which would include the
Spanish Viceroyalties of Venezuela, Colombia and Ecuador when
they would be liberated. This was the first step in a plan of continental proportions already taking shape in Bolívar's inmost
thoughts.

And today in Quito the design was moving toward completion.
Ecuador had been won.

Now he was nearing the plaza, and the little girls in their gaudy
angel costumes ran before him scattering flowers. From the overhanging balconies rose petals cascaded down like confetti, and
wreaths of laurel festooned with the colors of Gran Colombia fell
at his feet. Men saluted him, and women leaned forward to catch
the dark glance of his deep-set, disturbing eyes. Just ahead of him
was the great square, where the aldermen of the city were ready
to extend the official welcome. It was time to await his escort, the
long file of uniformed horsemen coming up behind him four
abreast, their drawn sabers flashing in the sun. He reined in the
impatient Pastor, and glanced idly at the Larrea balcony overhead, then at the cheering crowds at the highway's edge.

From her high place at Juan de Larrea's side, Manuela leaned
forward in sudden excitement. This was he at last — the greatest
man on the continent, the embodiment of all her dreams, her high
enthusiasm, the cause for which she had fought so long. A man of
fascination too, whose face showed suffering and thought, whose
supple body moved gracefully with every prancing half step of
his magnificent white horse. She took up a laurel wreath and
tossed it toward his feet — then watched in horror as the thing
veered crazily in the air and struck him full in the side of the face.

The Liberator's head jerked angrily toward the balcony. Then he saw the culprit — her dark eyes wide and luminous, the skin flushed a dull red, the white hands pressed to her white breast where hung the golden emblem of the Sun.

Bolívar bowed and smiled forgiveness into the eyes of Manuela Sáenz.

3

THE VICTORY BALL

THE LARREA HOUSE was ablaze. From the salon on the upper floor, flooded in light by a giant candelabrum, came the disorganized first notes of an orchestra tuning, and the sounds drifted across the Quito night. All afternoon, following the triumphant entrance of the Liberator, confusion had fallen on the mansion as servants bustled about arranging rooms and refreshments for the Victory Ball; but by the time vespers had come and gone everything was in readiness. Outside Indian lackeys with their black hair powdered, in satin waistcoats and knee breeches albeit barefooted, held torches to guide the guests over the unlighted cobblestone streets.

The streets of Quito in the early darkness were massed with celebrating people. Soldiers drunk on *chicha* careened down the gutters, wenching went on openly in the small plazas where in the light of the fireworks one could see love on display in every conceivable design; here and there were open brawls. The black-cloaked night watch tried to control the popular exuberance, but with scant success. This was a riotous night, and in the hurly-burly the nobility of Quito had to take their chances. The distinguished guests of the Victory Ball began to appear early. A few elderly ladies, still clinging with a certain autumnal poignancy to the things of the past, arrived in sedan chairs carried by Indians in livery, for in all the city there were no carriages. But most of the elite picked their way over the cobblestones guided by servants with small hurricane lamps while other lackeys held over their

heads heavily brocaded umbrellas, which this society affected
as a mark of distinction. Everyone of consequence was coming
to the ball — and in every style of dress that had flourished since
the halcyon times of Carlos III of Spain.

The old gentlemen wore the silk knee breeches and florid waistcoats of the eighteenth century, even the tricorne hat and powdered periwig. Those of middle years arrived in Spanish court
dress of 1795 — a narrow frock coat in striped fabric, with large
ornate buttons and broad flapping lapels. But the younger men,
the products of the revolutionary age, came *en frac*, in trousers
strapped under varnished boots, surtouts or caped overcoats, and
high beaver hats. These were the convinced republicans, and to
show their democratic sympathies, even on a night of such mob
license, they walked the crowded streets alone.

The women too reflected the same battle of the styles in their
gala costumes. Those who still dreamed the dreams of the old
regime came in stiff brocade, high heels, and powdered wigs with
walking sticks and quizzing glasses. All the young ladies, and those
who prided themselves on their modernity, wore daring dresses of
brocaded gauze or pink and white organdy; their small feet were
covered by satin ballet slippers, and their hair piled high in Grecian knots. There were even a few — scandalously daring these —
who tripped over the cobblestones dressed *à la sauvage,* their hair
cropped short — about as revolutionary a gesture as a woman
could make in Quito.

The doorway of the mansion was a huge nail-studded portal
over which the Larreas' arms were emblazoned Inside, the patio
was a beauty of flowers planted around a stone fountain on whose
crest a carved cherub embraced the neck of a swan. From its upturned beak poured a stream of cold water, piped down from the
snow fields high in the mountains around the city.

In the ballroom on the second floor, General Simón Bolívar and
his host stood ready to receive the arriving guests. A dignified
room this, long and wide, with tall latticed windows and a great
crystal chandelier bathing it in candle-glow. The chairs, settees

and small tables in straight-lined Directoire style, ornamented in
bronze against red damask, had been pushed back to clear the
floor for dancing Beside the door, the six liveried Indians who
were the orchestra sat ready with their strings and woodwinds. In
the adjoining room, cluttered with the ornamental baroque furniture heavily inlaid with gold for which Quito was famous, other
Indians presided over the wine bottles and punch bowl at a long
carved table.

From his place under a canopy of tricolored silk at the end of
the ballroom, Simón Bolívar watched the arriving guests with
interest. He had come with strict military punctilio, promptly at
eight and in excellent humor. For the festive occasion he had laid
aside his usual simple uniform, and instead wore a red military
jacket heavily braided with gold; on the epaulets that protruded
far beyond his shoulders were three golden stars, symbol of his
rank as Lieutenant General of the allied armies of liberation. His
hair was brushed up from his forehead, and his black lacquered
Wellington boots had extra-high heels; besides, he stood on a dais
raised above floor level, so that the illusion of tallness was complete.

Now, as guests streamed into the room, Bolívar, leaning lightly
on his dress sword, was fully at ease. A finished gentleman, raised
in luxury, well-traveled in Europe, and proficient in French, his
manners were exquisite. To each lady who was brought forward to
be presented, he gave full attention, kissing her hand and looking
at her with the warm eager intimacy of a man accustomed to con-
quests. Toward men he showed an easy camaraderie, a friendly
descent from the pinnacles of his fame. Well-known patriots whose
names he knew — for he had a prodigious memory — he greeted
with a Latin *abrazo*, folding his long arms about them gently
and patting their backs. For everyone he had a familiar word
or question, for his host and his aide-de-camp stood by, ready
to give him in hurried whispers his cue to every stranger.
There was little doubt about it; everyone was captivated by his
charm.

In the Larrea mansion this night Bolívar seemed to have achieved the heights of his ambition. Independence was all but won; and the glory of it was his. Still if he had any weakness it was his intoxication with the *aura popularis*. Yet here, for the first time in all those long years of fighting, he had a chance to relax. Here the atmosphere was something like that which he had known in Europe, with the refinements and small luxuries which years of campaigning had denied him. The room was filled with happy sounds — the murmur of violins, the rustle of women's dresses, and above all the sustained hum of laughter and talk in half a dozen different languages.

The war for independence had taken on an international flavor. For long it had been only an American affair — a matter of half-naked lancers, their long knives tied to bamboo shafts, against the well-armed legions of the Spanish army — and Bolívar himself was only an intelligent leader of wild guerrilla bands. But by the year of 1822 a great change had occurred. With his victories and the formation of Gran Colombia, Bolívar had stepped into the councils of Europe. Many veteran officers of the continental wars had sought employment with him after Waterloo, and they had found places in his army. His staff was now filled with Europeans — English, Scots, Irish, Germans, Poles and even Russians, all had commissions in his regiments.

All about the room now were handsome young leaders of the foreign contingent, dressed in the uniforms of their regiments — dark green jackets with cuffs and lapels edged in gold, and strapped dark green trousers piped with gold. There was Sowerby from Bremen, Duckbury from London, Captain Hallowes of Kent, all so young they had not yet been able to grow the bristling mustaches considered necessary for an officer. The Irish were there in force — O'Connor of the fighting O'Connors of Dublin, very attractive to the ladies because of his blond hair; and William Fergusson, impetuous and courageous, with a heart as huge as his appetite for Irish whisky, a man whose rashness made Bolívar no end of difficulties, but still one much liked for all that. "A good friend," Bolívar called him, "obliging and generous . . . also with much affection for me."

But O'Leary was the favorite. As trim as a bantam fighting cock, Daniel O'Leary of Belfast had been on Bolívar's staff since arriving at nineteen with the green of Ireland still on him. It was Captain O'Leary who, white flag in hand, had entered the royalist lines during the recent battle for Quito carrying the demand for surrender. Although he was the calmest of the Irish contingent, he could when aroused forget his Spanish and scream the vulgarities of a Belfast brothel-keeper. O'Leary was now only twenty-two, yet he had the grasp of Bolívar's greatness; he was already assembling all of the leader's papers so as to preserve this glory.

The foreign legionnaires were giving the war a needed professional direction and a touch of glamour, but Bolívar's field commanders were all South Americans. Such a one was Antonio de Sucre, whom he could now see leading a formal polonaise with the attractive Mariana, daughter of the Marquis de Solanda.

Sucre, the victor of the battle for Quito, was only twenty-seven and already a field marshal, yet his delicate face was more that of a courtier than a fighter. The huge sideburns coming down almost to his lips did not hide the finely penciled features which showed something of his heritage, for his family originally came from Flanders and belonged to the Walloon nobility. Sucre, a native of Venezuela, had left the university at sixteen to ride with Bolívar's guerrillas, and had risen rapidly through merit. He was the revolution's greatest field general, the white knight of the wars for independence. He would never lose a battle, except the one with himself. He was capable, quiet, fastidious; disliking the tropical luxuriance of his companions-in-arms, he had a delicate spirit, and was as sensitive as mimosa. And now even more. He was terribly in love with Mariana.

Here naturally enough was Córdoba, young José María Córdoba, a general at twenty-three, whose heroic charge a month ago had broken the resistance of the *godos* and brought victory.

A magnificent and dangerous man, a man made for war, aggressive and violent despite his finely chiseled face and his gentle, melancholy eyes. He had become a soldier at fourteen; he rode with the *llaneros*, learned war, loved it and fought it with frenzy He was a Colombian, and immensely proud; but he lacked balance and imagination, and these were fatal flaws. And near him, talking and laughing over a glass of port, stood that other polished man of violence, Scottish Rupert Hand.

Simón Bolívar from the vantage point of the dais could see them all, these men who had been, in one way or another, the elements of his glory Many had been his comrades-in-arms during the terrible years of struggle; many others, now met for the first time, he knew by reputation or through long correspondence It was a strange and wonderful gathering, for here before him — as he later recalled — was the entire cast that was to enact the drama of his life in the coming years. They were all here, save one. And then she came.

The Victory Ball was at its height, enough wine had flowed to break down the stiffness of a society unused to the free and easy ways of off-duty soldiers. Suddenly there was a stir at the entrance, a break in the rhythm of laughter and voices. The dancers continued the stately steps of the *contredanse*, but mechanically now; for all eyes had turned toward the door. Someone was just arriving, pushing into the room through the onlookers near the doorway — a woman marked by her easy, full laughter.

As she came toward him now, weaving her way between the dancing couples, Bolívar saw it was a young woman, twenty-odd years of age perhaps, in the full burst of her irregular beauty. She walked light and erect, her every movement smooth and graceful, with more than a hint of sensuousness, even abandon, underlying the controlled delicacy of step and gesture. She wore a light organdy in the modern mode, the skirt falling in long half-revealing folds from the high waistline to the tips of her satin ballet slippers. Across the low *décolletage*, half hiding the lovely ivory of her breasts, was the red and white *moiré* ribbon of her decoration; and under her left breast glittered the golden Order of the Sun. Her complexion too was clear ivory, her cheeks touched with color by the excitement of the moment. Her long hair lay across her head like a tiara, in braids interwoven with fresh white flowers.

Juan de Larrea, in black tailcoat and knee breeches, bowed his withdrawal to Bolívar and hurried forward to meet her. On his arm she came toward the dais to be presented, honoring the hero with a supple curtsy as he bowed over her slender fingers.

"Your Excellency . . . La Señora Manuela Sáenz de Thorne."

Manuela looked on him with open admiration; and he, always alive to lure of women, did nothing to hide his interest in her. But there were others waiting to be presented to the Liberator. As he kissed her hand and looked into the dark, mischievous eyes, this might have been just another attractive woman in his woman-filled life. But Manuela was twenty-four and he was thirty-nine; it was a dangerous conjuncture of ages.

As the evening wore on and Bolívar exhausted his stock of panegyrics to those being presented, his eyes picked out Manuela — first dancing a polonaise, and very cleverly, then later mixing with the group around the wine table. She was speaking to the legionnaires in their native English — and of course they loved it. She had learned the language at her husband's side and, since he entertained sea captains, Manuela's English was spiced with piquant expressions. She told droll and risqué stories; and one of them was so couched as to cause Fergusson to explode in his Irish whisky. Manuela was drawing attention to herself as usual and enjoying it thoroughly. Now to the horror of the other ladies she was dancing — not with a partner on the ballroom floor, but alone, for the benefit of the officers around her. Her skirt held high in both hands, her body twisting in sinuous suggestion, she began to writhe the notorious *ñapanga.* "That is not a dance," said the Bishop of Quito, who once witnessed it, "that should be called the resurrection of the flesh."

It was obvious that Bolívar would be drawn to this unpredictable woman. Since her half brother Colonel José María Sáenz was now a member of his staff, he already knew something about her — that she was born in Quito, that she was illegitimate, that she had served the patriot cause with distinction. If he wanted to know more — and he entered into love affairs as he entered into war, with extravagant attention to details and without doubts or scruples — there was one at hand who could tell him. This was Colonel Andrés Santa Cruz, the tall young commander of the Peruvian Legion, a native of Lima.

Santa Cruz could indeed tell much about Manuela's life in Lima society, and about her important place in the revolutionary movement. But of that possibly significant figure, Manuela's husband, he knew little, or little of nothing.

James Thorne, in fact, was somewhat of a mystery to everyone; no one knew more of him than it pleased him to tell of himself, and that was not much. It was known that he had met Manuela through her father in Panama in 1816, that a marriage contract had been arranged, that Simón Sáenz had provided her a dowry, after which he sailed to Spain, and that Thorne and Manuela had gone to Lima in 1817 to be married.

Santa Cruz could add little more to this picture. Lima had been Thorne's home since 1812, when he had arrived from Cadiz — a prisoner, people said, though for what cause no one ever knew. He was a native of Aylesbury in England, a short stocky man with gray eyes, and oddly enough a devout Catholic. His age he never revealed, but he was obviously some twenty years older than his wife. His business affairs were slightly mysterious too. In some fashion he had gained the favor of the Viceroy; he acquired property and ships, and traded all along the coast from Panama southward to Valparaiso in Chile. He had become, by the time of his marriage, a man of substance and influence but he remained a cold and enigmatic personality, formal, correct, and aloof.

Now Thorne had gone on a matter of business to Panama, and here was his lovely young wife gracing the Victory Ball in Quito, and attracting Bolívar's notice; but it was only later in the evening, after he had danced with all the ladies as the decorum of the occasion demanded, that he caught up with her Bolívar loved to dance. He could spend whole days in the saddle and then find relaxation in dancing half the night. On the ballroom floor as on horseback, he was skillful, graceful and at ease. Besides, he used the dance — the physical contact, the heightened emotions, the press of hand and body — for its original purpose, as a prelude to love. While dancing he could make casual exploratory caresses, to be disowned if the woman objected, or followed by more explicit advances if she did not.

In Manuela he found his ideal, and they danced, danced for hours to the minuets and the *contredanses* of the thin-toned six-piece orchestra. They were fully aware, they must have been, that all eyes were upon them. But seemingly they did not care, this perfect rapport, this complementing of one another, was new to both of them, and far too precious to bring to an end so soon. Manuela too loved the dance; she was in turn gay, serious, inconsequential, tender, risquée, revealing at every moment a new and startling pattern of her kaleidoscopic personality. Bolívar immediately became aware that this was no ordinary woman. Her speech, her repartee, her bearing, her personal history, even her acute summation of the people about them, were not the usual equipment of the women he had known.

And he had known women, for women were vital to Simón Bolívar. He was never without them — at home, abroad, even on his military expeditions. After the death of his wife, he said, "I shall never marry again." And he had kept that vow, giving himself freely to passion, but avoiding any semblance of a lasting emotional tie.

The names of his women had been legion, and some of them were well known. In Paris, when he was a rich young man, he had cuckolded one of Napoleon's generals and brought such joy to the lady, Fanny du Villars, that twenty years later she sent him her portrait and recalled their love. In Venezuela, while he alternately chased and was pursued by the *godos,* his mistress had been the lovely Isabel Soublette, and her brother, who had been a mere subaltern in the army, rose spectacularly in the train of Eros. Then there had been Josefina Nuñez, his beloved "Pepita," who rode beside him through all the terrible campaigns in the llanos. After that, during the lull of battle, it had been Anita Lenoit, seduced in a hammock, who remembered him vividly and sought him out years later.

He made love as the Russians operated their military commissary: he lived off the country, and one could follow his loves by a map of his campaigns. In the fortress city of Cartagena it was this young lady, in Bogotá it was someone else In Cali, when he was on his way to Quito, it was Bernardina — "You are the only one in the world for me," he wrote to his "celestial angel." But no sooner had the ink dried on this letter than he found another "angel" in Popayán. The catalogue of them was long and detailed and in his fashion Bolívar had loved them all, writing them all the fervent love letters, and whispering much of the same things into their ears. But never once had he fallen into their cleverly laid snares. And now this Manuela. . . .

They danced together almost continuously, weaving in and out among the other couples, losing themselves as much as possible in the crowd, avoiding the walls where sat the onlookers who looked at them disapprovingly from their quizzing glasses. Yet as the evening wore on, their very inconspicuousness became conspicuous. The ancient dowagers, in wigs and patches, nodded and whispered behind their fans, for here was the hero of the hour paying all his attention — and very personal attention — to that notorious little trull, that Manuela.

Then suddenly they were gone. They had danced, talked, laughed together half the night; they had gone in together to the wines and sweetmeats of the midnight supper; they had returned together to the ballroom. Everyone had watched them, no one had seen them go. Simón Bolívar and Manuela had vanished.

4

TRIUMPHS OF A HETAIRA

THEIR *amoretto* was all over Quito the next morning.

It set in motion all the loose-lipped volubility of little Quito, where nothing, not even matters as secretive as love, could be hidden from the all-knowing gossips of its provincial society. They had eagerly discussed every step of Manuela's earlier affairs, inventing what they did not know; now they found in this new affair (and she a married woman too) complete harmony with her *demimondaine* past. So she was after all the same Manuela. All the patina of respectability — the fine clothes, her marriage to a wealthy merchant, her new position in Lima society, the decorations and the honors — none of these could hide her true nature. She was little else than a trollop. Now she had taken the hero from under their very noses; and the women were furious. And jealous, too; for there were many in Quito that morning who would have liked to have Manuela's place as the chosen object of Bolívar's love-making.

Manuela was well aware of prying eyes as, in the late morning, she made her way to the hospital to do her share in tending the wounded. She tried not to be obvious, yet she knew that her inward glow was apparent to anyone — that people were watching her — that they were talking. For they were repeating that morning the old wives' tale: like mother, like daughter. They had seen the same pattern before, and they were remembering Joaquina Aispuru and her love affair with Simón Sáenz.

It had been Joaquina's one peccadillo, yet it brought shame to the whole Aispuru family, and they hated Manuela thereafter, regarding her as the living symbol of her mother's dishonor. Poor Joaquina's life, after Manuela's birth, had been a dismal succession of days in church and nights in prayer; a mildewy scriptural aura pervaded her room, making it reek of Jeroboam and Saint John. And although she had long since died in the odor of sanctity, Manuela remained, a perfect target for the venomous tongues of her relatives.

Even as Señora de Thorne went about her work at the hospital, with her black slave Jonotás always at hand, the malignant suggestions followed her path. She was, it was whispered, a wanton who could not pass up any man, she was sterile and insatiable. It was Jonotás, the pock-marked, frizzled-headed slave with the libidinous eyes, who gave substance to these calumnies; she adored her mistress, bathed her, dressed her, and gave all the outward evidences of idolatry. She accompanied Manuela everywhere, and the odd figure of the Negro woman in her soldier's uniform, red turban, and jeweled earrings was becoming one of the sights of the city. In her off hours she gathered the gossip of the capital and carried it to Manuela in lurid detail; there was reason for people to say, "Jonotás is a mirror of Manuela." She was also gaining a reputation in the low-class houses as a mimic, and it seeped out that many a *grande dame* of Quito had been pilloried by her caricature. With a borrowed lorgnette, a swathe of muslin resembling a wig, and an amazing ear for turns of speech and voice, Jonotás could ridicule the most dignified of aristocrats. It was scandalous to allow one's slave — and her obscenities, they were revolting enough to make a sergeant major blush. . . .

All of this was, naturally, fuel for the Aispurus. The real reason for their malice they never disclosed: Manuela was bringing legal proceedings against them.

Simón Bolívar was unaware of the complications that his casual love-making had brought on. Nothing had happened that was unusual to him; he had encountered an attractive woman, he had been lavish in his praises of love, and she had succumbed. It was not a situation demanding special attention. Besides, he was immersed in affairs of state.

In the Escorial-cold rooms that had once been the royal offices, Bolívar was busily creating a new order. All day long he paced up and down, dictating to three secretaries at once, while complaining in his soft patois that they could not keep up with him. A stream of decrees left his chambers: reformation of the educational system, revision of the Treasury, appointments of new governors, new judges, new laws, new names for the streets. Letters were being dispatched to the far points of South America: to Lima, to thank General San Martín for the contingent of Peruvian troops that had aided in the victory at Quito; to Bogotá, a thousand miles north, demanding of his Vice-President money and yet more money to complete the military operations. There were interrupted consultations with General Sucre, Military Governor of the Province, and lengthy discussions with Church fathers disturbed by Bolívar's demand for their store of silver plate to help pay for wars still to be fought. Bolívar acted like Prometheus unbound; his energy flowed out in all directions. Every letter that reached him was answered, no matter how lowly the writer. Did a wounded soldier beg for money? He was paid from Bolívar's personal funds. Was there evidence against an unworthy judge? He was dragged out to the gibbet. Thus it went all day long, until he left everyone about him in a state of exhaustion.

Only when night closed in, and the cold of a city two miles high began to penetrate the unheated rooms, did Bolívar allow himself rest. A glass of wine brought by his major-domo, and he drifted into a sensuous languor, then his thoughts went to Manuela. It was time to call José Palacios — his servant since boyhood, bodyguard, watchdog of his silver service — and send him with his mastiffs to carry the simple, meaningful message: "Come to me. Come. Come now."

And Manuela came, disguised in an immense cloak, guided by José Palacios's hurricane lamp, flanked by the two huge dogs.

The streets were dark, and empty, save for a few figures in the shadows. The only sounds were the splash of water in the fountains, and the distant call of the night watch — "Ave Maria, a serene night: all is well."

Quito by night was none too safe for the wayfarer, but with the straw-colored mastiffs for protection, and the great-hearted Palacios leading the way, Manuela had nothing to fear. At the hour of her love tryst the plaza was silent, save for the gentle drip of water from the carved stone trumpet of Fame into the fountain pool beneath. No figure moved on the broad pavement which had seen so much carnage in the last decade, the palace, the Tuscany-styled residence of the Royal Audience, was deserted too. All dark except for one room — Bolívar's room — where the candles burned fiercely.

There was something feverish in their affair. Perhaps it was the insistent presence of war which gave their love a sense of suppressed excitement; perhaps it was the knowledge that the end must come too soon. And yet more. Manuela could love without consequences, she knew that now. She was sterile, "a woman of singular conformation," said a Scottish doctor who once examined her; she would never know the normal fulfillment of motherhood, and so her deepest impulses insistently demanded other outlets.

Bolívar too was driven by powerful urges, and he was habitually prodigal with his energies, in this direction as in all others. Besides, he was already in the first stage of tuberculosis, a lethal disease which exaggerated his passions. It had killed his mother, and he was predisposed to it. Now, after the privations of his warring life, the ceaseless drawing on the capital of his energy for these past years, all this allowed the disease to take hold. Even his face suggested it at times; a touch of fever made his eyes glitter like jewels, and his skin had a dry, almost varnished look.

Theirs was the ardor of a man and a woman who had met in tropical violence. In the cold Quito night, with only a brass brazier to heat the frigid room, oblivious for the moment to all else, two revolutionaries exchanged their burning kisses. And in those naked battles by night Bolívar for once met his equal. It was not alone her physical passion, draining energies sapped by punishing days of work, it was something deeper than that, more lasting — some inward need of hers, crying out to something he had scarcely known was in him.

He had not seen it at first, but now Bolívar knew that the love Manuela offered was a love that could engulf him. It suggested a relationship that, since the death of his wife, he had endeavored with all his being to avoid. And he was adept at avoiding it. He had been through all this many times before, and he had a proper sense of proportion. Manuela was mere woman, and he was after bigger game; he was out to seduce a continent.

From now on Manuela's problems suddenly multiplied. When she had arrived in Quito, in a manner triumphant, there had been only a single battle to wage — the skirmish with the Aispuru family. Now the immediate consequences of her love affair with Simón Bolívar were upon her: the skirmish with the Aispurus had become a pitched battle; and she would have to face, in one form or another, the violent reaction of her husband when he heard the scandal. Yet all these personal dilemmas had to be put aside now to make way for the really salient one — the war.

Manuela was needed now. In Lima, she had organized the women into war units; she had collected money to build ships; she had managed a house-to-house canvass for cloth for uniforms. Here in her native land she drew on that experience. Accompanied by Jonotás in her red turban and pretty Natan in a modish coiffure, she descended on the ladies of Quito. Every house was turned into a factory where noblewoman and Indian servant worked side by side on uniforms for the new army. Then there was the collection of money, of jewels, of silver plate for the financing of the next campaign. Manuela was everywhere, organizing, pleading, cajoling, even forcing contributions with her sharp tongue, her knowledge of ancient Quito scandals, and her skilled use of social blackmail. It brought many precious heirlooms to the public war chest, but it did not help La Sáenz in public esteem.

Meanwhile rumors of war filled the Quito air. The army was going to march to the coast, to take Guayaquil by force in the face of Peru's opposition — no, it was going north to Bogotá, or over the mountains to the Amazon. General San Martín was coming up to meet Bolívar — no, he was going to Europe to find a German prince for a nebulous Peruvian throne. There would be peace in Peru — no, there would be war, for the royalists were poised back of Lima with ten thousand seasoned troops. So went the talk, while new recruits were coming into the city every day; and they all had to be uniformed.

Manuela had been through all this before. She knew what the fight for independence cost, what it meant in the disruption of private life, in sacrifices, in blood and tears. In war she was a realist; and she was aware of its urgency. She sent to the Aispuru estate for eight mules — whether legally hers or not was little to the point — for the transport service of General Sucre. Jonotás in her soldier's uniform, riding the lead mule bareback, delivered them to Sucre along with a letter from her mistress:

> What I regret most is that our brave soldiers do not have all that is needed. Nevertheless you may count on the slender resources I possess; which, despite the fact that they are small, are always at your disposal. I shall not call this a sacrifice, knowing it to be only my duty.

Sucre was deeply touched, as much by the letter as he was by the gift of the animals. He dismissed his secretary, and in his own hand addressed her:

> MY GRACIOUS LADY —
> The noble offer of your possessions for the defense of the state is already suggested by your generosity. . . . Please accept the gratitude of the whole corps of the Army of Liberation, in whose name I am able to assure you that nothing gives them greater pleasure than to know that there are heroines, such as yourself, with whom they can share their glories. . . .

But if Sucre called her a heroine, her relatives the Aispurus called her something else. It had become a social war of attrition. And for a reason obvious to Manuela: it was the legal action she was bringing against them. Since her mother's death, and the reading of her will, they had hated Manuela and feared her too. For Joaquina, although conveniently married shortly before her death, had retained her right to a share in the large family land-holdings outside Quito, and that share she had left to Manuela by a secret *comunicato* in her will. By the laws of Toledo, such a *comunicato* was inviolable. When Manuela came of age, she demanded the ten thousand pesos which was the value of her inheritance. The Aispurus ignored her; they would have had to sell the estate to raise the money for her. Still Manuela was a born fighter, whose bent it was to defend her rights under all circumstances. Even while in Lima she began proceedings in the courts to force a settlement, and she had come to Quito to press her suit in person.

Her love affair with General Bolívar would eventually become known to her husband by this insistent family campaign. That would doubtless mean trouble. Thorne was terribly possessive — and "more jealous than a Portuguese," she had already said of him — and he took marriage with the stiff propriety of an Englishman, rather than the casual grace of a Latin. For him, it was a binding contract with the strictest of rules: the husband was undisputed master of home and family, the wife a mere chattel, with no more rights than her spouse chose to allow. For her, reared in licentious Quito and matured in the easy atmosphere of Lima society, it was an arrangement of great social and economic convenience, strict fidelity was not among its obligations. Divorce was impossible, but in the spirit of the times (and in Manuela's own words), "Marriage — marriage pledges one to nothing."

So Manuela did not believe it wrong to give herself to Simón Bolívar; it was doubtless a greater wrong to live a marriage without love. She did not approve of looseness, she never took casual lovers; no matter what the scandalmongers said of her affairs, they always sprang from real passion. Love was the touchstone in matters of this sort, love alone the justification. And Bolívar's fascination was tremendous; she did not question at all her right to be his mistress. But Thorne would scarcely sympathize with that, or forgive it. To come to an understanding with him, to patch up a pattern for living — this was the disturbing prospect. And she would have to face it. Complete separation from her husband had not yet entered into the matter, and she could not force things. For there was Simón Bolívar — he could be terribly impersonal and devious, and he gave not the slightest encouragement to any ideas that this would be a permanent relationship.

The twelve evenings — for their love was always discreetly nocturnal — were complete and satisfying. Manuela complemented his needs so fully that he did not, in this time in Quito, look upon another woman. But these were only the surface elements of love. Something different, more profound, began to creep into their relationship, something which gave balance and depth to desire Manuela knew — as few of Bolívar's women had known — the value of empty space. She sensed instinctively when to be tender and passionate, and when to listen in silence as talking restored equipoise to his passion-sated body Bolívar gradually discovered that Manuela was the only person in Quito to whom he could speak with ease and perfect freedom of his inmost intentions and motives. She would not betray him, since she wanted nothing; it seemed, and it was true, that his hopes, his aspirations, his fears were becoming also hers. So it was that after their passion had been tranquilized in the cold apartment of the late royalist administrator of Quito, Bolívar would pace up and down, throwing out his thoughts as he walked. It was then that Manuela really began to learn something about him and his ideals.

At first, these interminable wars for independence had had no real meaning to her. She had first conceived them as an expression of resentment against the *godos*, to whom she ascribed all the difficulties of her childhood. They became in turn a blood revenge against those who killed, imprisoned, exiled the ones she loved,

then a game to outwit the ponderous majesty of government; then
a desperate struggle for survival. But the essential reason for it
all, the intellectual background of the revolution had never
touched her — until now.

After three hundred years of fidelity to Spain, the colonies had
revolted. The origins of the independence movement were complex; there were commercial reasons rising from limitation of
trade; there were social motives too, for only the Spanish-born
were given high offices. Besides, the idea of independence was
in the air, the successful revolt of the North American colonies
against England, the Revolution in France, infected all those of a
liberal caste of thought with the virus of freedom. There had been
abortive movements toward liberty as early as the 1780's. But
strangely enough it was Napoleon, an offspring of these revolutions, who unintentionally initiated the South American revolt.
When his armies invaded Spain, forcing the reigning Bourbon off
the throne, he crowned his brother, Joseph Bonaparte, king; it was
then that the patriots in South America launched a protest — they
refused to become vassals of a foreign prince. But Spain, even in
the throes of foreign occupation at home, revealed herself as an
implacable enemy of liberalism; she put down this mild-tempered
movement in her colonies with a display of carnage; the conserva-
tive revolution was choked in blood. Manuela knew how the war
had gone after that; she had lived through it here in Quito. But in
Venezuela, where Bolívar had fought, it had been war to the
death. For thirteen years he had fought through the plains, the
mountains, the jungles, and out of it all had come at last the thing
he had dreamed of, the thing Humboldt's words had touched off
nearly two decades earlier: a great Republic, the provinces of
Venezuela, Colombia, Panama and now Ecuador united into the
federation called Gran Colombia.

It was clear to her now what Bolívar wanted. First, Spain must
be decisively defeated throughout the Americas. Then, out of
battle and the liberty of these many free states, a great empire
arising out of the Andes, half democratic, half feudal, which

through a common policy would become one day the United States of South America. And with the new form of government, a new race: "The bond that united us to Spain has been severed and we are neither Indians nor Europeans, yet are part of each"

It would not be easy to achieve. It would take men, treasure, supplies; it would demand courage, sacrifices, persistence. And the first requisite was unity: unity in feeling, unity in purpose, unity in command.

> As long as we do not unify our American government, I believe that our enemies will have the advantage. We shall be inextricably caught in a web of civil war, and be shamefully beaten by little gangs of bandits which pollute our country.

In order to obtain unity, then, there had to be a strong central government, with strongly established power, to keep the state from sinking into incompetence. That meant sharp limitations on popular sovereignty. It was plain that Bolívar mistrusted the instincts of the masses, especially the race that was "becoming." They were not like the homogeneous people that formed the United States in North America, who were almost wholly Anglo-Saxon. Here in South America more than half were Indians. One third of the land was the Amazon Valley, where savages still lived as they lived before the conquest. Throughout the Andes, the base of the human equation was the *cholo,* half Spaniard, half Indian, containing within himself the conflicting emotions of each race. Those who constituted the governing class were mainly of Spanish descent, a thin veneer of competent officials who had survived the civil wars. Discipline and authority the government must have to put down the inconstancy of the masses. Manuela gathered, then, that Bolívar believed in the nation, but he did not at this time believe wholly in the people. He did not believe they were yet able to rule themselves. He disliked the politicians who appealed to them; he hated the pettiness, the *mesquinerie,* the idiocy of those who pushed the doctrines of "regionalism" by appealing to the prejudices of the masses:

The individual fights against the mass; the mass fights against authority. . . In every government there must be a neutral body, which stands apart from the attack and disarms the attacker.

What form should the new government take? In view of the fact that the mass of people had not yet learned to govern themselves, what machinery should rule them? First, a president elected for life; this would give the government time, without the repeated crises of elections, to train the people in the elements of democracy Then, following the English system, Bolívar would have a hereditary senate, corresponding to the House of Lords. He did not think in terms of a new nobility, but he wanted to develop a new American patriciate, a senate composed of people grown used to power and its traditions, those who were above the commercial battle and could thus use all their prestige for the public good. The lower house would be popularly elected, and would freely express the popular will. The ideal government must be strong, there must be discipline; the leadership must spring from the intellectual and moral elite. If not, there would be anarchy on which the petty politicians would feed; this would bring disunion, and Spain would again return to power: "Not the Spaniards but our own disunity shall lead us back into slavery."

Yet was it not chimerical to think at this time of unifying the whole continent and making it a nation with a single purpose? After all — and even Manuela knew this — the continent was in chaos; no one thought of it in such terms as these. To the south, Argentina was free, but chaotic; and the Indian state of Paraguay that bordered her was locked behind a green curtain of jungle. Chile, which had been liberated from Spain in 1817, had already fallen into just the sort of anarchy that Bolívar had described as a result of disunity.

And Peru! Only the capital city of Lima and a small section of the coast were in patriot hands. In the hinterland, in the Andes, was a huge royalist army, moving at will throughout the mountains, it threatened at any moment to sweep down upon Lima. Peru was hostile to the Republic, because freedom had been imposed upon it from without. Now few Limeños supported it, and only a very few had really participated in the earlier phases of the revolution. Lima set the pattern for the country, and Lima was the metropolis of the aristocratic classes, three centuries of colonialism had effaced Peru's will for independence. Precisely. Well this, then, this was the mission of Gran Colombia.

Simón Bolívar went up to a huge wall map. There, across the top of South America was Gran Colombia, on its Atlantic side stood Venezuela, sprawling with extended borders to Brazil; facing the Caribbean Sea was Colombia, which had as its citizens the best legal minds in South America (it had forged the Republic following Bolivar's concept); to the north was Panama, the entrepot of the Pacific; and to the south, completing the four-state union of Gran Colombia and holding the key to the continent, was Ecuador. Even though the Republic was rent here and there by local squabbles, it exhibited what political unity could do. Gran Colombia must be the sun around which the lesser South American planets revolved. Even now, before actuality betrayed the dream, Bolívar was sending an envoy to Mexico and an ambassador to Peru to win them to the idea of continental solidarity; and in the realm of the practical he had hired Swedish engineers to survey the isthmus and report on the possibilities of cutting a Panama canal. Of course, he admitted, ofttimes he did the necessary things with great expedition, and inquired afterwards as to their legality. Furthermore he had to concede that there were not too many politicians in Gran Colombia who believed in this grandiose conception. Yet he would press for fulfillment, he would pursue his ideal just as Don Quixote battled with windmills in the pursuit of his. Still there were many problems which had to be solved; and one of them was immediate and pressing.

Manuela well knew what it was, the large map hanging on the General's wall explained it graphically; it was the southern frontier of Gran Colombia, it was Ecuador. The country's Andean sections were already linked to the Republic; to the east lay the vast track-

less Amazon; to the south was Peru; and on the fringe of the tropical Pacific coast was the city of Guayaquil. It was a squalid port,
its houses of split bamboo raised on stilts lining streets that were
quagmires. Three centuries of ravage by termites and pirates had
left it with the formless character of a tropical abattoir, it was a
notable pesthole — unsightly, unsanitary, dangerous. But it was
built some distance from the Pacific on the edge of a deep river,
formed by a skein of smaller streams. Ships were built there;
lumbering was a sizable trade; chocolate, cotton, and rubber
poured through it. Guayaquil was not only the port that handled
all the country's commerce, it was the only good port within a
thousand miles. Whoever controlled it, controlled the whole of
Ecuador. Bolívar knew its importance, to Ecuador and to the
whole of Gran Colombia; he was determined to have it: "I have
not had time for anything, for I have been meditating how to acquire Guayaquil's adhesion to us; to win Guayaquil and yet to
preserve harmony with Peru."

Yet to preserve harmony with Peru! that was the heart of the
problem. General San Martín, victor of Lima and its Protector,
held the reins of power there — and he too was pledged to his government to gain Guayaquil. San Martín must not be alienated, nor
his prestige lowered; that would weaken Peru, and cause it to
collapse into the arms of the royalists, who even now were hover-
ing outside Lima with a force of ten thousand soldiers. He had
better confer with General San Martín. Such a meeting was long
overdue between the two leaders, and San Martín too looked anx-
iously forward to it:

> I shall meet the Liberator of Colombia. The common interests
> of Peru and Colombia, the effective conclusion of the war we are
> waging, and the stability of the political form toward which
> America is rapidly approaching make our meeting necessary.

Manuela's chance was here, and she knew it. These two great
men had never met. And about San Martín, Don Simón showed an
obvious uneasiness. He disliked entering into any action without
first having exhaustive intelligence of the matter in hand, the

strengths and weaknesses of his adversary. And he had no information on recent developments in Peru, or on the Protector himself. In fact there was only one person in Quito who did, and that was herself, Manuela.

It was scarcely six weeks since she had left Lima, where for five years she had known everyone who was anyone: royalists, patriots, priests, foreigners, fools, soldiers and even trulls. Her relations had cut through all the divisions of Lima's society. Her slaves had brought her the scuttlebutt of the people, from the wine shops and *picanterias;* she had picked up rumors, hints, plans, suggestions from midnight *tertulias* in the houses of people of quality; she had items of intelligence from the sea captains who frequented her husband's table. Nothing of import happened in Lima without her learning of it sooner or later. Besides, she had a wonderful faculty of being able to evaluate friends or enemies, and with a few strokes of pointed language she could sketch the character of men. She knew intimately the people with whom one had to deal in these delicate matters: the titled and reactionary aristocrats of Lima; the confused patriot Marquis de Torre Tagle; the volatile and sensitive José de la Riva Agüero, who already was tearing apart the fabric of the newly woven Republic of Peru; Bernardo Monteagudo, the intellectual force of the revolution. And she knew — this was most important — General José de San Martín; in fact Rosita Campusano, his mistress, was one of her intimates. Yes — Manuela, reclining on a high-backed couch in the pose made famous by Madame Récamier, would be happy to place all her knowledge at Bolívar's disposal.

A new Manuela was emerging, and Bolívar was quick to note it. Here was a creature who was more than a desirable woman; she had many facets to her and here was one which could be put to fundamental use. Manuela was well aware of this too. She realized that love in itself was not enough for Bolívar. That was what the long course of his casual loves had given him, and one by one he had moved out of their lives forever. To hold him, some depth must be given to the relationship, some third dimension added.

Manuela would bind Simón Bolívar to her by the bonds of shared creation.

And now of San Martín· let there be enough of him to explain his reputation. Well — in his essence San Martín was a soldier; a functional soldier without heroics, and — what was in these times almost an enigma — a man without personal ambition. He was tall, erect and reserved, a handsome man with a large aquiline nose and sweeping side whiskers, his military knowledge and leadership were outstanding.

San Martín, like Bolívar, was American — born in the little village of Yapeyú in Argentina Schooled at the Seminary for Aristocrats in Spain and enrolled in a Spanish regiment when his age allowed, he fought with distinction in the Peninsular Wars against Napoleon's invasion. At twenty-two he was a full colonel and a member of the Spanish commander's staff, but when the revolution broke out in Argentina he resigned his command and offered his services to his native land.

Arriving in Argentina in 1812, San Martín organized a corps of mounted grenadiers, molded a tough fighting army around them, and embarked on one of the boldest campaigns in military history. He knew, as did Simón Bolívar, that the center of Spanish resistance would be in Peru; and he resolved to attack Peru from the south. The heaven-scraping, snow-filled Andes barred the way, and the narrow length of Chile; but he marched forward. He crossed the Andes in twenty horrendous days, fell on the *godos* in the rear, and made himself master of Chile. Then he slowly moved on Lima. The patriot fleet, several ships of the line commanded by the British sailor of fortune, Lord Cochrane, controlled the seas. Within the city the patriot underground was effectively sowing disunion and undermining the defenses, and the Spanish had no stomach for battle. On June 26, 1821, they abandoned Lima without a fight, and retreated to the Andes to build up their army anew, while San Martín entered the gates of the walled city. But once Lima and the adjoining coast were in patriot hands, a strange lethargy seemed to settle on San Martín. His activities be-

came political rather than military. He was made Protector of
Peru, with Bernardo Monteagudo as Minister of State, a congress
was selected, a new democratic nobility, the Order of the Sun,
was created. He even attempted to reorganize the financial structure. Yet the lethargy persisted. It was said he was ill, weakened
by the privations of the past five years. He was racked with
rheumatism, he had sharp pains in his stomach (Manuela had this
from Rosita Campusano, who saw more of him than anyone else),
and he was compelled to take opium in small doses to ease the
hurt. Already he was abusing this malevolent anodyne beyond the
danger point.

Yet whatever the cause, military inaction was feeding the flames
of discord. The *godos* marched back and forth along the coast,
almost at will, Admiral Cochrane — "his metallic Lordship" — had
deserted the cause in an argument over prize money; behind the
walls of Lima spies and *agents provocateurs* were undermining the
Republic. There were defeats in the field, plots and revolts within
the city walls, betrayal and perfidy everywhere. For this chaotic
situation, Bernardo Monteagudo as Secretary of State had a single
panacea — the terror. Royalist sympathizers were hanged, many
were sent into exile, chattels were confiscated right and left. The
terror cut down through all ages and all sentiments; even ardent
patriots quaked before this revolution. The patriotic movement
had begun to disintegrate, and high-ranking officers were talking
openly of a rival republic. To make matters worse, an epidemic of
yellow fever had swept the city. San Martín now realized that
without Bolívar he could not raise an army of sufficient strength
to fight the Spaniards; thus he would be coming to Ecuador with
a poor bargaining position.

All this was precisely what Bolívar needed to know. There was
now no uncertainty about Guayaquil; he was ready to make his
decision: "These are the days to take advantage of charm and surprise . . . so I propose to enter Guayaquil at the head of the
allied armies."

As always with Bolívar the action swiftly followed the thought.

He perfected his plans, called his staff together, and gave the orders: "March to Guayaquil and arrange that I enter as its Liberator." Then he himself made ready to leave on the morning of July 4th. His twelfth night in Quito had come to an end.

Bolívar doubtless believed that he was riding out of Manuela's life, as he had ridden out of the life of many a woman, and that there would be no emotional complications here. He had already felt Manuela's strength — felt in her passion something which would swallow him whole if he allowed it; felt the force of her mind which could, if not guarded against, assume lasting importance in his councils. He did not want this to happen. The expedition to the coast, to Guayaquil, could not have come at a more propitious moment. He had found a good excuse to escape Manuela.

As he mounted to go down the same path that had brought Manuela to this heaven-bound city, she knew, as she watched him, his great fear of permanence. Even men as astute as Bolívar believed that women made no choices of their own; that they merely echoed the choices men had first selected.

At this thought a remembered smile crossed Manuela's face, a strange, enigmatic smile which held both challenge and promise. It would have frightened Bolívar half to death had he seen it.

5

THE PRICE OF GAINING

In the months that followed there were no letters from Bolívar. It upset Manuela, and angered her, for she had wrung a promise from him that he would write, no matter how complicated his movements. It would have been, of course, immeasurably reassuring to have had letters from him. Like most women, she was not fully satisfied with protestations of love; she needed the sense of permanence that came with the written word. But like all promises given under duress — there is coercion in passion — this was only a half promise; and Bolívar did not keep it.

Yet if there was no direct word from Bolívar, there was no lack of detail about what was occurring down in the hot lands of Guayaquil. All sorts of rumors boiled up from the cauldron of the tropic port, every newly arrived traveler to Quito brought his own version of the events. On one point all seemed agreed. Bolívar arrived at the port without incident, rode into the city as Liberator, and led his troops in a victory march through the mud-filled streets. Before this show of force the agents of Peru, who had hoped to win the city for their side before his influence could be felt, fled the political field, leaving it to Bolívar. He had used "charm and surprise," as he said he would, to win the leaders of Guayaquil. The city and its provinces were nailed to the jack staff of the Republic; Guayaquil was part of Gran Colombia.

Everything was in readiness when the schooner *Macedonia*, coming up from Peru with General San Martín, dropped anchor in front of the city's mudbanks. The gonfalons of Gran Colombia

flew beside the red and white banners of Peru, triumphant arch-
ways of palm leaves festooned the streets, people in festive clothes
lined the waterfront to witness the historic meeting, a band stood
ready with polished brass instruments to strike up a patriotic air.
The whole performance waited only for the cue from its supreme
director.

Bolívar, jackbooted, spurred, and accoutered in dress uniform,
waited on the landing, surrounded by his gold-braided officers.
The General from Peru stepped ashore. He had expected that one
of the topics of their conversations would be the future of the
province of Guayaquil, and he came fully armed with a dossier of
suggestions. Instead of which . . .

Instead of which General Bolívar met him with an ingratiating
smile, signaled the band to begin its playing and the claque its
cheering, and above the *vivas* and the music he spoke:

"Welcome, my General, to the soil of Gran Colombia."

No one could fully agree on what had happened after that meeting. Manuela was fortunate enough to have an official source of
information — her half brother, Captain José María Sáenz. He
was the same age as Manuela and looked like her, he had the
same alabaster complexion, the same brown eyes, dark and lively;
he reflected her spirit, her loyalty, and the unequivocal openness
of manner. Alone of his sisters and brothers, José María adored
Manuela. Her loyalties were now his loyalties, for only he of the
legitimate Sáenz family was a fervent patriot. Manuela had converted him to the revolutionary cause when they were both in
Lima; he had fought for the liberation of Quito; he now held a
command of trust in his native city. In a world alive with rumors,
José María allowed nothing to impose itself on his credulity.
Through his hands passed the official statements; and these facts,
few as they were, he passed on to Manuela.

It seemed that after the official reception and formal dinner,
the two generals retired alone to a guarded room. Manuela, who
knew both of them intimately, realized the basic opposition of
these two distinct characters, who were created to fill different

niches in the political puzzle. San Martín, Manuela knew, was formal, correct, and austere, with a soldier's rigidity and a high sense of honor and purpose. Bolívar — her Simón — was gay and light, with a disarming charm which disguised his Machiavellian maneuvers. He could play out the human comedy with periods of humor, but he was, and none knew it better than she, devious in his campaigns to triumph where triumph he must.

In their political concepts of America, the two had no common meeting ground. San Martín's collision with the problem of democracy in Peru — where three quarters of the people were illiterate — had reversed his earlier feeling for a strictly democratic government. He now sincerely believed that an interim form of monarchy was the only solution; and he was, as he admitted, in actual contact with a princely house in Germany, to seek a candidate for the throne of Peru. Bolívar abhorred the idea of kingship, and although he concurred with San Martín on the unreadiness for democracy of the bulk of the people, he still believed in a society of free American nations, to be governed at first by a lifetime president on the model of Gran Colombia, with a gradual extending of the democratic base. Their fundamental political disagreement was established quickly, San Martín then turned to the immediate military picture in Peru.

It was terrifying enough. The royalist army was constantly growing larger, while the patriot force was shrinking by desertions. Battle must soon be offered, yet Peru had not the necessary troops. San Martín pointedly suggested that Bolívar send forces to Peru for its liberation, just as he had sent a brigade to Bolívar to aid in the freeing of Quito. But Bolívar did not wish to be drawn into a political maelstrom. He offered the precise number of troops — one thousand and sixty-two soldiers — that had been sent to him from Peru, although it was obvious to them both that the whole Colombian army was needed. Again San Martín was stalemated. He then made offer to serve under Bolívar if he could lead his army into Peru. It was a generous and humbling gesture. Bolívar would not hear of it. He refused it, as Manuela well knew, because he had no power to accept it; he had yet to be given authority to leave the domain of the Republic. But there was still another reason. Peru lacked unity, it was divided, and Bolívar was afraid of it.

> I do not wish to go to Peru if glory does not follow me. . . . I do not wish to lose the fruits of eleven years of war through one defeat, and I do not wish San Martín to see me other than as I deserve to be seen, namely, as the chosen son.

It was an ineffectual, disappointing first meeting. General San Martín retired to his delegation and worked late into the night on new proposals, while Bolívar danced. The next day they met again. As at the first meeting, no one else was present, no one took notes. San Martín, away from Bolívar's dominating personality, had marshaled his arguments, and now presented a series of demands that sounded almost like an ultimatum. Bolívar did not bother to give them rebuttal, he reached into his military tunic and pulled out a letter just received from his ambassador in Peru. There had been a palace revolution in Lima. The day after the General had left for the Guayaquil meeting, the other members of the government had seized his Minister, the hated little dandy Bernardo Monteagudo, thrown him on a vessel bound for Panama, and installed a provisional government. San Martín was clearly in no political position to insist on any conditions. It was a terrible moment for this man, who had given so much of his life to the wars for independence only to be disowned as soon as his back was turned. Silently he emerged from the conference room, silently he embraced Bolívar; and with lowered head he walked in sorrow from the house.

That night there was a grand ball in their joint honor, with the usual flood of gold lace and bold *décolletage*, the flow of wine, and a spontaneous, vibrant gaiety Only whispered rumors moved about the grand hall, for no one else knew what had taken place in the conference room. Bolívar and San Martín gave no hint of it, yet those who observed them could guess by their attitudes who had won. Bolívar was gay and careless, he danced with abandon to a waltz newly arrived from Europe, and between dances trifled with the three Garaycoa sisters. General San Martín was taciturn almost to the point of rudeness; he danced several times, stiff and wooden, trying heroically through the evening to hide the bitterness that was consuming him. At last he could stand it no more; he quickly gathered up his cape and his patent-leather bicorned hat, kissed the hand of his hostess, and slid out unobtrusively into the darkness.

But General Bolívar saw him leave, and abruptly abandoned his charming lady of the moment to follow San Martín out into the night. They met on the pier at the edge of the river, and they talked long and quietly there. Each admired the other's greatness, yet they had now reached an impasse and — since genius is egocentric — someone had to yield. It was to be San Martín. He had been in Guayaquil only thirty-six hours, and in that short space of time all that he had worked for through these past years had crumpled like a pricked balloon. He was going back to Peru to resign from his office; he would eclipse himself at the height of his glory; and he would leave the field — the entire stage of South America — to his rival. They silently embraced. Bolívar stepped back to salute him, but San Martín stayed his arm and quietly said: "I have finished my public life. . . . I shall go to France and live out the days of my life in retirement. Only time and events will say which of us has seen the future with more clarity."

Manuela knew that Simón Bolívar had won. Guayaquil and the whole tropical province had been gathered into the Republic of Gran Colombia; its frontiers now ran from the Atlantic to the Caribbean, and from that stormy sea to the Pacific and the bleak coasts of Peru. Bolívar had won, but she knew too that winning sometimes consists in losing, for he had brought about precisely what he had wanted to avoid. He had lowered the prestige of San Martín, weakened Peru, and brought it closer than ever to the devouring maw of the royalists' forces.

If corroboration was needed, it was not long in coming. Manuela had a weeping letter from Rosita Campusano which, in purely personal terms, told almost everything. San Martín had returned, resigned his offices, and departed for Europe — leaving her, once the first lady of Lima, in obscurity. Everything was chaotic in Peru. An issue of paper money had depressed the currency, and prices were astronomical. Those who could, fled with their silver plate; there were no luxuries for those who stayed. And the blood-thirsty *godos* were making raids right up to the walls of Lima, pillaging, burning, killing everyone who had shown republican sympathies. The government, which was really a wrangling coun-cil, could agree on nothing; the armies they raised to defeat the royalists were decimated before they even reached the battlefield; the Argentine contingent of the Peruvian army had melted away; and unpaid soldiers were ravaging the farms of the coast. The Colombian troops sent down by General Bolívar had been re-ceived with open hostility, so that their officers had quickly em-barked the men and sent them back to Guayaquil. So it went. And all the while the royalist army hovered over the walled city, wait-ing like a carrion bird until the city's lifeblood ran out from the self-inflicted wounds of anarchy. And of course the scandal of Manuela and her affair with Bolívar was all over Lima. . . .

But Rosita did not have to tell her that; there were letters from her husband. The *Macedonia* had carried back to Peru more than a disillusioned General San Martín.

The impact of the love affair must have been horrible to James Thorne; there had always been gossip about Manuela, and he was a jealous man. Love affairs were viewed with tolerant amusement in Lima, but not by Thorne. He was English, and he was pre-occupied with the form as well as the substance of marriage; he had made a morality out of his incompetence. The shock of hav-ing been made a cuckold wounded his self-esteem, and put him at a disadvantage in business. Besides, he was terribly in love with Manuela. Still Thorne had learned something during his five years of marriage. He did not threaten or cajole her, he did not insist on his rights. Instead he hung his arguments on the theme of honor. Divorce was impossible. There was no way in which she could bring about a permanent relationship. Even time would not give sanction to the affair, so affair it could only be. The honorable thing, the wise thing, would be to bring it to an end.

Manuela's reaction was immediate and unequivocal: No.

On November 16, more than four months after he had left it, Simón Bolívar rode back unannounced into Quito. It was those passion-swept June days all over again. During the mornings and afternoons there were conferences with his officers, visits to the wounded, petitions of soldiers to be answered, letters to write. The comings and going of couriers at all hours filled the little white stone city of Quito with the sharp tattoo of horses clanking over cobblestone streets.

Then at night it was Manuela. But it was not quite as it had been before. She had stormed and raved over his neglect of her, and over his casual affairs with other women during their separation. They filled her with anger and disgust. She was, Bolívar soon found, not a woman to be trifled with; when aroused she had the temper of a tigress. But their violent quarrels were short-lived, and the reconciliations were delicious. Once the anger of Manuela was transmuted and her fierceness quelled and rechanneled into love, the moment of violence passed, and tenderness entwined them.

Manuela's personal affairs were now pressing heavily on her. She had no wish to burden Simón Bolívar with one more individual problem, but her affairs were complicated. It was the Aispurus again. They had somehow discovered another legal delay to keep her from her inheritance; she was just as far away from its possession as she had been five years before. The estate was hers by law, by every moral right; and to have these people standing in the way with their tricks and lawyers' quibbles — she was determined to beat them at all costs. Besides, at this moment, when the security which marriage had given her seemed about to be eclipsed, the modicum of security her estate would yield would be helpful.

When Manuela's thoughts were these, she forgot all else: the war, the soldiers, her husband, her lover. The possession of her inheritance became an obsession. Bolívar felt its urgency for her; he promised that he would personally intervene with the courts to get the matter settled, and so began the needed steps; but when one is living in a revolution, life is fraught with uncertainties. Before anything decisive could be done, a counterrevolution in a far corner of Ecuador blew up right in his face.

"Ah, these days," Bolívar sighed, "they have left me completely fatigued. . . . The insurrection at Pasto has alarmed all the patriots here in Quito."

The nerves of the people had been fretted. The chaos in Lima, the discontent in Colombia, and the insurrection here in recently liberated Ecuador alarmed everyone. Bolívar acted with alacrity. He sent young General Sucre ahead with a flying column of lancers to quell the uprising, while he followed with the foot troops. It was a long ride, five hundred miles across the dreaded snow-swept plateau of the Andes. Bolívar did not relish it. But go he must, to win back the province with honeyed words, or if need be with blood and iron. So suddenly, and without a moment of farewell to Manuela, he was gone.

It was only days later, after Sucre had put down the rebellion and he had reached the wretched little mountain village of Yucanquer, that Bolívar remembered Manuela. He had forgotten his promise to her. In a small, cold, grass-thatched mud hut, bored beyond measure, without a fire or friends or his Manuela, he sat down by the light of a candle and wrote his first letter to her. He apologized for not being able to fulfill his promise, told her of the victory here at Yucanquer, and dilated on his boredom. "What do we do here? We conjugate the verb *ennuyer* . . ."

Manuela answered his letter on December 28; her reply carried in it some of the penetrating cold of the high Andes:

Sir:
   In your much appreciated letter, dated December 23, you have shown me the interest you have taken in my affairs. I give you thanks for all this, although you deserve more than mere grati-

tude, for you have been so very considerate toward me in my
present position. If you had only been nearer when this happened.
What will it serve now, that you are sixty leagues from here? The
victory at Yucanquer has cost me dearly. Now you will tell me
that I am not a patriot for saying what I am going to say: "I would
much rather that I had won [the victory over the Aispurus] than
that you had gained ten victories at Pasto."

I know the boredom you must suffer in that town; but no matter how desperate you find yourself, it is not as bad for you as for
the most fervent of your friends, who is

MANUELA

The bells of Quito were tolling the New Year of 1823 when
Simón Bolívar, tired and worn, walked his horse into the city.
Manuela did not wait this time for his message: "Come to me.
Come. Come now." She was already there, waiting on the steps.
Bolívar was completely exhausted; and that fact was amazing in
itself, for he was thought to be tireless. In earlier years he could
ride three thousand miles through the jungles and plains, and
arrive at the journey's end as fresh as when he began; his soldiers
called him Old Iron-Ass. His personal physician, Dr. Charles
Moore of the British Legion, suggested rest as the best possible
remedy. But how could he rest? And Bolívar heaped on Dr. Moore
("a good man but triflingly timid") all the irritations of his impatience. However, Manuela took charge; she saw that the doctor's
orders were followed, and herself assumed the duties of his confidential secretary. She decided who would and who would not see
the Liberator, ordered the staff about, and emerged in this moment of his illness as the dominant person in his circle, part
amazon and part hetaira — "the ideal woman," said Dublin-born
Captain Fergusson, for a fighter such as Bolívar.

Bolívar did not accept this new arrangement willingly. He hated
the feeling of being swallowed up by a woman, especially by such
a capable, passionate, and determined young woman as Manuela.
He fought against her as much as his illness allowed. Yet she had
her way, and he improved noticeably with his days of rest. He was
still convalescent when she brought him a distinguished visitor.

He was a spruce, pock-marked, cat-faced dandy, a sturdily built man with a fine resonant voice. His leaden complexion, thick lips, and tightly curled dark hair, clubbed in a cadogan, suggested Negro blood. He was dressed in the latest Beau Brummel fashion, with trousers strapped under polished boots and high-collared coat of stylish London brown. Diamond studs stayed his cambric shirt, a diamond ring flashed on his finger, the jeweled watch in his florid waistcoat carried a golden chain with a gold nugget still buried in the quartz of its birth. His hands were manicured like those of a duchess, and the scent of eau de cologne was heavy about him. Yet there was more about him than this: he was the intellectual force of the revolution, and his name was Bernardo Monteagudo. He had come to claim Bolívar's protection.

So this was the man whose applied revolutionary metaphysics had brought down the house of General San Martín; Bolívar could feel his charm. His mind had the knife-sharpness of a guillotine, and he expressed himself eloquently and persuasively. As the great formulator of revolutionary thought — the Tom Paine of South America, so to speak — he was a man of importance, and his plea for protection demanded the most careful consideration. He was another of those whom Manuela had known so well in Lima. She would supply information about him — his personality, his background, his political career — when it was needed.

Monteagudo was a patriot, an Argentinian, he had been San Martín's man since the beginning. As a university student he had become involved in the Lautaro Masonic lodge, a hotbed of revolt; had been sentenced to death, pardoned, and exiled. Throwing in his lot with San Martín, he had returned to Argentina in 1812, written the manifestos, raised the troops, organized the civilian revolutionaries — and emerged the most important man in the movement, after its field commander. When Lima was occupied, he became *the* power in Peru; and he used that power ruthlessly in the carrying out of his ideals.

Everything Spanish was anathema to him, and he was always

in a hurry. To bring the new order to birth — and he, like Bolívar, thought in terms of an entire continent freed and reorganized — everything old must go. There must be a new organization of society, a new economy, new political forms; new names for the cities, the streets, and buildings; even new calendars and new emotions; morals too must change, echoing the extremes of the French Revolution. And all who opposed these reforms must be eliminated.

Obsessed with power, he executed his plans without scruple. He confiscated estates, banished many hundreds of well-liked royalists, sent even more to the gallows — including some who were undoubted patriots, but of a different stamp from this charming mulatto. His utter indifference to personalities and past services brought inevitable discord. He created a host of enemies, and soon they were actively plotting against him. Only his high office as Minister of State in San Martín's government saved him from assassinations; and his reply to such plots, as to all opposition, was an ever greater application of the terror. Soon all the factions in Lima, differing in all else, agreed on one single fact — their uncompromising hatred of Monteagudo.

When San Martín sailed for Guayaquil their chance came. They seized him, trussed him up like cotton in a bale, and bundled him onto a ship for Panama; he was proscribed and he would be executed if he should ever set foot in Peru again.

Now here he was in Quito. His future presented a serious problem, and so Manuela, while she liked him personally and had felt the influence of many of his ideas, still was against making him a political ally. She knew the people of Lima would resent it bitterly; they would feel that, in protecting Monteagudo, Bolívar was setting himself up against them. It would be political imprudence of the worst sort. But Bolívar was not convinced by her arguments. He was desperate for men of Monteagudo's intellectual capacity. He had field commanders, ambassadors, precise legal minds to draft laws and constitutions, all these in abundance. But men of vision, men who could see America in broad terms, men who thought as he did of a united continent—of them, there were hardly any. Monteagudo was such a man.

Besides, Monteagudo agreed that something must be done about Peru. The country would inevitably be reconquered by royalist arms unless help was despatched promptly. There was only one way to save Peru, and at the same time implement Bolívar's vision of a united South America. That was for him personally to lead his army south, and defeat the *godos* in a last great battle. The whole plan was filled with jeopardy yet he would have to take the risk. And he would have to find an excuse for immediate action.

The excuse was not long in appearing. A delegation from Peru arrived in Quito bearing urgent messages from the *junta*. Their strength was fast ebbing, the Spaniards were pressing ever closer, the situation was desperate for Peru, and for the entire continent. Would the Republic of Gran Colombia, would Simón Bolívar himself, intervene in their war and save their independence? Here was the opportunity he had wanted, the end to all uncertainty. He took his pen, and to its leaders he wrote: "I have decided to save your country from the tyrants."

Throughout the spring and the summer of 1823 men and material poured down to Guayaquil, the port of embarkation. The city swarmed with royalist spies, yet no attempt was made to hide the operation. Bolívar was preparing his army for service in Peru. Here were lancers from Venezuela in their jaguar-skin shakos, hard-riding *llaneros* who rode their horses into battle barefoot, and who could live on strips of sun-dried beef and fight in all climates. There were grenadiers from Colombia, seasoned troops efficient in mass attack, and the British Legion's "Rifles Regiment," sprinkled with Scots, English, German, Russian and Irish veterans of Waterloo. There were Ecuadorian regiments, newly uniformed in green homespuns piped with red, who had been hardened by the Andean campaigns. All of these, the flower of the allied armies, came down in a steady stream to the port of Guayaquil. Transportation problems were enormous. The patriot fleet was small, but it was being increased by the daring attacks of two English *condottiere* sea captains, Illingsworth and Wright. They raided the seas for Spanish ships, disposed of the crews by cheerfully dumping them into the placid Pacific or hanging them at the yardarms, and added their prizes to the allied fleet. Yes, inexorably each problem was being resolved. General Sucre was chosen as field commander of the armies, to precede Bolívar to Peru with the main body of the troops. Food, uniforms, munitions were arriving daily; everything was abundant. Everything except one thing — money.

Simón Bolívar had little concept of high finance. His family had once been the richest in all South America, he had been reared as a gentleman, money had always been available. Now, even though the wars had consumed almost all of his inheritance, he still lived as he had been taught to live, with no thought to expense. He was generous to excess, giving away most of his presidential salary as pensions to war widows or gifts to wounded veterans, spending the rest for purposes of state. Most of the financing for the war had to come from Colombia, which was impoverished by years of struggle. With its entire commerce dislocated, its famous haciendas ruined by the holocaust of battle, the Republic found it a fearful financial burden. Yet it was from Bogotá that Bolívar demanded funds for the continuation of the war. Money, money, money: these were the three elements of final victory.

"And speaking of money," wrote his Vice-President in answer to one of Bolívar's petulant requests for additional funds, "today there is not a centavo in the Treasury. The budget of this government alone consumes 1500 to 2000 pesos daily. You need money urgently. What do we do now, my general?"

Francisco de Paula Santander, the Vice-President of Gran Colombia, had been writing to Bolívar more and more in this vein. He was clearly irritated by the demands put upon him, and he did not like what he called the "Peruvian adventure." Even now, in the midst of final preparations for the campaign, he kept urging Bolívar to return to Colombia. The country needed the unifying effect of his presence. To all such requests Bolívar remained adamant:

> But realize this . . . I now belong not only to the Colombians . . . nor do I belong to Caracas. I belong to the whole nation; besides there is still the royalist army, which wants to conquer Peru.

In the end Bolívar's arguments prevailed; funds did arrive from Colombia. But there were still delays that affected the whole campaign. Dispatches sent him from the Congress in Bogotá seemed over-long in coming, even allowing for the six weeks it ordinarily took a messenger to ride the thousand intervening miles of Andean upland, precipitous river valley, and tropical jungle. He needed news, reports, copies of the latest decrees, and they came too slowly. He needed an "Enabling Act" to permit him to leave the territory of Gran Colombia and lead the expedition to Peru; it did not come at all. Gradually it dawned on Bolívar that all this delay was no mere accident; it was made by a man, not a god, and that man was Santander.

He knew Santander well — very well. He could remember the day, years before, when Santander had been one of his military officers and they were battling the *godos*. He had ordered an attack, the other had refused to obey — until Bolívar, turning on him with drawn pistol, had shouted, "You will give the order to charge; otherwise you will shoot me, for I will most certainly shoot you."

Yet Santander had been brave enough on other occasions, and he actually enjoyed the sight of bloodletting. He always attended executions, relished the sight of a body squirming at the end of a rope, and made formal appointments with captured royalist agents to "celebrate our meeting in the public square."

Perhaps his mixed heritage had something to do with this, for in his veins he had the blood of the conquistador Diego de Colmenares which mingled with that of an Indian cacique's daughter. He was a real American. He had done great work in the civil sphere, organizing the Republic, drafting its Constitution, con-

solidating the victory, administering the thousand and one details
of the nation's financial and legal management. Yet he had no
grasp whatever of Bolívar's continental visions; his own horizon
was limited by the skyline of Gran Colombia, he was not adven-
turous, and he thoroughly disliked Bolívar's form of personalized
government. He was a perfect bureaucrat, dominating and imperi-
ous — "a man of laws," as Bolívar contemptuously described him
to Manuela

While he fulfilled the presidential functions in Bolívar's absence from the capital, he became enamored of power. Now he
was trying to contain Bolívar in the orbit of the Republic, and
this when anyone but a clodpoll could see that Gran Colombia
had no safety as long as a huge enemy army stood undefeated on
its borders. As it was, Santander already gave signs of emerging as
a serious rival for Bolívar's authority.

Manuela did not know Santander, except as Bolívar had described him to her, and as he was pictured in those posters and
broadsides which, printed on Quito's one press, were already
bringing to the whole country the portraits of the heroes of the
revolution. These portraits, steel engravings for the most part,
showed the Vice-President as a handsome man of good bearing,
whose dark, slightly slanted eyes suggested his Indian blood.
Black hair accentuated the pallor of his skin, giving it an almost
gangrenous look, his expression was one of hauteur. She did not
like that face; it showed a character proficient in the dilatory arts
of negotiation, in scheming, in underhanded trickery. To her,
whose reactions were prompt and profound, it was very simple.
She did not like Santander. She hated him He was the enemy. He
was Manuela's personal enemy; for he stood in the path of Bolívar's
plans for final victory, and Bolívar's loves were now her loves, his
hates her hates. She began to hate Santander with vehemence; and
since she could never distinguish between a personality and an
argument, and as she had no special gift of reticence, she began
to say cutting things about him in public.

This, of course, got back to Bogotá; and it little advanced Bolívar's cause, for Santander could now point out that the President flouted the sacred tenets of marriage just as he ignored the Constitution. As for Manuela, he dismissed her contemptuously as "La Sáenz," and asserted that she was little better than a whore. He could not know it then, but he was clashing, at a thousand miles' distance, with one of the Furies.

Time had spun out to August of 1823. The transports had been sailing south to Peru throughout all the season. General Sucre with an army of five thousand troops was now in Lima. The dispatches coming up from him were full of foreboding, the royalists were on the march, and they had no intention of allowing a fully equipped allied army to gain further foothold. The chaotic political conditions in Lima made it impossible to carry on military operations. Without the magic of Bolívar's presence, all would be lost. He must come to Peru at once.

Bolívar in hectic impotence made another plea to Santander: "The commandant of the transports said that if I do not go to Peru it is useless to send another single soldier."

And still the Enabling Act did not come.

At length he decided to defy the Congress; he would go without the Enabling Act; he ordered the frigate *Chimborazo* to prepare to sail, and instructed his staff and a contingent of hussars to embark. And there was a final skirmish. It was with Manuela. She expected to accompany the military transports back to Lima, for she now felt herself an integral part of Bolívar's official circle. But it was not to be; Bolívar cherished his freedom too dearly. He had regained his old strength, and Manuela was no match for him. She remained behind.

Then, just before the *Chimborazo* lifted anchor, a courier galloped up on a mud-spattered mule with an official dispatch from the Congress of the Republic. It contained Bolívar's Enabling Act; he was now legally free to leave the country and to take command of the allied armies for the liberation of Peru.

As the frigate sailed from Guayaquil on August 8, 1823, Simón

Bolívar had reason to congratulate himself. He had triumphed over space, and time, and the titanic difficulties of nature. He had won over Santander, and the Congress. He was going to Peru on his own terms. And he had slipped out of the terrifying tentacles of Manuela. These were all victories, and he could list them with some of his best-fought battles. He had taken the measure of everything, he had considered everything, and he had triumphed over everything.

Everything except a single undefinable element — love. He had not counted on the power of that ambiguous monosyllable.

He still had to contend with Manuela.

Summer

The Years 1823–1827

PART TWO
Lima

6

LIMA, CITY OF CHAOS

Bolívar was the idol of Lima the moment he set foot in Peru. He was its one hope. To the patriots, those who massed along the tree-shaded highway that ran the seven miles from the Pacific to the walled city, Bolívar was the savior, the hero who would assure final victory. To others, who had grown lukewarm toward the Republic, he was at least the symbol of order, order out of chaos. He was received like a king. On that sun-splashed day of September 3, 1823, the Lord Mayor of Lima appeared to welcome him wearing a coat of sanguine red; a salute of twenty-one guns was fired from the fortress that dominated the port of Callao, and the sumptuous blue and gold six-wheeled coach of the Viceroy, with lackeys in powdered perukes and silk knee breeches, was offered to the Liberator for his triumphant entry. All along the tree-embowered highway, the green-uniformed soldiers of his Colombian army stood guard, under orders to cheer his coming like a claque. But there was no need of it. The welcome was spontaneous, delirious. The dashing quality of his past victories, the sacrifice of his personal fortune, his creative manipulation of human lives, his passion for America, the lyrical quality of his logic, the all-encompassing humanity which seemed to exude from him, captured the imagination of everyone who lined the route.

It was Bolívar's first glimpse of Peru. Since the days of his youth he had heard about the capital of the most important viceroyalty of America. It was the center of luxury and culture; its women were famed for their small feet and enchanting manners and the men for the opulence of their dress. It was the Paris of South America.

The land was immense and captured his imagination. For as soon as his ship had left the jungle-fringed shores of Ecuador and passed into Peruvian waters, the scene had changed abruptly. It was as his pilot had said it would be· "When you no longer see any trees you will be in Peru." The aridity of the land was almost impossible to believe. Along the coast it was not only dead — for dead implied having once lived — the land was unliving. Without trees, grass, or even cactus. Back of the coastal desert was the overwhelming eminence of the Andes, its immense rock walls veiled in a blue haze, gigantic, overpowering.

Yet the air was chilled; and a cold ocean current prevented the fall of rain, transforming a thousand miles of coastline into wasteland. Lima, which lay inland from the sea, seven miles from its port of Callao, was actually an oasis in the vast Peruvian desert. The gleaming whiteness of Lima's towers with the Andes as a backdrop, and the high crescent-shaped walls that encircled them, could be seen miles away Between Lima and the sea was the desert; here was none of the perfume of the tropics, nothing of the smell of dank earth or the musical swish of palm fronds; it was savage and waterless.

As Bolívar rode along the three-lane highway under the gossamer shadow of trees planted at mathematical distances, his experienced military eyes took in the strategic problems of the land, the arena in which he must fight. At the harbor was the gray-stoned fortress, its walls lashed by the sea; it had never been taken by storm, and was considered impregnable Then here was the highway which could bring troops in a rapid three-hour march to the walls of Lima. Back of the city, from one of the five fortress-gateways, a road led up to the interior of the Andes. All around it was the desert

As he passed along the highway, crowds left their places at the roadside and poured in behind the coach, overwhelming him with humanity. Ahead, the bastions of Lima were crowded with people, who draped themselves over the parapets, and thronged beside the Callao Gate.

This massive portal was the most direct gate to the sea. Over the entrance were the sculptured arms of Carlos IV, King of Spain, which five years of siege and countersiege had not yet effaced, to their left, the escutcheon of the City of Lima, a crowned double eagle with black outstretched wings, on a blue field with three golden stars, to their right, the symbol of the Board of Trade.

In front of the gateway stood the guard of honor, soldiers of the Peruvian Legion uniformed in blue with red facings and top-heavy bearskin shakos. A saber flashed in the sun, and above the cheers a bugler sounded the blast that ceremoniously opened the gates of the city.

Once inside the city walls, Lima took on for Bolívar the air of a sensuous Seville; Moorish balconies carved in arabesques over-hung the cobblestone streets, giving it much of the atmosphere of cities of southern Spain. Lima avenues, quaintly named — Street of the Egg, Street of the Scriveners, Seven Sins, Saber-makers, But-ton-makers — were laid down by exact plan, like a chessboard. And above the houses of limited horizon rose the turrets, cupolas and barbicans of the churches, towering over the flat dwellings. Taller than all the rest rose the spire of Santo Domingo, from whose pinnacle the bronze figure of Fame blew his trumpet into Lima's cloudless heavens.

Bolívar instantly noted this was not the Lima described to him so often by Manuela. The Moloch of war had taken its toll. When Manuela was first there in 1817, the city was filled with the car-riages of the nobility, who lived within the richly designed ba-roque of their châteaux with paneled rooms echoing the *hôtels* of Chantilly. Now Bolívar saw the great houses fallen into neglect; the avenues were filled with filth, and the water which ran down the gutters in the center of the streets was dammed by a concentra-tion of litter.

There was a shabby gentility about Lima, even though the people had done their utmost to present its best side to the man who was to restore order. Still this disorder was understandable. For the royalists, taking advantage of the confusion caused by General San Martín's self-imposed exile, had moved on Lima just before Bolívar sailed to Peru. They forced the defenders to flee to the fortress at Callao; they took the city, and systematically looted it. The royalists remained only five days — long enough, however, to hang a few of the patriot leaders they caught within the city, and to extract a huge sum from the inhabitants. The venerable Judge Prevost, United States Consul, wrote to John Quincy Adams·

> The rear guard under the Royalist General Canterac left their encampment in Lima on the night of the 16th of July . . . Except in the destruction of a few Private Houses . . . of Individuals distinguished by their adherence to the revolution the Spaniards have deviated from their usual savage mode of Warfare . . . 300,-000 dollars were levied in the first contribution and about 200,000 in value carried away in Merchandise.

The *godos* had also carried away some lives A few patriots were left dangling like fruit from the trees of Lima. One of them was cut down from the gibbet, and trussed up by the arms to a cross near the plaza. A lantern was placed above his head to enable the passers-by to read an inscription: *Here dangles Besanilla until the insurgents enter Lima.*

When the official receptions were over, Bolívar found himself the military dictator of Peru. And with that, he stepped down from the enchanting pedestal of a demigod into the mire of political confusion.

There were, he reckoned up, four distinct republican armies in Lima — Peruvian, Chilean, Argentinian, Colombian — all obeying different commanders and all with different ideas of how the war should be waged. There were also, in addition to the dictator, two rival presidents fighting each other. One of these, a *ci-devant* marquis, José de Torre Tagle, was supposed to answer in the conduct of his offices to a non-functioning Congress, while the Congress answered to no one. Three hundred miles to the north another president held forth; this was the self-assured, sensitive Riva Aguero. He had held office legitimately, then had been deposed; but he refused to be put aside, and had set up a rival republican government of his own. Now even Bolívar was bewildered. "Peruvian affairs have reached a peak of anarchy . . . Only the enemy is well organized, united, strong, energetic and capable."

He had fallen into just the trap that he wanted to avoid. He had come to Peru to fight the Spaniards; but now, as "dictator," he was enmeshed in a civil war. Each faction was trying to persuade him to use his Colombian legions to crush the other It was an extremely delicate matter; the success of his mission, of the war, of his plans and even his glory, depended now on the direction of his decision. He was soon sick of the whole business, and within days of his arrival was saying to a friend, "I am already regretting that I came here."

Bolívar found it difficult to make decisions in the city; he felt a strange languor he had never felt before. What was this insidious undermining spell of Lima? Was it the atmosphere? He had to work with deliberation; he needed time to think, to plan, to work out his strategy; he could not do this in the heart of Lima. So he left the palace of the Viceroys, and retired to what had been their summer home outside the city walls.

Magdalena, a short distance from the sea, was a delightful little village, an oasis eight miles west of Lima. It lay in a tree-embowered swale which had been a choice and fashionable summer resort since the early eighteenth century. The viceregal villa was an informal structure built of sun-dried bricks; it had large open-grilled windows, and an imposing double stairway that led to the great entrance doors. In front was a little plaza, deeply shadowed by huge strangler-fig trees which dropped their pallid aerial roots all over the fruit-littered earth. About the patio, in back of the villa, there was a garden, planted with flowering shrubs and time-twisted olive trees. The rooms were nicely adapted to Bolívar's purposes, large and spacious rooms papered in a florid and agreeably patterned design. The furniture was in the French provincial style, and the floors were made of sienna-colored tile that echoed to the high-heeled boots of the staff members. Within days Bolívar was installed in the villa. Sentries were posted at the doors, hussars with long sabers that dragged on the ground were stationed around the square, and a nearby house was preempted as a stable for the horses of the couriers.

War councils were held daily. An intelligence office was set up; and the city was scoured for the rumors, the gossip, the tittle-tattle of informers and chatterers, from which could be sifted out the pattern of public opinion. *Agents provocateurs* were sent out to tempt members of the warring factions to reveal their plans. Much news, and more speculation, came in; but every piece of information seemed to lead Bolívar further into the morass of uncertainty.

Most of his old companions-at-arms moved out to the villa to give council on his decisions. General Sucre, showing the strain of political confusion, sat in on all the deliberations; he was best when he discussed the problems in purely military terms. Young Córdoba, now a general, who eternally vented his spleen at the inactivity, gave nothing but silence at the councils, he was in his element only when he was on the battlefield. It was Jacinto Lara who advised Bolívar to caution. Tall and formal, with none of the flamboyance of his fellow officers, Lara was a Venezuelan and a man of mature years. He was the only one from whom Bolívar would take any personal criticism; he was in essence Bolívar's conscience, a balance to the Liberator's impetuosity.

The Minister of War, Tomás de Heres, insisted that the real problem was the Spaniards. They had a force of nine thousand men which was daily being augmented by the deserters from the patriot forces. The *godos* were well trained, well equipped; and they were led by some of Spain's best officers, many of whom had seen service in the European wars. They controlled the mountains, the heartland of Peru, with eight squadrons of the best cavalry ever seen in the Americas; the foot soldiers were well fed, well paid, and well disciplined. Therefore, before the patriots

could move on them, they must first rebuild their army. The Irish
contingent attached to Bolívar's staff were of the same cast of
thought. Arthur Sandes, who had grown a bristling blond guards-
man's mustache since his elevation to the command of the Rifles,
knew that his men, originally a British legion, had to be reorganized for a campaign in the Andes. After him, O'Leary, O'Connor
and the good-natured William Fergusson expressed themselves in
turn. But these were military opinions The problem now was political. How could Bolívar find the ends of this tangled skein of
Peruvian politics?

And then to complicate matters Manuela arrived.

Bolívar had almost forgotten Manuela. Perhaps he had believed
that, when he left her in her native land, it would be the end of
their relationship. But now here she was again. She had come
down on the brig *Helena* in the middle of September, and had
been given the cabin usually reserved for the master's wife. Captain Simpson, a good judge of Irish whisky and women, and in the
service of the patriots, believed himself a servant of Eros in bringing her to Peru. In private, General Bolívar told him he was something else. In Quito there had been no problem of a husband; but
here in Peru . . . And even though James Thorne was in Chile,
the disagreeable fact was that this was Lima, where Thorne resided. Here there could be no subterfuge, no disguise; and with
everyone all-knowing . . .

General Lara, thinking of the moment, spoke his mind. Manuela's coming here was most inopportune. But Manuela was aware
of no "problem." She brought her slaves and her trunks of clothes,
and settled down only a few squares from Bolívar's villa, in "my
house . . . in the village of La Magdalena where I have always
resided."

Manuela then went about renewing her old friendships. She
ignored the "problem." She drove in her two-wheeled *calesa*
through the shabby streets of Lima; she moved casually in her
habit-pattern of months before, as if her life had not changed
since she left Lima a year ago. Her slaves, delighted to be in Lima,

circulated again among the strange fraternities which the Negro servants, freed and bound, were allowed Manuela picked up the business activities of her husband — she held his power of attorney — and within days she was back in the intimate circles of Lima society.

Casual affairs were commonplace in Lima, but there was an accepted protocol; they were conducted *en tapadillo* — on the quiet; a lady never flaunted her love affairs in the public face. It was socially unforgivable in Manuela even though her visits were nocturnal; for "it was usually at night that Manuelita went to the General's rooms."

This did not matter; it was known.

Once again Simón Bolívar was feeling the impact of Manuela's personality. Of course it was delightful to see her in a fashionable gown, the short sleeves puffed and the low *décolletage* showing the tantalizing ivory of her breasts. And she was exciting to be with, for she was a match for his passionate nature, and she knew how to discipline his natural polygamy with a suspense which no other woman that he had ever known possessed.

In some curious way, passion and utility had coalesced in her, and he found that he was more and more relying on her judgments of people. Manuela was in her element. Lima was, it seemed, created for her, it was a sympathetic milieu for her type of being. She had contact with the strangest congeries of people. She knew and was intimate with all of Lima's nobility; she knew the patriots, the vacillating and the strong, and the fact that she belonged to the Order of the Sun put her on an equal footing with Peru's most distinguished families. Then through her husband's contacts she knew all the English merchants, she spoke English with them, and judged by the barometer of their business how they estimated the success of the patriot cause. She kept her eyes and ears open at all times, to sense the drift of feelings and opinions. She knew intimately almost everyone with whom Bolívar had to deal, their weaknesses and their hidden scandals. And her two slaves, especially the irrepressible Jonotás of the barbarically colored turbans, brought her the talk, the rumors, the gossip of the lower echelons of society. All this became part of Bolívar's network of intelligence, and it was important. But more important still was Manuela herself. She was bound to him in fierce loyalty. He could depend on her, and in this immense land, divided against itself, where he could never be sure of his trust, it was good to have someone such as Manuela about: "I shall always be a foreigner to most people and I shall always arouse jealousy and distrust."

Manuela was liked by all of Bolívar's staff, the Irish, the English, the native Americans. They found that she could transmit to him many unpleasant truths which they could not tell him; she had his ear in more ways than one. And while she idolized him, she kept a sense of humor and proportion, and was never afraid to expatiate to him on his faults. Manuela had suddenly become a vital necessity to the Liberator.

By October, despite the objections of General Lara, Manuela was officially added to Bolívar's staff. At the suggestion of Colonel O'Leary, who in time became deeply attached to her, she was put in charge of his personal archives. She took her new duties seriously. And she dressed for the role. She gave herself the rank of colonel and appeared at headquarters in blue tunic with scarlet cuffs and collar, and on each golden epaulet, where a blue cloth strip carried the symbol of rank, she embroidered a silver laurel leaf. She flung herself into her duties with the fervor with which she did everything, and she soon made herself so much a part of the Liberator's *ménage* that it did not seem at all *outré* to have her attached to the general staff.

José Palacios, the General's major-domo, was delighted to have her with them. His two mastiffs remembered her from Quito, and when not walking beside the red-headed, blue-eyed José, they lay on the cool sienna-colored tile floor beside Manuela. Palacios, while he did not like her two slaves, was happy to share the responsibility of the Liberator's well-being with someone else. He had promised Bolívar's mother — whose maiden name of Palacios he bore — that he would never leave Simón's side; and he never did. Although he could neither read nor write, he was remarkably astute. His chromosomes had produced a startling pattern; with Spanish, Negro and Indian blood in his veins, he had, strangely enough, blue eyes and red curly hair. He was built like a gladiator, yet he was as simple as a child; he had a head that was hard as jacaranda and a heart as capacious as his big body. He and his dogs followed Bolívar everywhere — on long trips the two huge beasts rode in traveling baskets — and until Manuela came into their ménage he loved nothing else but these.

Manuela was now, as she wished, in the center of operations. There was a steady stream of visitors to headquarters: a general wanting more arms, an army paymaster complaining that he needed silver if the troops were not to go unpaid again, merchants, politicians, soldiers, mothers. Between audiences Bolívar, lying in a hammock or furiously pacing back and forth, dictated to his secretaries. His letters flooded South America and encircled the globe — letters to Italy, France, England, and North America. Manuela worked closely with the secretaries: young Diego Ibarra, a distant cousin of the General, José Pérez, whose reputation with the ladies was worse than hemlock; and Colonel Juan Santana, the principal amanuensis. Juan became an understanding friend to her, and there sprang up between them a lifelong tie, an indisputable connection without ambiguity. Santana, not much over twenty-five, had been born in Caracas, but he had gone to college in Baltimore and learned to speak English. It was difficult to serve one as protean as Bolívar, and the General found him wanting in enthusiasm:

> Everything is cold in Santana· his spirit, his heart, his morals . . . he has a melancholy humor and is already a young misanthrope. . . He is not a military man in spite of his title of Colonel, but he knows how to keep a secret. Such is Santana.

But Manuela liked him, and he adored her; and throughout the war she could always rely on Santana for intimate details of her lover. He gave her copies of all the Liberator's personal letters to keep in her archives, and she guarded them like a castellan. She allowed no exceptions to the ukase of Bolívar that no one should see his letters except at his command. Even Heres, the Minister of War, could not pry an important paper from her. At length he was forced to complain to Bolívar:

> I have need to publish an important document in facsimile. I asked for the letter from Manuelita, but she, following your orders, gave me great difficulty before I finally succeeded in obtaining it.

There had been in the weeks that followed some improvement in political affairs in Lima. Bolívar was able to convince the Congress, which met to hear of his plans, of the necessity for his full and complete control over Peru for the period of emergency. "I promise you," he said, "that my authority will not exceed the time necessary to prepare for victory."

His name remained the talisman of ultimate victory. Even in the darkest moments he never lost hope, and his optimism was reflected, for a time, in the people:

> I am now more delighted with Lima every day. So far, I have gotten along very well with everyone. The men respect me and the women love me. That is all very nice. They hold many pleasures for those who can pay for them. . . . Naturally I lack for nothing The food is excellent, the theater only fair, but adorned by beautiful eyes . . . the carriages, horses, excursions, Te Deums . . . nothing is lacking but money.

And unity. There had recently been more desertions; and in the walled city of Trujillo, three hundred miles to the north, the *soi-disant* President of Peru, the title-proud José de la Riva Agüero, was now in open traitorous rebellion; Bolívar's spies had intercepted his correspondence with the Viceroy. He was making overtures to the Spanish enemy. Bolívar tried compromise and he offered propitiation:

> The ruin of Peru, Sir, is inevitable, if under these circumstances you hesitate for a moment to accept my generous offer of amnesty.

The offer was refused. Bolívar knew now that he must move, but with caution; for this was no ordinary man. Riva Agüero was proud, capable, and as untouchable as a sensitive plant, he was an unquiet character, with frigid manners and heroic gestures. He had been born in Lima in 1783 of a blood so blue it could have been used as litmus paper; his mother was the daughter of the Marquis de Monte Alegre, his father a grandee of Spain. He was well educated and held several important posts under the Viceroy; but after the revolution began to take hold, he worked alongside Manuela as a secret agent of San Martín. He was the author of many of those seditious broadsides which republican agents plastered on Lima's walls at night. When the city fell to the patriots, he emerged as one of its leaders — which verified, said O'Leary, "the parable that those who come in at the eleventh hour receive as much as those who have borne the heat and burden of the day."

Riva Agüero belonged, however, to a class of men that is willing to sacrifice the principle for the form. After the self-exiling of San Martín he became the leader of Peru, and for the moment that followed he was indefatigable. He raised money, floated a loan in England, entered into an agreement with foreign merchants to fit out the troops, and invited Bolívar to Peru. But fatal strategic errors in sending out his troops to engage the royalists left the city open to attack, and after the Spaniards had occupied Lima and walked off with half a million dollars, the Congress tossed him out of office. But he refused to be tossed. He fled to Trujillo where he began to raise an army of his own — and to conspire with the royalist forces in the Andes. He was clever, but his very cleverness was his undoing. Bolívar now had his correspondence with the enemy. So, when Riva Agüero's aide-de-camp rode into the Liberator's headquarters ostensibly to carry on negotiations, he was shown the intercepted letters.

There was no doubt. The officer agreed to capture Riva Agüero for Bolívar. But Bolívar took no chances. As soon as the other had departed on his perfidious mission, he gave the marching orders to his troops and called up all his ships. Then on November 15th he left Lima for the north to crush the opposition.

Manuela was now the grand vizier of what had once been the Viceroy's villa. Lima, or at least its aristocratic society, was aghast at her metamorphosis into *the* woman of Peru; the ladies were shocked down to their silken ballet slippers. It was unthinkable. This notorious little bastard! She had now — was it really possible? — the same social power as a Viceroy's consort! With Bolívar gone, and she in the villa, she had become a sort of *maîtresse-en-titre* of the government! It was too much, quite too much.

A whispering campaign against her was already in progress. Manuela reacted to it precisely as expected: no shadings, no prudence, no balance. She made a point of going out of her way to shock society; she used her power in army circles; and to cap the climax she flung in the face of Josefa, the wife of the Marquis de Torre Tagle, her own loose morals. It was an unwise thing to do, even if it was Manuela's way.

"In Lima," said her confidant, "Manuelita behaved with startling imprudence. She became a Messalina. The aide-de-camp of the general told me some unbelievable things which Bolívar alone ignored. But then lovers, when they are in love, are as blind as husbands."

Then, to worsen matters, Bernardo Monteagudo returned to Lima.

It was an act that was either very brave or very stupid. For if the people of Lima could agree on nothing else, they agreed on Monteagudo; he was universally hated. He had been perpetually exiled from Peru, placed out of the protection of the law, yet now he was above the law for he had returned to Lima under Bolívar's protection. The public had full notice that to strike at little Dr. Monteagudo was to strike at Bolívar; and there was no one yet in Lima who could have nerved himself to raise a hand against the Liberator. The aristocrats, who had suffered most from Monteagudo, plotted his death openly, but fear stayed their hands.

Meanwhile, with money supplied to him by the Peruvian treasury, he kept up his opulent style of living. His table, thanks to the French chef he had brought with him, was the most exquisite in Lima, and coffee — few people drank it — was his passion. He exhibited his showy exterior — the diamond pin in his white stock, the golden chain on his waistcoat, the pungent smell of eau de cologne. Lima observed this with fury. No one was interested any longer in the concealed depths of Monteagudo; the razor-sharp intelligence, the fine prose style, the incisive phrases No one cared a fig for his visions of America and the history-making Congress of Panama, the League of American Nations, which he was now drafting. Hatred allows no shadings: Monteagudo, there could be no doubt, was marked for death.

The population of Lima had become a legion of discontent. A chorus of female voices bewailed the scarcity of food and the dearness of it. They cursed the royalists, the patriots, the army. They cried out at the cost of supporting eight thousand inactive troops, half of them foreigners. The people were sick of war. They were angry at the privations, and at the depredations committed by both sides. The soldiers within Lima, as well as those who held the fortress of Callao, demanded their wages, now six months in arrears. And there were rumors that a group of aristocrats, once ardent patriots, were plotting to change sides again.

All this news, with the added spice of personalia, Manuela put into her letters to Simón Bolívar.

At least Bolívar had been successful in one way. By the time he reached the walled city of Trujillo, Riva Agüero had been captured by his own officers, and the fear of civil war had been averted. Released from an odious undertaking, Bolívar was generous to the rebels. He incorporated the officers and the soldiers into his own army, and even though the Marquis de Torre Tagle in Lima wanted the head of his rival, the defeated rebel was allowed to go into exile. He eventually reached Belgium, where he found some comfort in marrying Carolina de Loos, a Flemish aristocrat.

While the army was being reorganized, Simón Bolívar traveled in the interior, trying to get an estimate of the supplies that he could obtain for an offensive against the Spanish army So Manuela's letters about the state of affairs in Lima never came to him. Instead Juan Santana answered:

My Esteemed Lady,

At this moment I have received your letter with which you have had the kindness to favor me, and I am all the more grateful to you, as I have not kept my word that I would keep you informed, having been absent from general headquarters and having rejoined it only four days ago. In proof of my gratitude, I want to be the first to give you the news that I know will be extremely agreeable to you.

Within four days the General marches toward Lima, and I think he will pass the whole summer in that city. The faction of Riva Aguero has been destroyed, his troops and this vast province obey the legitimate government of Peru; and I confess that never has the Liberator worked with such cleverness, with such political skill and judgment, as on this occasion. If Peru is grateful, it must give to this event all the credit of a brilliant victory; it prepares us for another that will seal the glory of the Liberator and the independence of this unhappy country. Ah, my señora Manuelita, what a country this is, and what men! With what sorrow I see the general taking it so much to heart, but I have confidence in his good fortune, and no one can be unhappy who gives so much happiness. Finally, señora, I would like to go on at length, there is much I could say to you about these things, but my destiny is to write a great deal, but nothing of my own . . .

For the first time I sign myself

Your affectionate friend,
Juan Santana

Bolívar was paying heavily for his activity. He had had several warnings, while he was riding up the Andes, that the strain was too much, and Dr. Moore had tried in his Irish way to explain the need for rest. Bolívar, as usual, would not listen. The inclination toward tuberculosis which he had inherited from his mother had already suggested itself, and Dr. Moore warned him of the "dreaded phthisis." Then it fell upon him. He coughed, spat up blood, vomited, and for days lay shivering in agonies of ague. He was brought aboard ship, but half way to Lima he had a coughing fit so terrible that the ship's master feared for his life. The vessel put into one of the desert harbors; and there at the village of Pativilca he was carried ashore in a state of collapse. Without doctor or medicine, he hovered for seven days between life and death. Rumors circulated in Lima that he was dying. Manuela was preparing to ride to him when a letter from Juan Santana stayed her trip:

14 January, 1824

MY GRACIOUS LADY,

At last I have the pleasure to tell you that the Liberator has improved so much from his illness that he is now in a state of convalescence. Nevertheless, I feel I should tell you at the same time that our return to Lima is not to be as soon as I promised it would, or as soon as all of us wish it to be My friend Medina is the bearer of this note and so he will be able to inform you of all you wish to know, and he will doubtless have much pleasure in doing so.

Here we are like souls carried off by the devil, dead from disgust and bored as we have never been bored before.

So Bolívar was out of danger. But Lima was not. Since the news of the Liberator's illness, there had been renewed activity among the dissidents. Manuela now had positive proof that the Marquis de Torre Tagle was in communication with the royalists. Bolívar had heard this from other sources too, and he raised himself from his sickbed to dictate a letter to the man he had once called "a gentleman in the whole extension of the word":

Believe me, believe me, the country will not be saved in this way. My own was liberated because we had unity and discipline. You cannot imagine what this war for liberty can be and can cost. We endured war to extinction for fourteen years, and you complain about black bread for four years. . . .

It had little effect, for José, Marquis de Torre Tagle, was only a remnant of the patriot that he had been. His pride was vast and puerile, and he was completely dominated by his wife, Josefa, who influenced him against Bolívar. She had been insulted by Manuela, by the rudeness of the Colombian troops, and by the ostentation of Monteagudo; and this, combined with the general discontent, had changed the sentiments of the Marquis. A stout, florid, handsome gentleman, who wore the blue uniform of a general of the Peruvian Legions, Torre Tagle had passed through all the phases of politics. Extravagant, indecisive, susceptible to every fleeting impression, he was as variable as a New England spring. He became a patriot when perfidy was in fashion; and when it seemed expedient to be a turncoat, he changed sides without scruples or doubts. The revolution had left him in possession of his offices, his emoluments, his estates, and his noble titles. Now the revolution had become inconvenient.

On the 4th of February at precisely 3 A.M., the fortress of Callao was betrayed. And a few days later the Marquis de Torre Tagle himself opened the gates of Lima to the royalists.

7

THE STEP OF CONQUERORS

THE *godos* were athirst.

They rode into Lima on February 12 through the East Gate, fanned out through the city, and within an hour threw a cordon around the five gates of its walls; Lima was hermetically sealed. Then, led by their informers, the blue-clad troops made a house-to-house search for the republican leaders.

It was fortunate for Manuela, for she was high on the lists of the wanted, that she was out at the villa. This allowed her the precious interval to effect an escape. As it was, had it not been for one of her slaves, she would have been caught completely unaware. Jonotás had been carrying on with a soldier of the Callao fortress, who had warned her of trouble in the offing. As a precaution Manuela had begun to box Bolívar's archives; she was deep in the process when the news reached her. Three hundred officials of the republican government went over with Torre Tagle to the royalists, and with them a cavalry battalion of the Peruvian Legions.

All was confusion at the villa. Many soldiers, fearing for their lives, ripped off their uniforms and slid into the rags of the peasants. No one paid any heed to the commands of the officers. It looked for the moment as though everyone would be lost. Then General Miller rode up with a corps of cavalry that he had managed to salvage from the betrayal, threw a cordon around

Magdalena to protect the villa, and allowed Manuela time to pack. Other officials who had escaped the royalist dragnet rode up to headquarters — General Lara, tall, calm and unruffled; Monteagudo, elegant in his English riding coat, bewailing the loss of his French chef; Heres, the War Minister, and all the rest of Bolívar's cabinet.

Judge Prevost, the United States Consul, hurrying by to take an American ship to Trujillo, said, "I am persuaded the whole plot is the work of those surrounding Torre Tagle." And he had a moment to make a report to President John Quincy Adams:

> SIR:
>
> On the 4th of the last month [February], the black troops of Bs. Ays. [Buenos Aires] to whom had been confided the Castle of Callao, in number of about 1100 mutinied, and hauling down the Flag of Peru, refused to acknowledge the further authority of the President and Congress, until their arrears in wages were paid ... At the expiration of a week, the Negroes liberated the Prisoners confined in that Fortress, hoisted the Spanish flag and sent an Agent to Canterac [General of the royalist forces] in order to advise him of the event ... and a Body of 1000 Spaniards followed to sustain the Conspirators.

And then he was gone to Trujillo, to put himself under the protection of Bolívar's troops. Manuela managed to pack all the archives, Bolívar's uniforms, his gold service plate, and some of her own clothes. Then, slipping into her uniform, she joined the squadron.

At night, under a crescent moon, they moved off across the desert. With no trees to give them cover, General Miller had to lead them in wavering patterns between the sand dunes so as to cut down their silhouette. Somewhere along the way they were joined by a group of guerrillas who formed part of Miller's cavalry. Quietly, with no sound except the swish of the sand under the horses' roofs, they made their way in the direction of the Pacific. Once off the main routes, they crossed the swollen Rimac River, made a wide detour around the little desert-bound villages, and changed their direction toward the east, riding all night until they came to the bare, inclining hills of the lower Andes.

The little squadron was dwarfed by the overwhelming Andes, a rock-hard world set on edge. The mule path they followed was so narrow that their stirruped feet scraped the overhanging cliffs; it wound round and round in caracoled ascent. Abysses yawned below them like the mouths of hell, and a slip of the horses' hoofs, a miscalculation of the rider, could cause one to slide off in fearful silence to eternity. The friable, naked rocks gave way, as the troops slowly mounted, to slopes covered with cactus. At a still higher elevation swathes of stunted trees sprang up from crannies of earth held in the interstices of rock, then these yielded, on the high plateaus, to sere grass clumps and gray-green, sharp-spined agave plants.

Two miles above sea level they rode between snow-covered mountains over a vast rolling plain, the dreaded *puna.* It was utterly deserted, lifeless and inert: a moonscape. In the incredibly blue sky dark silhouettes of condors glided, and from the chalice of a dainty red flower, growing beside an ice-cold rill, a hummingbird no larger than a human thumb was trying vainly to coax out a drop of honey. For hours, there was nothing else to see on the lonely *puna.*

The *montoneras* rode ahead of the squadron, constantly on the alert for the enemy. These mounted guerrillas tireless in the saddle had been taught by war instincts that were subhuman; they could scent the enemy before he appeared, and when pursued they could melt into the landscape of the static *puna* and vanish out of sight. They were of the dispossessed. They were men whose families had been butchered by the royalists, whose homes had been destroyed, and whose lands had been made desolate by this war without rules. In 1821 the town of Reyes on the shores of Lake Junín had been gutted by the enemy; of its four thousand people, only three hundred men survived. They formed themselves into a guerrilla band. Cutthroats, murderers, men on the run, the landless, the hungry, the disillusioned joined these *montoneras*. There were no qualifications, other than hate and the ability to ride a horse. Cruel and relentless, they served without pay, taking their money, and in no very pretty manner, from whatever *godos* they met. With their wide-brimmed felt hats, ponchos over the shoulders, and lances, cutlasses and cocked pistols, their mere appearance was enough to throw a passer-by into a frenzy of fear. They were of inestimable value to the patriot cause even while being a terror to the officials; and the only one in all Peru who did not fear them was William Miller, the general now riding beside Manuela.

This slender, blue-eyed Englishman would have seemed the last man in the world fit to command the *montoneras;* but Miller, in charge of all patriot cavalry, was a man who had earned their respect. The left hand that held his reins was permanently disabled from a bullet wound; his face was scarred by an explosion of powder that had occurred as he was preparing Congreve rockets to bomb the Spanish fleet in Callao harbor. He had lain in torment under a plaster-cast mask, fed for weeks through a silver straw before he again saw the light of day. He limped, from another wound he had got in Chile while fighting in the patriot cause. He was fearless, he was a good officer, and the *montoneras* idolized him. Miller had been born in Kent, had entered the English army at sixteen, and had fought in Spain against Napoleon's legions. As war was his forte, he came after Waterloo to Argentina to serve in the wars of independence. He was in every important action. He had fired the first shots of the campaign against the Spaniard in Peru, and he would fire the last. A gallant man, this General Miller, with his lithe figure almost feminine in its delicacy, his long nose, delicate eyebrows and light hair — and an intelligent one. It was this same warrior who would one day furnish the descriptions of the Andes over which they were now riding to William Prescott, for *The Conquest of Peru*. A discerning man, too — he liked Manuela.

For days the squadron rode northward over the *puna* in search of Bolívar. He was not in flight, as were they, but he kept shifting his headquarters so as to throw the royalists off his trail. He was also, with his staff, scouring the countryside for men, for food, for clothing, to be sent down to the army that was building on the desert coasts. No one was permitted to reveal his whereabouts or the exact location of his headquarters, so the squadron escorting Manuela, his personal papers, and his Ministers of State, Finance, and War — his "ambulatory government" — moved over the raw face of the Andes in search of him.

Now they learned what the army must face, once it left the warmer lands of the coast and mounted the Andes to do battle with the royalists. The world here was bleak and dun-colored, the temperature extreme. At night it fell below freezing. In the day the mercury rose to ninety degrees. There was no food except what the Indians raised for themselves. Cattle roamed the hills as untamed as lions; they had to be hunted like wild game. There was no place of refuge from the winds. Troops crossing the *puna* during a hailstorm had to cover their faces with their knapsacks, for a man could easily be flayed by the huge ice drops flying with the speed of a spent bullet. Manuela had seen the hands of a regiment caught in such a storm; they were raw, cut, and bleeding, like diced beefsteak. And there was the feared *soroche*, the swooning mountain sickness; for in the higher areas of the Andes, over two and a half miles above sea level, the rare atmosphere made each breath a conscious effort. Once a battalion of patriot troops passed Manuela on rapid march in the *puna*; and suddenly, as they breasted a rise in the ground, man after man toppled over as if cut down by an invisible scythe. Nowhere in world history had battles been fought on so inhospitable a terrain.

Manuela had been so numbed by the swift pace of events that not until now had she been able to appraise the disaster of Lima. The situation was appalling. With Lima and the fortress of Callao held by the Spaniards, it meant that only a thin strip of northern Peru was left in the hands of the patriots. The Andes were a no man's land. The country could support no large body of troops; the potatoes, the barley, the *quinoa* grown in these bare uplands

were barely enough to feed the Indians. Bolívar had lost the
capital, the treasury, the port that would have brought him supplies. His government was three men on horseback, his soldiers
were without the means to attack, and the enemy, ten thousand
strong, encircled him. He was faced with disaster; yet how had
Simón Bolívar replied to the question: "What will you do now,
my General?"

"I? I? Why, I will triumph."

The squadron protecting the "ambulatory government" divided
along the Andean way. Jacinto Lara, impatient at having to gear
his pace to the slow step of the pack mules carrying Manuela's
trunks and Bolívar's boxed archives — disgusted, too, with the
perfumy atmosphere of Dr. Monteagudo's eau de cologne — took
a troop of lancers, turned west, and headed toward the town of
Huarás.

The little village with its sienna-colored tile roofs lay in a protected valley below the serrated crests of the most magnificent
mountains in Peru. On both sides, east and west, four-mile-high
peaks covered by eternal glaciers held the storm winds in check
Soldiers in the blue and red uniform of the Peruvian Legion were
on guard in front of the largest house at the plaza, and at the
entrance flew the gonfalon of the Liberator.

General Lara found Bolívar paper-deep in administrative details. He had just returned from a personal survey in which he
had sequestered herds of cattle, cloth from the looms of the
Indians, and silver from the churches. After they had exchanged
views on the Lima situation, Lara announced in a voice of extreme
irritation: "Señora Manuelita and Doctor Monteagudo have arrived."

Bolívar received this news with little outward show of interest,
and turned back to the work on his desk. But General Lara would
not be stayed. "Here we are on the eve of cutting up the *godos*,
and Your Excellency is again carrying women with him" — and he
included Monteagudo among the "women."

"Well, they run the risks of the campaign."

"That is all very well," responded Lara, "but the truth is, Your Excellency, that someone will kill that little Monteagudo."

Bolívar rose up from behind the table, his voice shrill as it always was whenever he was angry:

"Just let them touch a hair of his head . . ."

And the subject was closed.

Despite the press of duties, Bolívar sent a letter to Manuela — for she had taken up residence in Huamachuco, a hundred miles distant — telling her of his delight that she had arrived safely, and expressing hope that soon the campaign would allow him to see her. Then he was off again with his staff, scouring the Andes for the sinews of war.

Along the way he decided to put up for some days at the village of San Ildefonso de Caras. It was like any other of the little villages in the Andes, houses of red tile clustering around a plaza dominated by a crumbling ancient church. The officers of the advance guard had their instructions. On their arrival in the village they sought out the Mayor, a rustic fellow whose flowing river of chins cascaded down into a soiled neckband.

In a curt military voice they repeated by rote the requirements of General Bolívar:

"There are to be rooms for His Excellency and staff, a house for a squadron of cavalry, good forage for the horses; and for personal consideration, a good room, a good table, a good bed, etcetera, etcetera, etcetera."

Did the Mayor understand? Yes, the Mayor understood. He knew how precise General Bolívar was about matters of this kind. Yes, he knew, he would follow word for word the request as given by the officers.

When they had gone, Don Pablo called in the town elders, who still wore the rural dress of the last century, coarse homespun stockings and knee breeches. To them he explained the desires of the General, who was to arrive that night. They understood all, or almost all, until they came to the "etceteras." Here an argument developed over just what was implied; but Don Pablo, who had once visited Lima and thus knew something of the world, believed that he knew what the General referred to.

That night, with the full moon reflecting its coldness on the snows of the Huarás Mountains and making the world as bright as day, Simón Bolívar clattered up to the village of San Ildefonso. Don Pablo, in a newly washed shirt, stood at the door as Bolívar strode into the apartment prepared for him. Don Pablo, rubbing his hands, itemized all that the General had required. When Bolívar entered his bedroom, there, standing in fearsome awe, with tears ready to spill from their eyes, were three of the best-looking young ladies that Don Pablo could scare up on short notice.

"And these," said Bolívar with a sweep of his hand, "who are they?"

Shaking all his six chins, Don Pablo shuffled his way to each of the three in turn.

"These, Your Excellency, are Etcetera, Etcetera, Etcetera."

The captive pigeons were released but another, named Manuel-ita Madroño, a little prize of eighteen years, of whom it was said that there was nothing else like her in the whole province, was singled out by the General. She bedded with Bolívar that night, and, as the wits at his headquarters had it, on all other nights until the full moon waned. Of course Manuela Sáenz heard of it; the episode could not be kept private even by a hundred miles of mountains. Alone, bored, angered by what she thought to have been a senseless affair, she sat down at Huamachuco and wrote her friend Juan Santana:

28th May

MY DEAR FRIEND:

Misfortune is with me, all things have their end; the General no longer thinks of me, in nineteen days he has scarcely written me twice. What is wrong? You have always professed to be my friend, can you tell me the reason? I believe you won't, because you will hold your tongue. And why should I ask *you*? But of whom shall I ask it? No one, only my own heart which is the best and only friend that I have I feel inclined to commit some absurdity; afterward I shall tell you what it is and you can tell me if what I do is not justified.

Remember in my absence her who is your very good friend,

MANUELA

P.S. Good-by until accident brings us together. I am very ill and could die, because now I no longer care to live — that is sufficient reason, don't you think?

These were rare moments in Manuela's life; she had unbounded confidence in the efficacy of her charm, and her grief was short-lived.

And soon Bolívar, in his interminable wandering, came to Huamachuco She welcomed him with passion. Their reconciliation was delicious. It was only a brief moment of love snatched from the turmoil of revolution; all the morrows were uncertain, yet the mingling of terror and delight intoxicated them.

And then Bolívar was gone.

So it went for weeks, months. They would correspond, then the break in the communications would be taken up by Santana; and Manuela, protected by a body of Colombian lancers, would follow the trail of Bolívar, dragging the boxes of archives across the indented face of the Andes.

As she took the path that led to the Huaràs headquarters, Manuela could see that preparations were already in progress for the crossing of the mountains. The strategy was so obvious, no one in the command made effort to hide it; Bolívar was going to lead his army right up the Andes into the regions commanded by the royalists, and there seek out a place for a decisive battle.

General Sucre was in charge of the Andean crossing. He knew what such an operation would entail; he had fought in the high ranges for fifteen years, and he knew that for every soldier that died in battle, a dozen died on the march. So all along the planned route of the army they were erecting wooden shelter sheds. Everything had to be brought up to this treeless land from the dry coast, or from the wet jungle. While carpenters put up the rude shelters, the soldiers kept off the royalist scouts. Indians were put to work to cut *champas,* the native peat, for fuel; other Andean dwellers were made to reveal the location of caves, where supplies could be cached. Into the caves, where the temperature was permanently at freezing, streams of Indians carried piles of *charqui,* the Andean sun-dried llama beef, rice, tobacco, salt, and sacks of cocaine-yielding coca leaves. The Indian laborers on the operation were taken under guard to the coast to be held until the army's ascent, to make certain that none would reveal the storage places to the royalists.

In the town of Huarás, Manuela was woman again. She flung off her riding uniform, selected her most feminine of dresses, and then gave herself over to Jonotás, who twisted the heavy strands of blue-black hair into a crown-like tiara, interwoven with freshly cut flowers. Now scented with verbena, wonderfully coiffed and gowned in an off-shoulder dress to reveal the alabaster of her flesh, Manuela was ready for the impromptu banquet.

Bolívar was gone, but his officers were preparing to give this terrible war one of its moments of pleasure. O'Connor, who shared a room with General Sucre, was there; so was Colonel Sandes, delighted that he could wear his dress uniform of blue trimmed with scarlet, its golden-fringed epaulets carrying the blue strap and golden laurel leaf of a full colonel. Others of Manuela's old friends were present — Captain Simpson, who had brought her down from Ecuador on the *Helena,* and the lively William Fergusson, his Spanish spiced with a Dublin brogue, who was already deep in the Irish whisky which Simpson had brought. It was the same Fergusson, but a bit subdued and chastened since his court-martial — he had been condemned to death for disobeying orders, and had been saved only at the last minute by Bolívar.

Charles Sowerby was especially gay. His men had ambushed a royalist supply train and had brought him back food and wines which had been intended for the Viceroy. He looked boyish and young, even though at twenty-nine he had seen every horror of war that could be created by man. He had marched halfway across Russia, fought with Napoleon's legions at Borodino, and in the

Americas had taken part in all the engagements. He had, and he always made a point of it, emerged from all of this without a scratch.

And so had Bruiz, who was trying to understand the French that Manuela was speaking to him. A gallant little Parisian with flamboyant manners, he had been a page to Napoleon. He too had seen service in Russia; he had been in the first contingent that swept into Moscow, and his handsome face showed a saber scar that ran from his ear to the corner of his mouth.

The evening as it went on gradually dissolved into a bacchanal. Jonotás demonstrated the lascivious *ñapanga*, Manuela enlivened it with the fashionable Peruvian *hondu*, a bolero which she danced to the tapping of Jonotás's fingers on a borrowed snare drum. Fergusson did an Irish jig. Even Sucre, who was always restrained at these gatherings, joined in and danced with Manuela.

Some time toward the end of the evening Sucre, "that complete gentleman," as O'Connor called him, turned in seriousness to Arthur Sandes. Everyone present knew that both Sucre and Sandes were in love with the same girl, the lovely eighteen-year-old Mariana, daughter of the Marquis de Solando, whom they had met at the Victory Ball in Quito.

"Don Arturo," challenged Sucre, "they say that you have the promise of marriage of the young daughter of the Marquis de Solando. I also want her. Now, if you will permit, let us try our luck to see who gets her. Let us toss a peso to see who gets the hand of the little Marquesa. If you lose, I will send my offer of marriage this very hour to Quito, even though it is a thousand miles away, so that I may marry her."

"Why not?" said Sandes. "Who knows that we might not both be killed in this bloody war, and it won't make any difference anyway."

O'Connor took a peso — tossed it into the air.

"Heads," shouted Sucre.

The coin showing the profile of the King of Spain — the Roman nose, the Hapsburg lip — on one side, the arms of Castile and Leon on the reverse, spun and fell, rolled about, then came to a tinkling halt on the floor. Staring upward was the imperial face of Charles IV.

Sucre had won.

Behind the walls of Trujillo, the third city of Peru, Bolívar had created his army. He had taken the remnants of the units from Argentina and Chile, joined them to the Peruvian Legions and the Colombian Corps, and put them under a unified command. Blue tunics trimmed with scarlet cuffs formed the official uniform, but cloth was so scarce that Bolívar was happy to buy up on credit — and therefore at fantastic prices — whatever was offered to him by English merchants. They had sent to Europe for every military garb that could be purchased. There were greatcoats designed to cover Frenchmen on their march to Moscow, hand-me-downs from the battle of Waterloo. Some officers wore patent-leather bicornes, some grenadiers wore the bearskin shakos of the Guard, others were fortunate to get in the distribution Wellington boots or thigh-high gaiters, but the army in general wore sandals, *jatas*, made from green leather. Each company was given a bullock's skin, and every soldier carved out his piece of hide to fashion his own boots. But despite the bizarre costumes it was a fine-looking army. General William Miller, who had command of the cavalry, stated to a friend, "I assure you that the Colombian infantry, as well as the cavalry, could hold a parade in St. James' Park and would attract attention."

Still, without Lima and its mint, Bolívar was troubled over money, or rather over the lack of money; so he put all ranks on quarter pay. A captain, who earned seventy-five dollars monthly, could draw only eighteen dollars. A private, whose pay was ten dollars, had to surrender four dollars for food and two for clothing, the remainder was halved, so the foot soldier received fifty cents a week. But at least he got it. And so a new spirit was coming into the army.

Bolívar had been ruthless in building and supplying his forces.

He impressed reluctant Peruvians into the ranks so as to make them take full share in the campaign for their own liberty; the levies were often cruel and unjust; but then so was the whole procedure of war. He stripped the churches of their silver, he took the ponchos of the Indians for his soldiers, he preëmpted cattle from their owners, sometimes with receipts, sometimes without acknowledgment.

But above all he wanted to keep up the spirit of his army, for his men were faced with one of the most horrible marches in the history of warfare. He personally saw to it that they were fed as well as possible. One large bullock was allotted daily for every hundred men. The hide was saved for sandals and the flesh divided. The soldiers squatted about fires, roasting their beef, washing it down with the corn-beer *chicha*. Two handfuls of dried corn, eaten roasted, replaced bread as part of the daily rations. Sometimes the food was augmented with rice, vegetables and *charqui*.

Still there were not enough trained soldiers for Bolívar's requirements and he again pleaded with his Vice-President in Bogotá for more men: "If I am sent troops, freedom will follow."

He had yet to win his rival Santander over to his over-all plan. Everything had happened thus far as Santander said it would. Peru was a political morass, and Bolívar had fallen into it because of his insistence that this must be the final battleground. So again Santander deliberately hesitated, and evaded the requests for more troops. Bolívar then accused him of trying to hide behind the letter of the Constitution, once again saw him as the "man of laws" who was purposely withholding the means of victory. After that the Liberator's letters grew increasingly abusive.

Santander, sitting at his desk in Bogotá far from the battlefields, his hands folded over the balloon of his belly, complained to all those who would listen, not counting those who would not: "The Liberator thinks I am like God and can say, 'Let it be done' and it will be done. So he asks pitilessly for arms and men, and the worst of it is Bolívar gets all the acclaim, while the Peruvians fail to recognize the efforts of the Colombian government." But to

Bolívar's taunts about being a mere "man of laws" he replied more directly:

> Nothing is so painful to me as your official letter in which you blame this government for all the Peruvian ills, because it regards your demands for more troops with seeming indifference I am an honorable man, my General, and my conduct in these matters deserves from no one, and least of all from you, such an unjust and deliberate censure I rule Colombia, not Peru. The laws that were given me, by which to rule this Republic, have nothing to do with Peru; and their character does not change because Colombia's President, Your Excellency, commands an army on foreign soil. Either there are laws, or there are none . . . And if there are, they must be kept and obeyed.

When copies of this correspondence came to Manuela to be put in Bolívar's archives, she was vehement. What sort of man was this Santander, to attack the Liberator's glory! Manuela fulminated against him as if he were the enemy, rather than those regiments of *godos* who were lying in wait in the security of the Andes. But soon all these specious arguments over the metaphysics of "laws" came to an end. The time for decision was at hand; the army was on the march.

All through the latter part of June, the soldiers came through the valley of Huarás on their way to climb the Andes. Day after day the troops, nine thousand in number — three divisions of foot, one of cavalry, one of mounted grenadiers — snaked up the mountain pass. From this point onward, the army advanced in three columns, each taking a different route. Thus, if the royalists attempted an ambuscade on the treacherous narrows of the mountains, the whole of the force would not be imperiled. The mounted *montoneras*, armed with funnel-shaped shotguns, went ahead of the columns to guard the passes; behind them the cavalry, each man mounted on a mule, and leading his fighting horse. In single file, so narrow were the passes, came the infantry, slowly mounting the defiles of the Andes. Far behind the soldiers followed the commissary, driving ahead of them six thousand head of cattle. And somewhere lost in this panoply of war was Manuela, mounted, dressed in her own colonel's uniform, over which she had flung a red and blue alpaca poncho. Her papers, her slaves and her equipage, despite the protests of General Lara, formed a small squadron of its own.

All day long trumpets as means of communication sounded through the valleys, their notes echoing back and forth between the rock walls, rolling down to the unseen bottoms. It was a slow and painful march. Day upon day the climb, then the restless night with its numbing cold. Those who were unable to reach one of the wooden shelters erected for this purpose died standing against the rock walls. And the mules, unable to forage among the inhospitable rocks, grew weak and lost their sureness of foot. Several times each day a mule would slip off the narrow ledge and plunge downward into space, dragging its rider with it. The terrified soldiers hugged the wall as they heard the screams of the falling man, the thud of a body as it hit the bottom, the rumble of falling stone, and then the eerie silence. . . . Once more the bark of command, and the soldiers continued their slow, almost funereal pace upward. . . .

Thus it went day upon day.

Graves now began to appear. With every mile gained, a soldier died. Yet the stirring news was that the bulk of the army had passed over the serrate Andes and had gained the flat cold lands of the *puna*. The royalists had failed to halt the columns. They did not know, because of the tactics of advancing in three columns, whether this was a reconnaissance in force, or the main effort; and when they discovered that Bolívar was moving up his whole army, nine thousand strong, it was too late to stop him.

Still the treeless wind-swept *puna* swarmed with royalist cavalry, and Manuela was in danger from them every foot of the way. She knew that she was high on the proscribed lists; that, woman or no, she would dangle from a gibbet should she be captured. As for Simón Bolívar, she had not seen him for weeks. He was to make his new headquarters at the ancient hamlet of

Huanuco in the central Andes, but she would be quartered elsewhere. So it was agreed between Santana and herself that, in their
letters, they would use the code word "Colonel" for Bolívar. Thus
if any letter fell into the hands of royalist scouts, they would not
be able to plot the location of the general. On June 23, she had
her first word from Santana:

MY ESTEEMED LADY:

At this moment Luis has presented himself to ask me for a passport I do not want to lose this chance to greet you and to ask you
a thousand things that I want to know; how was your journey?
You will forgive my curiosity; the interest that I have in everything that touches you obliges me to take this step that another
time would be indiscreet. I remember that many times you have
placed your confidence in me, and certainly it is what I appreciate
most. I do not know why I did not see you when you visited headquarters in Huamachuco. I went in search of you at the house of
the Colonel, but as you were speaking French, I went to mine
with the intention of returning in the morning; but upon leaving
I knew that you had not arisen. I shall speak of everything at one
time. The 28th we go to Cerro de Pasco, the 10th of August we
shall begin operations, and the army is reuniting. You will say
that I am an extravagant gentleman, but what would you have
me say, my lady? Certainly I shall not speak to you of snow, grate-
fulness, and duty.

Give me your orders because I want to serve you.

There was little for Manuela to do now but wait. Bolívar, who
usually turned out a torrent of letters even while on the march,
had no time for dictation; he was now the warrior searching for a
battleground. His three armies had reunited, and he was repairing
the damage they had sustained in the ascent. The royalists had
accepted the challenge; his scouts reported a build-up to the south
of the blue-and-gold-clad troops.

On the 18th of July, Santana again wrote her about the details
of headquarters, reported on Bolívar from the little village of
Huriaca, and managed to squeeze something amusing out of the
terrible moments of war:

My Esteemed Lady:

Three days ago we arrived in this town and we will be in it for some time. Things do not all go as the Colonel would like it. They follow their course, and in war things are always slow. Many here are despairing, but I arm myself with my philosophy. You will say that this phrase is long, but actually I have nothing to say to you, although I never lack desire to write you. Truly I have no head for anything, and to complete this letter I only lack some of your notes to excite my imagination You will say I am a very bad-humored gentleman. No, my lady, when I talk with you all this is dissipated, and I am a better man, and who would not be with you? You will say I am a flatterer No, I am frank, my friendship for you has something of gratitude, and is as disinterested as it is sincere I have always told you that the day I say good-by to Bolívar I shall ask nothing of him and shall be grateful for everything You understand, madame. As for English, you have never told me when you would like to write in that language. Do you think I am writing just to write?

Torre and Dr. Charles Moore arrived this morning, and yesterday came — Monteagudo. Tomorrow we expect the army. The Colonel is well although he has been somewhat ill. You have told me nothing about your letters from Quito. Have you received them? Did I fulfill my promise or not? All, all is for you, and for always.

On a hill commanding a wide view, General Bolívar was reviewing his troops. This was one of the finest armies that he had ever commanded; as far as his eyes could see to the clear unobstructed horizon, the troops were assembling. At this spot, twelve thousand feet high, he looked upon one of the most spectacular panoramas in the Americas. At his back, to the west, were the jagged peaks of the Andes over which he had led his troops; to the east, clouded by fogs, lay the Amazon, on the flat plain to the north was a large glacially cold lake, out of which flowed a stream which was the highest source of the Amazon River. The pampas surrounding that lake were to be Bolívar's battleground. He had chosen the place of action. The royalist divisions were coming to him, and his scouts reported that long columns of the enemy were converging here on the plains of Junín.

Nine thousand troops paraded in front of him. It was truly an allied army — veterans of the battles for Quito and Lima, others who had crossed the Andes with San Martín to fight in Chile, soldiers who had lived through the "war to the death" in Venezuela, and among the foreign legions survivors of the battles of the Rhine, of Moscow and of Paris.

General Miller himself led the cavalry. A fine powdered dust, raised by the thousands of hoofs, heralded their appearance, then they came thundering by. They were the best horsemen in the world: *gauchos* from the pampas of the Argentine, who could pick up a silver peso from the ground at full gallop, *guasos* of Chile, who had ridden since childhood; *llaneros* from the flat llanos of Venezuela, wearing their jaguar-skin shakos at a cocked angle; and, with the regular cavalry, the much-feared Peruvian *montoneras.*

The first test of strength was at hand. It was August. The royalists, misled by faulty intelligence, moved to the east of the lake, spending their endurance in a long march, for they believed they were to deal with only a division of the rebels. Instead they ran into the whole patriot army. A retreat was ordered. Bolívar then sent his troops on a forced march up the other side of the lake, in an attempt to cut off the whole army of royalists. In the afternoon patriot scouts on the heights overlooking the plains saw the retreating *godos* five miles away. The officers had difficulty in restraining their soldiers. The cavalry changed from their mules to their horses, took up their twelve-foot-long lances, and moved in swift pursuit, the whole army was put into movement to follow.

It was late, and the long shadows of the freezing night were already upon the earth. The mountain Indians came out of their grass-thatched mud huts, and climbed to places of vantage to watch the spectacle. Now the royalists had stopped their retreat, swung their numerically superior cavalry into line, and prepared for a rear-guard action.

And down on them poured the patriots, hoofs drumming the

plain and voices raised in savage yells. Then the royalist cavalry, responding to the trumpeters, spurred their horses forward in full gallop. The lines met with terrific impact. Lances were propelled with such force that even their shafts passed through enemy bodies. The force of the charge carried the patriots through the enemy formations, and in a moment the battle was a formless melee. Lances were dropped, and the two forces slashed at each other with sabers. Not a shot was fired. The patriots retreated, then rallied. Now a reserve of Peruvian cavalry thundered into action, and under the shock of this charge the *godos* broke and fled. After them came Miller's cavalry, hacking and slashing. Then the dark of night was upon them. The enemy had broken off the engagement and gone into full retreat; the patriots had defeated in one hour the flower of the imperial legions of Spain. Hundreds of dead lay around the field. Riderless horses, wounded horses, neighing in horror, trampled fallen men. The wounded, fearing the freezing night, kept screaming for their comrades. One royalist, pinned to the ground by the spear that had impaled him, kept sliding his body up and down the shaft until a passing soldier blew out his brains. All night long, in the light of candle lanterns, the patriots searched out the wounded, but the Indians had already stripped the fallen of their uniforms, and those who were not found at once died of the cold.

Inside an Indian hut, where the limp red gonfalon of Simón Bolívar hung on a lance, the staff officers were appraising their victory. They had lost seven officers and fifty soldiers dead, less than a hundred wounded; the enemy had lost six times that number. The effect, like the victory, would be as Simón Bolívar foresaw — enormous. It was the first time that the legions of Spain had met his allied armies in formal combat. The triumph gave heart to his army; to those who had passed to the royalist side it would give pause, and to the wavering it would bring strength. Now that his soldiers had smelled blood and won a battle from the highly vaunted *godos*, his orders were to follow the retreating enemy, pick out a suitable place, and there fight a decisive battle. In the light of a hurricane lamp the blood-smeared officers gave a toast to the victory.

There was only one officer present who did not lift his glass. He could not; an old acquaintance had stayed his hand. It was Sowerby, leaning against the wall, pale and silent. During the nocturnal staff meeting he had not spoken; a thin blood foam was gathering at the corners of his mouth. He had received two lance thrusts in the first shock of battle. Thinking them only flesh wounds, he had kept fighting until he toppled from his horse from loss of blood. Bandaged with one of General Miller's fine linen shirts, he now insisted on standing, as if he wanted to meet his old friend in fighting position. At last he spoke. He wanted to correct the figures of the wounded and the dead; the casualty list named seven officers killed. It was a mistake.

"It is eight," said Sowerby.

With that he quietly slid to the floor, leaving a path of blood on the wall to mark his fall.

Miller bent over him . . . Sowerby, who had fought under the banners of Napoleon and survived the horrors of the retreat from Moscow, now dying, in his twenty-ninth year, from a lance thrust in a battle fought at the top of the world.

"Miller," he whispered. "We have fought side by side. You are my oldest and best friend. I am too feeble to say much. Write to my mother and father and tell them I fell in a glorious cause."

Manuela followed the van of victory three days later. The army was far in advance, and even the dwindling walking commissary, the cattle, was days ahead of her. She stopped at the battle-ground of Junín just long enough to bury Colonel Sowerby at the Indian church at Carahuamayo, and to put up the grave-marker which General Miller had written. Then, moving southward, she was lost again in the snow-topped mountains. Now Bolívar was worried about her. They had lost all contact, until Santana addressed a letter which eventually caught up with her:

Huanta, 28 August, 1824

MY DEAREST FRIEND:

I have written many letters to you since I left Huarica. I must tell you that although I have not seen your letter I know about your halting-place, the state of your health and what has happened on your journey from the coast. I am always the same and conform to my eternal maxim of friendship. I am a hundred leagues from you but very close by in the good friendship which I have always offered you. Tell me where can I send my letter safely, because I would never want you to accuse me of being indifferent.

We are six leagues from Huamanga [Ayacucho] and tomorrow we shall enter this second city of Peru. The Spaniards are fleeing, we are pursuing them, and making them lose many men.

We shall not see the coast for a long time, because the circumstances of the war will lead us as far as upper Peru. To destroy the enemy before they can re-form their army is the principal object which now occupies us.

The campaign had now become one of position. There were skirmishes, retreats, advances. The suffering on both sides was horrible, but the patriots suffered most, since they were in hostile land. For five years the Viceroy had held this part of the mountains; and the Indians, finding among his troops a continuous market for their produce, favored the royalist side and were the base of its army. The patriots were constantly being led into ambush.

Once a company of patriots, trailing the enemy, were caught in a snow-filled pass; within hours they were suffering from the *surumpi*, snow blindness. Tiny tubercles formed on their eyeballs, the lids could not be closed except with excruciating pain; in two days they were completely blind. Indians found them huddled on the side of a precipice, and offered to lead them to safety. In single file they fell in behind the guide, each man grasping the poncho of the one ahead. In this way they slipped and slid down the icy slopes into the plain. When they recovered their sight, they were looking into the rifles of the *godos,* into whose hands the

Indians had delivered them A volley at close range, and they were made blind again. So went the war.

And Manuela waited.

She waited with all the impatience of a woman expecting her lover. She had followed Simón Bolívar and his armies for a thousand miles over one of the most terrifying landscapes in the world, solely to be with him between battles. In the start, when she did not have news of him, she would torture herself with imagining that something had happened to him, but slowly she gained confidence in his own belief that his glory would protect him. She settled down in the little valley of Jauja, not too far from Bolívar's headquarters, and waited. The earth was spinning around to spring, which in this land now meant only rain. Rills swollen by the heavy rains became raging rivers and overflowed their banks, roads were turned into quagmires; the days began with rain, ended in rain. Manuela could do nothing but gather in the gossip that she heard from travelers, and listen to the rumors, which fell about her like the incessant rain.

As Simon Bolívar had known, the victory of Junín, that bloody skirmish between two bodies of cavalry, had had an electrifying effect in Peru. Those who had changed sides now wondered if the royalists would win after all. Lima, occupied by the royalists, was uneasy. The United States Consul, writing to the Secretary of State, had expressed what most people were thinking:

> *Lima, August 24, 1824*
> On the 6th instant a combat took place between the patriots and Spaniards which ended in the triumph of the former. . . . It appears that General Canterac . . . moved forward . . . and the advanced divisions of both armies encountered each other and after an obstinate combat, the Spanish force was worsted with considerable loss. . . . It augurs badly for them that they should have been defeated. . . . In the contradictory and confident assertions of both sides, it is difficult to get at the truth, but the aspect of affairs has essentially changed in favor of the patriots within the last three months. The great exertions that have been

made by the patriot government of Colombia and the energy and
ability of General Bolívar have brought forward an army filled
with enthusiasm. . . .

The Spanish general commanding in this district has removed
all the public property from the Mint and elsewhere to the Castles
of Callao, and the small garrison that remains in the City is ready
to evacuate it at a moment's warning. The Montonera have made
incursions in its immediate vicinity the last two days for the purpose of pillage and the approach of some patriot force is now
daily expected.

And the consequences of Junín were being felt as far north as
the capital of Gran Colombia. Santander had received notices of
the victory. It meant something entirely different to him than to
others. So when night hung its blue veils over the narrow streets
of Bogotá, he lay awake — and thinking.

Manuela waited, and meanwhile she read. There was *Belisario*,
given to her by O'Connor; Tacitus, which O'Leary insisted that
she read if she would understand the nature of war, and then for
sheer pleasure she had the delectable adventures of Don Quixote,
a well-thumbed copy from Simón's library which he once carried in
his saddlebags. Reading, rain and rumors; so went Manuela's
private war. For weeks there was no word from Bolívar, until one
day a courier rode up and brought a water-stained message from
headquarters. It was from Juan Santana, dated from Huncayo on
October 24:

My Dearest Friend,
We have just arrived this moment. Here is a letter. The Colonel urges me to write this note since the courier rides. Will we see
you tomorrow?

But even before she could think of a reply, a corps of cavalry
rode up, and there was Simón Bolívar.

Something seemed to come between them during their two
nights together. It was not that Manuela had lost anything of her
fascination for Bolívar, for neither time nor war had stripped her
of a particle of her demanding passions — if anything, they had

multiplied them. But things were not as they had been Simón Bolívar was distraught when he arrived; soon he lapsed into moody and inattentive silence. Finally, in a fury, he poured out what had unnerved him. Manuela had been right. Something *had* come between them, to mar their few hours of happiness. That something was a someone, and his name was Santander: he had had the Colombian Congress revoke the Enabling Act.

What did that mean? It meant that Santander — for he was the real "Congress" — had been frightened about the victory of Junín. He had believed, when Bolívar insisted on leading his troops to Peru, that the Liberator would fall into a political swamp, and return with his reputation worn thin — whereupon he, Santander, would emerge as *the* power, and the Republic as he envisioned it would emerge. However, he had not counted on the hidden strength of Bolívar. The raising and training of that army out of chaos, the scaling of the Andes, the defeat of the legions of Spain in the first test of battle, augured ill for Santander's plans. If Simón Bolívar personally led the allied troops to final victory, his prestige would be so tremendous that there would be no containing him or his ambitions. So "Congress" had decreed that the General must, "for political reasons," give up active command of the army. He was not to be permitted to lead it into battle.

Manuela insisted that Bolívar should disregard Congress, ride out to war at the head of the army he had created. And to begin with, he should order Santander hanged as a traitor. But Bolívar would have none of this. There was too much talk already of his being a dictator. If he should disregard Congress now, no matter how justified, it might ruin his entire plan for America. He would yield; the whole business made him sick at heart.

Then he informed General Sucre of his decision. At first the whole staff threatened to resign. Sucre, on the point of tears, at first refused to take command of the army unless Bolívar were there himself to lead them to final victory. But at last Bolívar's views prevailed. The fate of Peru, the final outcome of the long years of struggle, lay in Sucre's hands. There remained only two final instructions: Sucre must find the right place in this upside-down mountain world for a last battle, and he must be careful not to tire out his troops by marching:

"Feet spared Peru, feet saved Peru, and feet will again cause Peru to be lost. . . . Since we cannot fly like our enemies, we must reserve our energies. . . . Sooner or later they will stop, and we shall defeat them."

Then, with only a squadron of cavalry as escort, Simón Bolívar was gone.

Manuela weeks later was already at the villa outside Lima, waiting for him, when Bolívar arrived. He had taken an indirect route, making a wide arc to the north to recruit more soldiers for General Sucre. As he neared the city, the mere word of his coming so frightened the few royalist troops behind the walls that they hurriedly flung open the gates, and with hundreds of turncoats fled in dismay to the fortress at Callao. Bolívar reached Lima on December 7th, 1824. "I have the honor to inform you," read a report, "that General Bolívar entered this city today accompanied with no other troops than a corps of cavalry."

Arriving in Lima, Bolívar became terribly distracted. He drank more than his usual glass of wine, he was irritated by Manuela's smoking, he fumed at the red-headed José; he paced up and down the floors of the villa, his heels clicking on the tiles, dimming the shrill chirp of the cicadas in the trees outside. His secretaries were worn out from lack of sleep, and their nerves flailed from the strain. Santana chewed the end of his goose quill until it was feathered like a plume. All this because news had come through that a battle was shaping up in the mountains. Bolívar, chafing at his loss of the command, was dictating a battle plan to General Sucre. Yet even as he was putting his signature to it, the battle action had begun.

December the 8th was dawning clear and cold. Through the night that preceded it, on the eleven-thousand-foot tableland over-

looking the ancient city of Ayacucho, the fires of the patriot troops
burned brightly. There was little sleep. Small groups of soldiers,
huddled in woolen ponchos, lazed about the fires which twinkled
in the cold night like myriads of stars. Some of the warriors were
sharpening their bayonets, others casting lead shot in bullet molds;
many just sat and stared blankly into the dancing flames. From far
off in the night came the sharp crack of rifle fire, and an occasionally louder noise as the one remaining piece of artillery left to the
patriot encampment was fired into the shadows. A mile away on
top of a hulk of land, called Condorcanqui, the "Condor's Neck,"
lay the enemy.

For two months the armies had pursued and retreated from
each other, trying desperately to feint one another into an area for
positional warfare. The marches had played havoc with the
patriot army. More than half the men had been lost through illness
and desertion, all of their artillery was gone except a single
twenty-four-pounder with a broken caisson, and this had been
hauled up to the heights of Quinua. There was only enough food
for two days and there was now no means of withdrawal. To the
north and south were deep ravines, at their backs hundreds of
Indians only waited for the moment of retreat to fall on them.
Fronting them was the whole of the royalist army, more than nine
thousand men, a thousand of whom were mounted — the famous
Spanish regiments of Burgos, Guias, Victoria, Gerona, Fernan-
dinas. The Viceroy too was there, and with him were his sixteen
generals. There was no choice left the patriots, it was victory or it
was death.

In spite of being outnumbered two to one, the council of war
of the allied armies that night had decided to give battle. In an
Indian hut, from which the smoke of a fire found its way out
through the grass thatch as best it could, sat the staff of General
Sucre. As they deliberated they ate cheese, hard bread and scrap-
ings of brown sugar.

"We won't die of overeating," said General La Mar, cutting a
piece from the sugar loaf.

La Mar was in command of the Peruvian Legions. The oldest general in the field, he had been born in Ecuador in 1777, and educated in Spain, where he fought against Napoleon. Commissioned a general by the King of Spain, he had been sent to Peru as military consultant to the Viceroy; but after the first fighting of the revolution he sent in his resignation and offered his person to his native land Córdoba, the handsome sloe-eyed young Colombian, a general at twenty-four, commanded the Colombian contingent. Jacinto Lara, reserved and erect, generaled the reserves.

At dawn the royalists were breaking camp. The long lines of pale blue uniforms could be seen descending from the heights to the battlefield. The bulk of their forces deployed in line of battle at the foot of cliffs, but one section moved down to the ravine on the left flank, bringing along with them several pieces of artillery. Scouts hurried back to report to Sucre that it was commanded by the famous General Valdes.

Sucre knew all about Valdes. Violent, abrupt and overbearing, he was feared by his officers and idolized by his men; although a field marshal, he dressed in an odd uniform of his own devising — a broad-brimmed beaver hat, a coarse gray homespun surtout, and long leggings. He performed the task of throat-cutting with honor. Sucre was sure of that. He himself, riding hard through a town to escape Valdes's pursuit, had once been struck by a rope hurled from a window by an ardent royalist.

"Here, Sucre, you nigger half-breed, here's a rope to hang yourself with," said the lady; and she urged her slave to throw a rock at him.

When General Valdes came into town she gloated over what she had done. Valdes promptly put a noose around the slave's neck.

"Madame," he said, "Sucre is as much a general as I am, although we are fighting on different sides. What your slave did to Sucre yesterday, he would do to me tomorrow. Sergeant! Hang this man."

As the enemy was organizing into formal position of attack, a group of horsemen detached themselves from the mass and galloped toward the patriot lines flying a white flag of truce. General Monet, resplendent in a parade uniform emblazoned with decorations, saluted the officers:

"Gentlemen, there are in your army, as in ours, officers fighting on opposite sides who are joined by bonds of family or close friendship. Would it be possible, before we knock each other's blocks off, to chat a little and exchange farewells?"

While the knightly honors were going on, the royalist troops slowly maneuvered into position. At eight o'clock the officers returned to their own lines, and the patriots moved up to attack. The royalists had already opened fire with their artillery, and cannon balls were rolling down the field like bowling balls. Sucre, in a tight blue frock coat with a row of gilt buttons, wore neither sash nor medals. He took off his cocked hat festooned with white feathers and made a brief speech — only a dozen words, but unforgettable:

"Soldiers, the fate of South America depends on how you fight today."

The troops began to cross the half mile that separated them from the enemy, whose long-range fire soon gave them trouble. Córdoba, at the head of the Colombians, called a halt; drawing a long knife, he dismounted, approached his animal's head, and killed it with a single well-aimed thrust.

"I want no horse to flee from this battle," he said

Then, raising his wide-brimmed Panama hat on the tip of his saber, he roared, "Forward! Arms at discretion."

A captain, already wounded by a spent bullet, shouted:

"What step, General?"

"What step? Why, the step of conquerors!"

The patriots rushed forward again, not even pausing in their advance to take aim. From his fixed position the enemy poured a withering fire into their ranks. Cannon balls rolled down on them, carrying off heads and legs; shot from the rifles belched at close range into their lines. They wavered, fell back, recovered. Their dead piled higher and higher. But they kept on, and drove a wedge into the royalist center. Now onto the field came Miller, leading his cavalry, and into the hole that had been punctured by the infantry rode the saber-swinging guerrillas, cutting down the halbardiers who defended the guns and trampling their broken bodies into bloody pulp. The patriot foot soldiers swarmed over the guns and turned them against the ranks of the enemy.

Now the battle tide turned with a rush: the royalist retreat became a rout. Soldiers threw away their rifles and ran to the cliffs, trying to climb to safety. Cannon balls splintered against the rock walls, killing as many by flying stone fragments as by the shot and shell. The cavalrymen hacked at them, and the infantry sat below picking them off as if they were clay dummies in a shooting gallery. The slaughter was awesome It was no longer a battle, but a morning in a mountain abattoir. On the field, the royalists left fourteen hundred men killed and seven hundred wounded. Those who escaped the butchery to reach the heights were brought into a semblance of formation, but their spirit was gone. Those who survived on the plain were soon captured — among them the Viceroy, La Serna, his gray hair matted with blood and his strength sapped by a head wound At the very moment La Serna was affixing his signature to the articles of capitulation, his King in faraway Spain was rewarding his past victories with the resounding title of "Count of the Andes."

Within an hour the battle was over. It was one of the most decisive engagements in world history, this battle in which the last of the imperial armies in America was defeated.

All afternoon the prisoners came in; sixteen generals, sixteen colonels, the whole residue of the army that had not been destroyed. General Sucre went at once to his squalid headquarters, and on an upturned brandy cask wrote to Bolívar of the victory at Ayacucho. Two identical copies of the dispatch were made. One was given to Manuela's friend, Colonel Medina, the other to Captain Alarcón, their orders, to ride like Pegasus over the fearful dis-

tances and reach Lima as soon as possible. Medina set out first.
He was just over the first hill when a well-directed rock hit him
on the head; he was knocked to the ground, and was instantly cut
to pieces by Indian scavengers. The diversion allowed Alarcón to
slip by, and down he went carrying the news to Lima.

They were alone that night in the villa. Simón Bolívar had been
unwell the whole day, coughing fitfully into his cambric handkerchief. Wrapped in a large blue cape with embroidered high-stand-
ing scarlet collar, he rested his feet in the warmth of a bronze
brazier. His eyes were half closed as he listened to Manuela reading to him in her soft Quito lisp. Outside, there was a scuffling
movement, a welling rise of sound, and shouts from the sentinels;
then a pounding at the door. Juan Santana burst in, bootless, but-
toning up his red jacket as he came forward. There was news, important news, a battle had been fought — and Captain Alarcón
stumbled into the room. He had ridden from the battlefield of
Ayacucho in eight days, and he gave the General the dispatch.

Bolívar read it unbelievingly. For a moment, he stared before
him; then, waving the dispatch in his hand like one intoxicated, he
leaped over chairs, bounded onto a table with one jump, and
danced about shouting, "Victory! Victory! Victory!"

8

THE THREE-CORNERED AFFAIR

Manuela had now her own private war to wage. For a time, with the distractions of war absorbing her whole being, she had forgotten, or at least had given little thought to her personal conflict. Now it was upon her; James Thorne was on his way back to Lima. Nothing could be hidden, nothing glossed over. Her husband already knew, for the letters that waited her return were proof of the logomachy that would ensue, the moment he set foot in Lima.

Manuela could not dissimulate, she was incapable of it. She wore her hates and her loves on her forehead for everyone to see, yet now she faced a decision. She knew, for he had said so, that he was coming back with all the prerogatives of her husband. They lived, he pointed out, under rigid Catholic law. Divorce was granted only in the most extreme of circumstances; husbands could — and many did — shut their wives in convents when their public conduct was disapproved by the bishop. A husband's rights over property and children were absolute. Manuela was Thorne's heir; she held his power of attorney which she could use for his ill or his good, depending on her caprice. Moreover it was Thorne, after all, who had to face the innuendoes that entered the conversation every time the name of Bolívar was spoken.

Manuela had once said of matrimony, "Marriage pledges one to nothing." Perhaps. But there were pledges to society, which in a place such as Lima could not be easily broken.

Her marriage was actually one of the few conventional things she had ever done, even though the bishop hurried it up so that James Thorne could "arrange his conscience." Still in 1817 he had offered her all the things she most wanted — security, position, respectability; by marriage she at once "belonged." And that was after Panama.

When Manuela arrived in Panama in 1815 to be with her father after her scandalous affair with Fausto in Quito, the entire isthmus was in ferment. Spain had decided to put down the rebellion of the American colonies and was sending a stream of men and materials across the isthmian jungles. Ships arrived constantly in the Atlantic ports, and mule trains in a steady stream carried their cargo over mountain trails to the city of Panama on the Pacific side, to be reloaded and sent to destinations down the coast. There, among the honeypots of business, Simón Sáenz was trying to recoup his fortunes. Into this easy, undisciplined life Manuela slipped, and there put the finishing touches to her education. She aided her father in his work, for she had inherited his good head for business and his inclination for money-making. She acquired two personal slaves, learned to smoke — which every woman, no matter what her family position, seemed to do in Panama — and developed a taste for liquor. Moreover, under the spell of the tropical luxuriance of the land, she discovered what was later called "a secret charm to make herself adored." Not that she needed any aphrodisiacal devices; her manner, her walk, her movements aroused in most men only a desire to possess her. Behind her father's counting tables, she must have seemed an alluring nymph to the ships' captains who frequented the place.

So at least she appeared to one merchant who often called there to transact business with Don Simón. If his blue eyes and reserved manner did not betray him as an Englishman, then his language did; his Spanish, although grammatically correct, was flat and unmusical. He had none of the persuasive tongue of the officers who paid her insistent court, nor was poetry his métier; he could make no pretty speeches to turn girls' heads, and so ripen them for the gentle fall. Still this *Inglés* was in love with Manuela — his name was James Thorne.

James Thorne — the Spanish called him Don Jaime — was a paradox within a paradox. An Englishman who was a Roman Catholic, living in Lima, when the English were proscribed and excluded. He was a friend of the Viceroy, and a mystery to everyone. . . . Thorne made his proposal to Simón Sáenz; and in the manner of the day the marriage was arranged, he was given eight thousand golden pesos as dowry, and then the only remaining part of the transaction was to inform Manuela.

One never knew about Manuela, particularly in a matter like this proposal. Thorne was more than twice her age; he was correct, she unconventional. He was an Anglo-Saxon; she was Latin. Yet there were certain advantages to the marriage. She could instead go abroad with her father, but this held no appeal; she was an American, and all her emotions were ranged against Spain. Her reputation had preceded her to Panama, and this virtually cut her off from an advantageous marriage. The only alternative would be to remain on the isthmus and become the mistress of some well-placed man, with the possibilities of a slow drift into prostitution.

So the marriage was arranged. Simón Sáenz gave his blessings to the union and left for Spain. James Thorne filled his coffers with the eight thousand golden pesos and sailed with his Manuela for Lima. There they took up residence in different houses in the parish of San Sebastián, to fulfill the laws of the city that one had to be married from the place of residence.

San Sebastián, founded in 1561, was one of the oldest of the parishes of Lima. Bounded by the noisy, turbulent Rimac River, which cascaded down from the Andes, its limits ended two blocks from the heart of the city. It was noted then for the quality of its citizens; there were numerous titled *Limeños* in residence. The Counts of Casa Boza occupied the most imposing of the houses, the Count of Fuerte González had his mansion on the Street of the Palms. Close by was the famous sixteenth-century pharmacy "At the Sign of the Six Palms," to which all Lima's doctors made their

way, since it had the reputation of never adulterating the medi-
cines. The rakes also knew the "Sign of the Six Palms," for there
they got certain elixirs of love. San Sebastián was doubtless a district of consequence.

James Thorne had been invited to spend the days preceding
the marriage at the home of Domingo Orué, now in business with
him. Manuela, disdaining her distant relatives the Sáenz y Tejadas,
went to stay at the home of Don Toribio Aceval, secretary to the
Viceroy. He was a friend of Manuela's father, had been knighted
in the Military Order of Calatrava, and owned a coach — which
only the most noble possessed and which gives more index to his
importance than any name or rank.

On July 22, 1817, Manuela, in black veil, flowing skirt and satin
ballet slippers, went with James Thorne to the Archbishop's Palace
for their premarital examination. There was much about Thorne
that Manuela did not yet know. He had never told her his exact
age, although she judged that it must be at least twice her own.
He never explained why he, an Englishman, was allowed to live
in Lima when most of his countrymen were excluded, nor had he
ever said how he had arrived in America. He already had excellent connections; he could gain an audience with the Viceroy
when he wished it; he was friendly with many well-placed Spaniards, and his business as a factor and merchant-ship owner was
far flung. Here, as witness to their marriage, was León de Alto-
aguirre, principal accountant to the King's Treasury. How had
James Thorne, Englishman, managed to plunge ahead so quickly
in the closed society of Lima? She thought that she would learn
the answers to such questions from his replies to the Vicar-Gen-
eral. But his age he did not give; he merely said that he was over
twenty-five years old. He had been born in the village of Aylesbury
(the Spanish notary wrote it Ayleburis) in Buckinghamshire, a
county that was full of Thornes, "villeins in breed and tenure."

There was one thing Manuela did discover about him. One of
his witnesses testified, "I arrived from Cádiz with James Thorne in
1812 as a prisoner." Why was he a prisoner? And of whom? Had

he been arrested while doing business in Spain during the Peninsular Wars, and sent in one of the galleys to the New World? If so, then how had he managed to extricate himself from this predicament, make his way to Lima, set himself up in business, and within five years become so prosperous that he could command as witness to his marriage no less a personage than an official of the Viceroy's suite? It was an unanswered question. She never found out either his age or what had happened to him in Cádiz

On the night of July 27 they were married at the Church of San Sebastián. Manuela, "veiled and anointed," gave her marriage vows to James Thorne, the knight, Don Toribio Aceval, stood as her sponsor, as he had promised her father, and gave the bride away. They exchanged their vows; and as they were both Catholics, it was presumably for all eternity.

The marriage at first worked out well. Despite the vacuity of his love, Manuela was helpful to him; she kept her eyes open, she had a sense of the drift of things, and her opinion was extremely shrewd. In entertaining the sea captains who came to their table, she learned English, turning her Spanish thoughts easily enough into piquant if not always grammatical terms. For a time she was amazed at how she settled down to being "Mrs. Thorne." Then came the irritants. Thorne was wholly unsatisfying to her. He approached her without art or imagination, and once in an argument she flung at him, "As a husband you are clumsy. You love without pleasure. Believe me, the monotonous life is reserved for your nation."

Then, as early as 1819, the revolutionary movement became activated. Manuela took an active part in it, endangering both their lives and his business. There was constant argument over this, and over her two slaves with their penchant for dressing in men's clothing. Thorne disliked them and their intimacy with Manuela. It seemed to him that every time he wished to see her they were present; they hung about like the shadows of her soul. Thus the discords in their marriage increased with the cacophony of war.

Now in this year of victory, 1825, the time for decision had arrived. She had been away from her husband for many months, first in Quito, then for almost a year riding the frigid *puna* in the Liberator's circle. In all that time, she had given little thought to her lawful spouse or her marital obligations. But this was Lima, where Thorne's friends and interests were centered, where all her movements were known — and where he himself might return at almost any time. What about the future? What should be her next step?

Simón Bolívar, absorbed in his grandiose dreams of America, had given her no encouragement to believe that he would some day offer her marriage; he could be, when he wished, terribly impersonal and devious. James Thorne had told her that she and Bolívar could not be united under the rules of honor — which meant, of course, that he would not consent to a divorce even if it could be arranged. Should she then insist on a final break on Thorne's return?

Manuela did not believe it wrong to have given herself to Simón Bolívar; there was a doubt if it was more wrong than living what was at best only a fragmentary marriage. Still she did not approve of looseness, she never had casual liaisons — no matter what the scandalmongers said of her affairs, they always sprang from real passion. Love was the touchstone in matters of this sort, love alone the justification She did not question at all her right to be the mistress of Simón Bolívar. The conflict sprang, at least within her, from no moral issue: it would be merely inconvenient.

Inconvenient. And difficult. For no one could make decisions in Lima now. Manuela was not alone in her search for an answer to personal problems. The very air was tremulous with short tempers, and for good reason. Victory had not brought victory, and the war's end did not end the war. The fortress of Callao still held out under siege.

Everyone had expected the Spanish General Rodil to be reasonable. But then war is often illogical; so José Ramon Rodil, commandant of the fortress that guarded the approaches to Callao, would not let go. He was offered generous terms. His garrison would be given all the honors of war, and amnesty was offered to most of the four thousand royalists who had taken refuge in the fort Bolívar wanted to end the war and get on with his plans of reorganizing the Americas, so his terms were magnanimous. Rodil could see for himself — for all he needed was to mount the ramparts with a telescope to note that Bolívar was keeping to the terms of the peace treaty. All captured Spanish officers were being repatriated and going onto the decks of the frigates in full range of the guns of the fortress General Rodil responded to the peace offer with savage indifference. The patriots got back their first courier with the offer of peace pinioned to him by a knife; another was tossed into the sea.

Bolívar reacted vigorously to the challenge. Four thousand troops invested the fortress; siege guns were brought off their ships; the battle of attrition began. The fortress had never been taken by storm. One side of the castle rested in the sea, great stone walls lashed by the unquiet Pacific; the other sides were protected by a moat and high walls. A huge gate with a drawbridge was the only entrance. Supplies were smuggled in to the beleaguered garrison by those who had the stomach to run risks for payment in Spanish silver.

The siege went on day and night. Although seven miles way, the guns sounded in Lima as if an unlocked door was slamming in the wind. At first the siege about Lima lent a spice of excitement, but then as casualties mounted and the wounded soldiers began to come back, and the incessant firing went on, the tempers of everyone grew taut. Don Basilio, the septuagenarian night watch, who for fifty years had made his nocturnal cry, "Ave Maria, all is serene," one night threw his lantern at the head of a priest; the next morning he was found sitting naked in the fountain at the Plaza de Armas. It was "the siege." Robbery increased, masses were well attended, hens stopped laying — all of this was "the siege." But it was only when the *verdugo*, the public hangman, pushed aside the man he was supposed to hang, slipped the noose over his own head and flung himself from the gibbet, that officials recognized the seriousness of the public neurosis. Festivals were arranged to distract the people; bullfighting, which had been curtailed because there was a scarcity of fighting bulls, was resumed; cockfighting was again permitted; and the Old Comedy Theater, where once the famous La Perrichóli strode the boards, was open again to the buffoonery of strolling players. And a sumptuous victory ball was arranged in honor of General Simón Bolívar.

But on that very Friday of January 28, in a night as clear as day, Bernardo Monteagudo was murdered. He was discovered lying in the street near the Plazuela of San Juan, stabbed in the back. Many people saw him lying there and passed by, thinking him only some gentleman who had drunk too much *pisco.* Then someone turned the body over, and found himself staring into the fixed open eyes of the whilom Minister of State. Everything marked his opulence: the signet ring on his finger, the golden watch with the golden chain and nugget, the diamond-studded buttons on the linen shirt front The news spread quickly. Some citizens wanted to charge his death to the nerves of "the siege," but it was obvious to most that its origin sprang from something else. More, this murder was to have serious consequences.

Bolívar was called away from the Victory Ball, the Minister of War was summoned, and within an hour every man with the reputation of being a cutthroat was thrown into jail. Bolívar was in a fury, first that anyone should have the nerve to attack a man so close to his person, and then that this death had robbed him of one who shared his vision of the Americas Monteagudo had been working on the program of the great Panama Congress of American Nations, and was to have been the chief delegate; his death created a vacancy that could not be easily filled. So it was a remark by one of the aristocrats of Lima, overheard by one of the secret police, that gave the murder a political cast: "Whoever killed Monteagudo deserves a prize for putting away a pestiferous enemy of peace and liberty."

Bolívar had not forgotten that the murdered Monteagudo had

a regiment of enemies among the aristocracy. The first suspects flushed out proved to be the freed slaves of the Count de San Isidro, one of the distinguished patriots of Lima. Although the Count insisted that he had no connection with the murder, he had, unfortunately for himself, publicly denounced Monteagudo. Despite this, most believed in his innocence, and even the United States Consul reported, "The assassination of Monteagudo seems to have been an isolated crime unconnected with any conspiracy and owing undoubtedly to the hatred which was felt for him by the people of Lima."

Bolívar, however, was certain of a conspiracy, and for the first time he used his dictatorial powers ruthlessly. He seized the personal papers of those who had been implicated, and at the slightest resistance to law he clapped several of the well-born gentlemen into jail and held them incommunicado. The first weeks of February 1825 were taken up completely by the investigation. Bolívar hung onto the processing of the crime with the same tenacious spirit with which he had pursued the *godos* across the Andes. At last, after a fortnight of supreme assiduity, the police finally extracted from three rakehells a full confession. It was simple robbery after all. They had seen the well-dressed Don Bernardo walking in front of the Church of San Juan, the moonlight flashing on his diamonds — he was, it appeared, accustomed to visit a married woman in that neighborhood, a señora who lived in the first house on the Street of Bethlehem. They confronted him, trying to seize some of his diamond shirt studs. He resisted. One of the thieves tried to fire his pistol, but it flashed in the pan; then another stabbed him in the back. If there was an indication of a conspiracy against Bolívar, the police had not been able to worm it out of the prisoners They were led off to the gallows, and the imprisoned gentlemen were released.

But *l'affaire Monteagudo* left deep scars. After that, although Bolívar was always revered in public, behind his back a caterwauling chorus of resentment was taking form.

The siege went on. Day upon day, night upon night, the dull

thump of exploding cannons drifted back to Lima. An assault on the fort was ordered, but it was repulsed with terrible carnage. Again there was an offer of honorable surrender, and again it was pushed aside by Rodil. The siege lines were tightened. And death began to stalk within the fortress. Every night the besieged lowered their dead into the sea; hundreds of bodies drifted up on the shores, and long lines of weeping relatives walked the waterfront to identify their kin. Of the four thousand royalist sympathizers who had taken refuge there, hundreds died in the first months, including the Marquis de Torre Tagle.

The siege wore on endlessly, and nerves in Lima stretched. People developed nervous tics; every time a cannon went off, their shoulders jerked in spasms, and it soon appeared that the whole city was afflicted with St. Vitus's dance. Even Simón Bolívar did not escape. At the villa, the country house of the Viceroy in tree-embowered Magdalena, he was preparing an "account of his deeds" for the Peruvian Congress. The noise bothered him, the atmosphere upset him, at times he grew abusive to his secretaries, and Juan Santana often emerged from a day's dictation completely worn out by the Liberator's temper. And there were quarrels with Manuela. Her smoking bothered him (no one else was ever allowed to smoke in his presence) and she was becoming entirely too possessive. He was naturally besieged by women, and adored by a constantly widening circle of amorously dressed ladies who directed upon him luminous glances. This infuriated Manuela. There was many a scene between them at the villa; for she was an animal when aroused, and the merest hint of replacement awoke all her untamable pride.

> One night [the story ran] she went to the villa when she was not expected. And what did she find in Bolívar's bed, but a magnificent diamond earring.
> There was then an indescribable scene: Manuelita, furious, wanted to tear out the Liberator's eyes She was then a vigorous woman. She attacked her unfaithful lover so savagely that the unfortunate great man was obliged to cry out for help. Two aides-

de-camp had all the trouble in the world to rid him of this tigress
As for Bolívar, he never ceased saying to her· "Manuelita, you
are bewildered, bewildered"

Manuela's nails — "very pretty nails" — made such scratches on
Bolívar's face that he had to remain in his room for eight days.
The official story said it was the grippe — "the General has a heavy
cold." But during those eight days the scratched one received the
most zealous and touching care from his dear little cat.

A week later, his "grippe" cured and his scratched face healed,
General Bolívar appeared before the Peruvian Congress to give
full account of his deeds.

They were the deeds of a new Iliad. He arrived in Lima, he recalled to them, when it was torn by civil war. Then a huge royalist
army was poised in the mountains back of the capital, threatening
to push the patriot forces into the sea. He had put down the fac-
tionalists, and even with Lima in enemy hands he had raised an
army, equipped it and then marched it across the Andes. Eventually, as they all knew, the whole of the royalist force was defeated
at the Battle of Ayacucho. His work therefore was ended in Peru
. . . he would resign his dictatorship. Immediately all the delegates sprang to their feet, and in one voice urged him to continue
in power. Bolívar, in his dress uniform, with a single medal, stood
dramatically before them, drinking in the scene. Then, with a
gracious bow of acquiescence, he agreed to remain until the political reforms that he felt necessary to the establishment of a democratic order in Peru were carried out. Even the United States
Consul, who attended these sessions, observed that "the Congress
have wisely continued the political power in the hands of General
Bolívar for another year, which appears indispensable for the
safety of Peru."

So Congress broke up, having delegated its powers to Bolívar,
but not before they voted him a million pesos — which he refused
to accept. So instead they made elaborate plans for monuments to
be erected to his glory, and ordered medals to be struck off in
celebration of the victory over the Spanish.

Naturally Simón Bolívar had to explain his equivocal position to his Vice-President, Santander. How could he be President of Gran Colombia and, at the same time, Dictator of Peru?

> Here they compare me with Mercury's staff which had the power to link in friendship all the serpents which might have devoured each other. Nobody gets along with anybody, but everyone gets along with me.

As for his strange dual role of President and Dictator, he explained, "Every day I become more convinced that it is necessary to give our life a foundation of security."

The diplomatic rewards of Bolívar's victories were already being prepared in Europe. He had grown to statesmanlike proportions, and those in the councils who had before regarded him as merely an intelligent leader of a band of guerrillas now were extravagant in their praise of him, and proposed diplomatic missions. In North America, by January, 1825, the United States at long last gave recognition to the new republics created by Bolívar, and dispatched the frigate *United States* to Peruvian waters. When the battle-scarred warship dropped anchor, the Liberator was invited aboard for an official dinner.

Commodore Isaac Hull was in command. He was a gruff old sea dog, a hero of the War of 1812, famous enough to have been painted by Gilbert Stuart, and diplomat enough to have been selected for the Peruvian mission. He had suggested that General Bolívar set his own date for the dinner; and thus on February 22 Bolívar with his English-speaking staff was piped aboard the *United States* — without Manuela, for this was an occasion of state. The ship's log:

> On the 22nd, the Liberator partook of a collation on board the frigate *United States;* he selected the day himself as being George Washington's birthday. The Americans present took the opportunity to echo the voice of their country as they had done in the reception to General La Fayette. General Bolívar afterwards rose, gave La Fayette a toast, and made a very complimentary speech.

Yet his most particular flourishes he saved for the young lady at the end of the table. Her face was interesting — eyes dark and inquisitive, brown hair arranged in ringlets dropping down to her bare shoulders. She was dressed in a Regency gown, laced high under a revealing bosom; she wore the fashionable satin ballet slippers. Bolívar had watched the way she fingered her wine glass, and appraised her face and figure. When they met she came forward, curtsied, and in perfect French presented herself: "Jeannette Hart of Saybrook, Connecticut, Your Excellency's obedient servant."

She was the daughter of Captain Elisha Hart, whose ships sailed from Saybrook to the East Indies, and she had been born in 1794 in that village on the Boston Post Road. As the mission of the *United States* was diplomatic, Jeannette had been invited to join her sister and her brother-in-law Commodore Hull. She was fresh and eager, she spoke a beautiful French, to Bolívar's obvious delight, and her full wistful eyes were luminous with admiration for the great man.

A few days later she returned his visit ashore; and afterwards, stirred by the outpouring of his romantic speech, she wrote him a letter in poetic form Bolívar answered in French:

> I would like, mademoiselle, to be able to answer you in a language worthy of the Muses, and worthy of you, but I am, alas, only a soldier I must thus speak to you in military French. Your charming verses are so flattering to me that I do not hesitate to find them more sweet than the divine song of the lyre of Orpheus. O wonder! A young beauty singing of a warrior. It is too much, mademoiselle. Your kindnesses precipitate me to humility. Only gratitude saves me from annihilation and gives me speech to interpret my admiration and my attachment to you.

How deeply attached? He gave her a miniature of himself, and this she preserved, with a few faded letters, all the rest of her life. She never married. And to the horror of her Puritan family, she joined the Catholic Church.

When this light romance came to Manuela's ears, she did not

pause to wonder whether it was serious, or just Bolívar the poet, again composing in human flesh. She merely decided to stop it. Her chance came at a formal ball given in honor of the officers of the *United States.*

It was a gala affair, and Simón Bolívar was in high spirits. Again he was paying extravagant court to Jeannette Hart. So, during a pause in the dancing, Manuela bore down on her.

"How long do you intend to be here?" she asked.

"I do not know."

"It would be better if you departed soon — and meanwhile much better if you associated with your own countrymen, or with the English."

Jeannette, affronted by this, responded, "And who are you, to give me such advice without having been asked?"

"I," replied Manuela, "I am La Sáenz."

It was now April, and the moment that Manuela had dreaded most: she was to part from Bolívar. The mere thought of it had so distracted her that for days she had scarcely noticed the intense activity about the villa. A detachment of newly uniformed cavalry had arrived, several riding horses had been brought out for Bolívar's inspection, most of the staff were packing their dress uniforms. José Palacios, Bolívar's old servant, was readying the baskets in which his two mastiffs would go on the journey with him. Preparations were nearing completion for the Liberator's expedition, for Simón Bolívar was to make a visit of state into Upper Peru.

At first Manuela insisted on accompanying him, and there was the usual storm. But soon it was obvious that on this occasion Manuela was not to have her way. General Jacinto Lara was adamant on the subject. He had told Bolívar this before — now he said it again with greater emphasis. Manuela must go. In this critical period of his career, with the future of Peru and Colombia in the balance, with everything for which he and thousands of others had sacrificed so much to be gained, the Liberator could not allow a scandal, such as attended his love affair with Manuelita, to disrupt his plans. Did Bolívar know what people were saying — that he had ordered her husband, James Thorne, from Peru, not to return except under pain of official displeasure?

Yes, Bolívar knew it. It made him fearfully unhappy that he had placed Manuelita in so equivocal a position. She had grown so necessary to him, but events now made impossible a continuation of their relationship It was a hard decision for them both, but by that April day when Bolívar was ready to begin his thousand-mile tour of inspection, he had made his decision. They must part.

Then Bolívar was gone.

Juan Santana kept his word. When he tearfully embraced Manuela, he promised that he would keep her fully informed about the General. Within four days she had the first letter.

Mataratones, April 14, 1825

MY DEAR FRIEND:
   Yesterday afternoon we arrived at the hacienda Mataratones after a long and arduous journey. Is it not utterly wonderful that we are still crossing deserts, mounting stupid beasts, and arriving now at Mataratones? ["Rat-killers."] And all this after leaving a beautiful capital where they speak more French than in Paris, leaving behind such inestimable friends. All of us are well and day after tomorrow we shall be in Pisco and next in Ica There we shall rest and later continue to Arequipa.
   The post is leaving and I close my letter. Greet everyone at your house and believe me your good friend,

SANTANA

Three days later Manuela rode out in her own *calesa* to meet her husband. It would have been even in normal times a difficult situation. And to Manuela, swept back and forth by passion, her interest chilled by years of separation, the meeting with her husband was not easy. Love for Bolívar was deep in her soul and it was not to be damped out at once by the mere "rights" of marriage.

James Thorne was patient. Too patient, Manuela must have

thought, for it is good at times to be in a passion. It was all very well for him to display those distinctive qualities of the Englishman: dignity, serenity, reticence. But in this Latin world, where every human act was parabolic, only a violent response to pain or pleasure was real: all else was folderol.

James Thorne, however, scarcely would think of himself in such a light. He wanted a complete Manuela body and soul, and despite the differences in their ages he was passionately bound to her. He was willing to forget her love affair with Bolívar, to swallow his pride, and to act is if, like a man of the world, he did not care if his pond had been fished in by another man But he wanted Manuela completely. He disliked her fierce independence. He feared her inner life, those varied impulses of her flesh and her spirit that made her something apart from him. This passionate, sensuous Manuela, whom he could not fully possess, gave a pathological twist to his jealousy and filled his mind with odious imaginings.

And yet at first he suppressed all this — on the condition that Manuela end her love affair with Bolívar abruptly, never mention it, and permit no welling up of the juices of resentment. But how could Manuela do it? How could she, with a turn of the screw, dislodge one such as Bolívar from her thoughts? Everything here, everything in her world, was part of him. When she went riding with her husband in an open *calesa*, she could see the passing women observing them, exchanging glances, the single eyes framed by the *saya* and *manto* vibrant with understanding.

Yet apart from this, time and circumstances had done well by James Thorne. Now approaching fifty years of age, stocky, blue-eyed and precise, and decidedly a man of importance, he relaxed a little in the choice of his clothes. His high-collared frock coat was the latest *bleu céleste*, made fashionable by Beau Brummell, and his cambric waistcoats were impeccable in their patterns. The wars too had been kind to him. At first his ships had carried for both factions, royalists or patriots, the elements of war. Now that the wars had ended — except for that interminable siege at Callao — they were carrying materials to reconstruct the ruined cities.

With his shipping business, his factories, his great haciendas, his villa outside the walls of Lima, his mansion in the parish of San Sebastián, life would have been complete — if only he could have one thing he could not control .   . Manuela

The art of reconciliation was not something at which Manuela was adept. She did not know compromise. The duties that marriage imposed upon her she did mechanically. She would not let her slaves go; in fact, they became her one link to the past she had known, for these faithful Negro women — these "mirrors of Manuela" — had shared all her joys and her sorrows throughout those eventful years. Thorne did not like them. It did not matter; they remained. Perhaps if times had been normal . . .

But they were not. The siege went on day and night, night and day. The patriot army investing the fortress was suffering from the constant exposure, for in these spring months the opaque *garua*, the thin eternal mist, fell on them, chilling them to the bone marrow. There were epidemics of yellow fever and then smallpox; the hospitals were filled with the dying and the unburied. And always, there was the incessant jarring sound of the cannons.

Then one day Manuela had a letter from Bolívar — and in his own hand. It had been written from the town of Ica, on the north desert coast:

MY BEAUTIFUL AND ADORABLE MANUELA,

Each moment I am thinking of you and the fate which has touched you. I see that nothing can unite us under the auspices of innocence and honor. I see well, and deplore, the horrible situation for you. You must be reconciled with one you do not love and I must be separated from one I adore. Yes, I adore you, today more than ever before. Tearing myself from you and your love has multiplied in me all the sentiments which bound me to your heart, your soul and heart, that heart without equal.

When you were mine, I loved you more for your enchanting nature than for the delicious attraction of your body. Now it seems to me that an eternity separates us. In the future you will be only at the side of your husband, I will be alone in the midst of the world. . . . Only the glory of having conquered ourselves will be our consolation!

It was a beautiful letter, but what did it mean — "Only the glory of having conquered ourselves will be our consolation"? There was a ring of finality in it, even though the letter had been couched in the most tender of tones And then, at the very moment that Manuela was making an effort to be "at the side of her husband," Jonotás brought her a note from Colonel O'Leary. It was short and full of meaning· "Samuel Robinson has arrived."

Manuela felt that she had known "Samuel Robinson" all her life. Under his true name of Simón Rodríguez, he had been Simón Bolívar's beloved master, and she had heard much of this learned Bohemian with whom the young Bolívar had traveled in Italy and in France. On a hot August afternoon in 1805 they had climbed Monte Sacro, overlooking Rome, and in the chrome-yellow light of a sunset had looked down on the Eternal City at their feet They had been speaking of liberty, of revolt, of the history of Rome with its tyrants and its Caesars. Then, with tears in his eyes, Simón got to his feet and faced Rodríguez:

"I swear before you, I swear by the God of my father and mother, I shall not give respite to my arm nor rest to my soul till I have broken the chains which oppress us by the will of Spanish power." That day with the man who later took his sobriquet from *The Swiss Family Robinson* was a well-remembered moment in Bolívar's life.

How Manuela had laughed and wept over this teacher's foibles; born in Caracas, he had been sired out of wedlock by one Carreño, but he took the name of his mother and became Simón Rodríguez. Dabbling in revolution while a priest, he was caught up, tried and exiled. After that he lived by his wits. He had some of the attributes of genius. He had a prodigious memory for names (although he frequently changed his own), a gift for languages, a droll manner, and an inventive mind. But he was beautifully inept, and completely unable to turn anything of this to advantage. He became a translator in Jamaica, a typesetter in Baltimore, a tutor in Paris, a circus performer in Russia, a candlemaker in Germany, and a bookseller in London. Employed in the claque at Covent Garden, he could applaud like ten. Although a rake and a hellbender, he kept his innocence, and women adored him. He had read all the French Encyclopedists, devoured Spinoza and Holbach, and worshiped the philosophy of Jean-Jacques Rousseau. He wanted to live like the "natural man," and had with enthusiasm read *Émile* aloud under the trees to the fifteen-year-old Bolívar. He believed with Jean-Jacques that men are born innocent and that society alone corrupts them, so he set off in this realm of incoherence to follow Rousseau's precepts. He developed the "ambulatory mania," just as it was suggested by the master. When Bolívar was in Paris, at the impressionable age of nineteen, he met Simón Rodríguez again, and together they traveled to Italy. Of him Bolívar said, "Rodríguez formed in my heart the ideas of liberty, justice, greatness and beauty."

Yet they had lost track of each other for many eventful years, until one day, while Bolívar was recovering from an illness, he heard that Simón Rodríguez had returned to Bogotá. Immediately he sent an urgent message: "Oh! My teacher, my friend, my Robinson, you are in Colombia and you have not told me." And he urged Rodríguez to come to Peru, for "instead of a mistress, I am in need of a philosopher. For the present I prefer Socrates to Aspasia." Bolívar provided the money for the trip ("This man might become very useful to me"), and soon after he had left for Upper Peru, Rodríguez arrived in Lima.

> Mr. Robinson [said a Frenchman recalling him] was the pseudonym of an original type; he was first known as Father Antonio, a Franciscan monk of Caracas, who was Bolívar's teacher. One fine day in January 1824 Robinson appeared suddenly in Bogotá in search of his old pupil, who, unfortunately for him, was in Lima.
>
> Robinson, getting on toward sixty, had a young wife, a very nice girl and a good laundress, whom he had married in Paris. She had brought back from Europe a small alembic to make table liqueurs which she peddled. This gave me the occasion to meet her and her husband, a man still in the green of manhood, with a spiritual face, a worn black suit, indicating a state of semi-poverty.

He . . . possessed a high degree of learning: he had lived in France, England, Russia. and was a master of languages. . . . There was certainly some disequilibrium about his personality . . . that caused this poverty. Yet he spoke well on all subjects, and he had concerned himself with the applications of the sciences to industry. . . . Robinson left for Lima with his wife and her alembic; unfortunately the Parisian chippy contracted the fever while descending the Magdalena and succumbed in Cartagena.

Such was the "natural man" who dismounted at the villa in Magdalena, not knowing what sort of reception he would have. He was surprised out of his wits at the welcoming He was a small man with twinkling eyes, and several majestic chins falling over a soiled neckpiece. His face was open and disarming with a fresh pink glow like a baby's bottom, and his hair was gray and curled around the ears, giving it the look of a freshly crimped and powdered wig, and his generous nose with its network of filaments had a purplish tint, put there by the wines of Burgundy to which he was addicted. Manuela and Simón Rodríguez were instantly drawn to each other. Apart from their natural sympathies, they both loved Simón Bolívar. Rodríguez was installed at the villa and acquired, despite his threescore years, a nice mistress the color of *café au lait*. He was gentle, gay, learned — a little mad perhaps, but as enthusiastic about knowledge as when he had first turned the leaves of Rousseau's books. Living had been difficult at times, and he once said to Manuela in a rare moment of melancholy, "I, who wanted to make the world into a paradise for all, have made it into a hell for myself."

By the orders of Bolívar, he was to become Director and Inspector General of Public Instruction in the new republic called Bolivia. So he was presently off again, mounted with obvious effort on an outsized mule. With his books and instruments on one pack beast, his mistress on another, and a packet of letters from Manuela to Bolívar in his pocket, he set off like Don Quixote to tilt with the windmills of the Liberator's America. Director of public education in a land he had never known, carrying advanced

European ideas of teaching to a people mostly unlettered, office-holder at sixty in a treeless windswept world three miles above the level of the sea, public instructor to a land that he had left forty years before — as Manuela watched him go off into the coastal desert, she must have wondered at the wisdom of Simón Bolívar in this. Poor Rodríguez, he would provide the only comic relief to the universal carnage in the months to come.

> The siege of Callao continues . . . General Rodil has not 900 effective men, and misery and dissatisfaction are daily increasing in Callao, and the mortality is very considerable. How long he may hold out is uncertain. His vigilance is incessant, and he exerts all the talents of an able commander.

So wrote the United States Consul to Henry Clay, and weeks later he added:

> General Rodil still holds out in the castles of Callao. His situation becomes every day more critical. He has lately shot . . . three or four in close arrest, this danger of disaffection is more imminent than even famine or the cannon balls of the besiegers

And still the guns thundered. No longer was the sun the arbiter of the life movements of Lima. The siege guns marked the day's hours; their first salvo became the *diana*, their cessation the vespers. Everything was geared to them. And the specter of death continued to stalk within the fortress. The defenders ate their mules, then rats, and then each other, the four thousand refugees were reduced to less than a thousand. The beaches of Callao became noisome with the unburied bodies, and over them slack-winged vultures darkened the skies. Only the coffinmakers seemed to gain anything from all of this. There was a constant flow of funeral corteges through the streets; the tolling of church bells and masses for the dead went on twenty hours a day.

By now James Thorne at last had lost his patience. He was, in turn, pleading and insistent with Manuela, then violent, contrite, threatening. He knew that despite his vigilance she was carrying on a correspondence with Bolívar, and somehow getting letters

in reply. He began to feel that, as long as the harassing shadow of
the Liberator was between him and Manuela, he could not win.
He suggested a trip to London. Manuela wrote Bolívar about it,
for thus she might test the finality of the separation implied in his
letters. From the top of the world, from Bolivia, came his answer:

> DARLING, MY ADORED ONE.
> Your answer is not clear about that terrible trip to London. Is
> this possible, my darling? Don't give me mysterious riddles to
> solve Tell the truth, that you don't want to go anywhere. Answer
> what I recently asked you, so that I know your intentions defi-
> nitely and surely. You want to see me . . . at least with your own
> eyes. Well, I want to see you again, to touch you, feel you, taste
> you, join myself with you in every sense. You don't love as much
> as I do? Well, that is the realest and most honest thing you can
> say. Don't go away, even with God himself.

That responsive answer was enough for Manuela: she told
Thorne she would not make the trip. And now their relationship
took a nasty turn. Thorne became abusive, and once completely
losing his poise he struck her — a dangerous thing to do to someone
as inflammable as Manuela. Throughout the months, to the drum-
beat of the siege guns, their quarrels grew in number and in
violence. Her only solace, for the moment, was to write to Simón
Bolívar; and he, despite the fact that he was immersed in affairs
of state, replied in considerable agitation:

> MY LOVE,
> Do you know how much pleasure your beautiful letter has
> given me? It is very charming and was brought to me by Salazar.
> The style of it makes me adore you for your wonderful spirit.
> What you tell me of your husband makes me at once sad and
> happy. I want to see you free, but innocent at the same time; for
> I cannot bear the thought of being the thief of a heart that was
> virtuous and is no longer thus, by my fault. I do not know how
> to reconcile my position with yours; your duty with mine. I do
> not know how to cut this knot which even Alexander would only
> complicate the more with his sword; for it is not a matter of
> weapons or of force, but of pure and guilty love, of duty and
> error; of my love, in short, for my beautiful Manuela.

After that letter, silence dropped on Manuela. Weeks passed, and Bolívar had no letters, no news. The situation seemed desperate enough for him to write to his Minister of War: "I have heard nothing from my Manuela. I beg that you visit her, and ask her for me just how she is."

General Tomás de Heres did so at once. He was an imposing man, an Argentinian who had come to Lima with San Martín's army and remained to serve Bolívar. He rode up to Thorne's villa with a bodyguard, visited Manuela, and like a good officer reported to the Liberator:

> Manuela says that she has written to you incessantly through the medium of Cayetano Freyre, and through him has received letters from you. She is well and is living with her simpleton of a husband — "simpleton," those are her words.

So it was Freyre who had to run the gantlet of James Thorne's violence. One of Manuela's oldest friends in Lima, he was now, thanks to her intervention with Bolívar, Chief of Police. He idolized Manuela and would do anything for her. Freyre was a hunchback, his gargoyle-like head large on his small misshapen body, his bandy legs emphasized by his military uniform. Trained for the law, he had met Manuela in the secret conclaves of the early revolutionary plotters, and she had helped him to win and marry his imperiously bosomed love. Trusted by both Bolívar and Manuela, he frequently acted as their courier; now he had to transmit the disquieting news that James Thorne was becoming very threatening:

> I enclose a letter for you from Doña Manuelita, who gave it to me just before her husband arrived. I told her that in case of any trouble she should come to my house, where she can be taken care of by my wife and placed in safety.

Bolívar had her letter in the fabulous silver town of Potosí, in frigid Bolivia, and from there he replied:

> Manuela — I am in bed and have read your letter. I do not know which surprises me most: the bad treatment you have received

because of me, or the force of your sentiments which I at once admire and applaud. On the road to this city I wrote you that if you wish to fly from the things you fear, come to Arequipa, where I have friends who will protect you.

He was not always able to write her personally, for he had to attend to the birth of a new republic, a state carved out of the territory of Upper Peru, to be named "Bolivia" in his honor. "Please forgive me for not writing to you in my own hand, but you are used to this by now." And so Juan Santana became the amanuensis of love. Manuela chided him:

> Why is it, that you forget to seal the letters that you write me for the Liberator? You should not be so distracted, my little friend, that you do not care if they are read by others or not. And yet another — why, when the Colonel orders you to write to me, do you not wish to salute me, now that you no longer care to write to me personally? What a rogue you are, but I shall punish you. . . .

Those in Bolívar's suite understood the relation, and most of all Juan Santana. He felt her problems as if he were emotionally involved in them, and when she did not reply to his letters, he wrote little Freyre to be sure that he had not, in some way, injured her. Freyre answered:

> I have spoken of you to Manuelita; this gracious lady esteems you. The difficulty of talking to her is getting around some of the inconveniences. I do not go much to her house because of that brute of a husband. Having been told that I am a friend of the Liberator, every time I go around there, he gives me looks that would singe the devil; for this reason she cannot always write to repeat her assurances of her interest in you.

Life for Manuela had by now become a nightmare. The atmosphere in Lima seemed poisoned, the siege dragged on in mounting horror, and her marriage had long since ceased to be a marriage. It was now reduced to open warfare, and by all indications Manuela had enough. If there resided any efficacy in hope, then she hoped for Bolívar's return. Down from the Andean waste-

lands, a thousand miles over the rise and fall of mountains, rode
a courier with a letter from Bolívar:

> I am desperate to return to Lima. If I do not do anything else,
> then I think constantly throughout the day and the entire night
> of your loveliness and of my love for you — and about my return —
> and what you will do — and what I shall do when we see each
> other again

Manuela had left James Thorne. This was known all about Lima
before the act was actually accomplished. She did not precisely
leave their house, but when he had to go from Lima on business
she refused to accompany him. When next James Thorne had news
of Manuela, she was living in her own house in Magdalena. As
the exigencies of business held him and he could not come personally, he wrote her. She did not answer. Then he multiplied his
attentions, begging, urging, demanding, then pleading that she
return to him. He flooded her with letters; they poured down on
her night and day, more insistent a motif, it seemed, than the
bombardment of the fortress. At last Manuela could stand it no
longer:

> No, no, no more, man, for God's sake say no more! Why do you
> try to force me to change my resolution? A thousand times, No!
> Sir, you are excellent, you are inimitable. But, my friend, it is no
> small matter that I leave you for General Bolívar, to leave a hus-
> band without your qualities would be nothing. Do you think for
> a moment that, after being beloved of this General for years, and
> with the security that I possessed his heart, I would choose to be
> the wife even of the Father, Son, or the Holy Ghost, or of all
> three? I know very well that I cannot be united with him under
> the laws of honor, as you call them, but do you believe that I feel
> less or more honored because he is my lover and not my husband?
> Oh, I do not live for the prejudices of society, which were in-
> vented only that we might torture each other.
> Let me be, my dear Englishman. Let me be. Let us instead do
> something else. We shall marry when we get to heaven; but on
> this earth — NO! Do you think this arrangement is bad? In our
> heavenly home we shall lead entirely spiritual lives. There every-
> thing will be quite British, for monotony is reserved for your na-

tion (in love, that is, for they are much more avid in business). You love without pleasure. You converse without grace, you walk unhurried, you sit down with caution, you do not laugh even at your own jokes. These are divine attributes, but I, miserable mortal who can laugh at myself, laugh at you too, with all this English seriousness. How I shall suffer in heaven! Quite as much as though I were to go and live in England or Constantinople. You are more jealous than a Portuguese. That is why I do not love you. Am I in bad taste?

But enough of jesting Seriously and without levity and with all the conscientiousness, truth and purity of an Englishwoman, I say that I shall never return to you again. You are a Catholic, I am an atheist, and this is our greatest religious obstacle; that I am in love with someone else is a greater and still stronger reason. You see how exact is my reasoning?

Invariably yours,
MANUELA

9

THE LAWS OF HONOR

IT WAS SUMMER, 1826 All the battles had been won. Even the
terrible siege had come to an end; the ragged remnant of General
José Rodil's army had marched out of the fortress with full honors.
Once again, the ships filled the harbors and a stream of luxuries
once more was pouring into Lima. International bankers were on
the scene to make tempting offers of loan money. There was, on
the surface at least, peace over the land.

The city of Lima overwhelmed Simón Bolívar with gifts: a gold
service for his table, the former Viceroy's carriage with his own
arms painted on its doors, a jewel-studded sword embellished with
hundreds of diamonds and emeralds, and a dress uniform so richly
embroidered with gold that he could not even nerve himself to
wear it. Throughout all the churches of Lima, supplicants began
their prayers: "O Lord! All good things from thee. Thou hast given
us Bolívar . . ." Poets sang his praises, and one in so exaggerated
a rhetoric over the skirmish of Junín that Bolívar himself had to
protest:

> You have extolled me to such a degree that we are cast down
> into an abyss of oblivion. If you were not a poet, I could believe
> you wished to write a parody of the Iliad, using the heroes of our
> miserable farce as characters.

Yet only occasionally did he object. Bolívar loved it. For the
first time in fifteen years, he had been released from the pressing
details of administration that had made his life full of little hells.

These were the halcyon days — something like one of those ever-remembered summer evenings when day is no longer day and night not yet night, with the soft afterglow of the day's dying still pervading the sky. Such were the summer months of 1826.

Honors poured in on him from the outside world. His name was spoken with grave respect in European councils; to North America he was another liberator, and a member of George Washington's family sent him a medallion containing a lock of Washington's hair and graced by a miniature by Gilbert Stuart: "This portrait of the author of liberty of North America . . . to him who achieved equal glory in South America." With the medal came a touching letter from the old Marquis de La Fayette, addressed to the "Second Washington" of the New World: "Of all men living and even all men in history you are the one to whom Washington would have preferred to send this medallion."

On the Senate floor, Mr. Henry Clay placed him in the galaxy of a new Iliad. In Paris women wore hats *à la Bolivar*. In London the art shops on Conduit Street did good business in engravings showing Bolívar in military dress. In Italy he was universally acclaimed. Two years earlier Lord Byron, ennuied of women and writing, had christened his vessel *Bolívar* as he sailed to death and glory in Greece.

Bolívar had triumphed over everything — the elements, the mountains, time and distance. He had beaten the Spaniards, and routed his rival Santander. And to fill his life, he had Manuela.

The victory was complete. People no longer speculated — at least in the open — about their affair. Manuela's husband had been eclipsed, and by all those who surrounded the Liberator she was granted the respect they would have shown his wife. He no longer made an effort to put a diplomatic face on matters; time had given sanction, and Bolívar was above criticism. At dinners Manuela appeared, beautifully gowned and coiffed, as the mistress of the villa, reigning over a table which was the pride and the envy of Lima. Bolívar kept the best chefs, and entertained lavishly, although he usually dined privately on a dish or two and appeared only at the end of the meal to give the formal toasts. Meanwhile Manuela was allowed to preside.

She was there when Admiral Rosamel arrived on a delicate mission. He had been sent by the King of France with a proposal that Peru allow a number of its most promising youths to be trained in Paris at the expense of the Crown. It was flattering, but, to those in Lima who mistrusted Bolívar's political motives, highly suspicious. It was an open secret that France would like to see Bolívar crowned Simón I, king of an Andean empire — in whose affairs France hoped to play a leading role. In other parts of South America, too, the talk of monarchy came up with "suspicious frequency." From Venezuela an old companion-in-arms wrote to Bolívar: "You should now become the Napoleon Bonaparte of South America," and an envoy was sent from Caracas to minute the suggestion that he declare himself king. Bolívar's sister, María Antonia, vehemently urged him to refuse:

> They send you now a commission to offer you a crown. Receive them as they deserve to be received. This title of Liberator is your real one; it has extolled your name among the great of the earth. You should repudiate anyone who offers you a crown.

So there was trouble in the Peruvian paradise. It did not come alone from the talk of monarchy, or from Bolívar's magnificent style of life with its golden service and the endless bottles of eau de cologne, or even from the terrible fear that Manuela might become Queen of Peru. It came from his dream, his political dream. He wanted to form a series of Andean republics, with identical constitutions and a single purpose, an organized group which would embody his ideal of democracy. As a step in this direction, he proposed to break up Peru, for he thought it gigantic, too large and too powerful. He was going to separate Upper Peru from the rest of the country and form it into the new nation of Bolivia.

There was scarcely anyone in Peru who really liked the idea. There was opposition in Congress, but Bolívar snuffed this out by the mere threat of leaving the country. When they thought of the chaos that would follow his departure, they capitulated, and placed their seal of reluctant approval on the creation of the new republic. Afterwards, while Peru grumbled, Simón Bolívar lived in his villa seemingly oblivious to the growing discontent about him, dictating to his secretaries the ideal constitution of the state that was to bear his name.

Manuela, as usual because it was her nature, was nearer to the true nature of things. She heard and saw much that Bolívar either missed or chose to ignore. She saw the enemy where Bolívar saw only mild opposition, she scented obstacles where he sensed only minor irritants. What, for example, of the United States Consul? Was he not undermining Bolívar's prestige in North America? What was one to make of letters such as the following, which she discovered William Tudor was sending out?

> The Liberator is a very ardent, impetuous character; he has achieved such great things, has had such a sole direction of affairs that the jarring movements of civil governments are regarded by him too much in the light of military subordination. The officers about him are young men, and three of them Englishmen — O'Leary, Fergusson, Wilson, devotedly attached to him, and unconditionally submissive. He has no characters of weight and dignity near him, who can sustain a contrary opinion; and there is a tone of excessive adulation and absolute deference in those of this country who approach him. This state of things gives occasion to the enemies of Bolívar. A Frenchman of liberal thought and intelligent character said to me, "He will lose himself as Napoleon did."

William Tudor was a very proper Bostonian. He did not like the climate of Lima. He did not like Simón Bolívar. As for Manuela — especially as he was a bachelor — she was an unpredictable woman and beyond his comprehension. "Were I to repeat to you," he wrote Henry Clay, "some authentic anecdotes they would seem incredible." Tudor's ideas of democracy were firm and unalterable. He had, after all, been in Boston during *the* Revolution, and had imbibed revolutionary principles from his parents, who took an active part in it. Besides, he was a literary figure, and anyone who had not read his essays was certainly unlettered. He knew

the world, he had traveled widely with his brother the "Ice King,"
who had made a sizable fortune carrying ice from Boston to the
tropic West Indies islands. Tudor was small and precise, his high
white neckstock and lace jabot were crisply immaculate; he had
gray cold eyes, a cleft chin, a thick lower lip which he pushed out
when irritated, and a habit of cocking his right eye in disagreement. Both lip and eye were often seen in these positions — especially where Bolívar was concerned. But it was only after
Manuela had spoken out against him in public that he came out
openly against the Liberator. "His model," he said, "is now
Napoleon, and his ambition is equally unbounded!"

Simón Bolívar had just dispatched his constitution for Bolivia.
He planned it to combine the virtues of all political systems, but
what he did was to disregard Napoleon's dictum that a constitution should be short and vague. Instead of the virtues of all systems, said his detractors, he had brought together all their defects His plan called for a lifetime presidency — a scheme which,
if followed by other South American nations, would give him control of half the continent. So at least said his political opponents.
William Tudor interpreted it this way:

> It is in the highest degree painful to change a favorable opinion
> we have formed of any individual and how much more so when
> that individual is so eminent and his own great reputation is at
> stake and the hopes and credit of these new Republics are in-
> volved with it. The deep hypocrisy of General Bolívar has hitherto
> deceived the world, tho' many of his former friends have for more
> than a year past discovered his view and abandoned him.

It was difficult to keep any secrets in Lima. Though now there
were no newspapers, it mattered little, rumor was the lifeblood
of society. The lack of secrecy, the want of continuity made impossible any movement of genuine surprise. There was a plan for
a revolt against Bolívar in the higher echelons of society and it
was well hidden. Many prominent people in Lima were behind it,
but as usual the best intelligence of it came from Manuela's creatures, who picked up news of it at night in some of the *picanterias*.

For soldiers' tongues, loosened by rum, babbled everything they knew and much they did not know. By the end of July 1826, Manuela had at least enough to show that there was an organized movement to seize Bolívar, his aides and his generals, and banish them with the main body of the Colombian army from Peru When this was confirmed by Captain Espinosa, who acted as an *agent provocateur*, Bolívar moved with surprising suddenness. William Tudor reported:

> All the officers of the Peruvian corps stationed in the capital were arrested. It is said that 60 to 80 persons are in confinement in the Convents of St. Domingo . . . Bolívar was thrown in the most violent agitation by this event, and if prudence of the Ministers is not able to calm his feelings it is feared that executions will begin.

Bolívar had won again. Yet winning sometimes means losing, for now the summer evening of his life, those halcyon days, were gone. Night was upon him, night closed in on him with all the menacing shadows of tumult. Revolt in his native land of Venezuela threatened the whole fabric of Gran Colombia; Bogotá was a suppurating wound: and Vice-President Santander urged him to return at once to stanch the flow of blood. Geography was the monster, his real enemy. It assailed Bolívar on every side. He had to be at all places at the same time, but the distances were immense. It took two months for a letter to reach him from Colombia; Panama was fifty-five days away, Venezuela three months. Couriers had to go through jungles, ford raging rivers, ride up and over the swooning heights of the Andes, killing a dozen mounts before they could reach Bolívar in Lima. Because of this it was impossible for him to be kept correctly apprised of events; a minor problem was a disaster before he learned of it.

In high, heaven-bound Bolivia, his "ideal" republic was also coming apart at the seams. General Sucre, who had agreed to become "lifetime" president for only a limited period, was involved in the complexities of the new state. But even worse. It was the "natural man," Simón Rodríguez, the Minister of Public Education, who caused him his greatest worry. Rodríguez was in hot water with everyone at once — the governors, the mayors, the priests and the mothers of the children whom he instructed. He taught anatomy in his "natural school" by taking off his clothes and walking around the frigid classroom "so that the pupils could accustom themselves to the naked body." His discourse was so heavenly that no one understood him. Nor had age withered his interest in women. Although his "hair was white as snow, and he had an angelic face," he made a try for every woman who came within reach. When at last he was forced "because of circumstances" to marry little Manuela Gomez, the citizens of the capital would have no more of him. He was sent, with his girl wife, scurrying into Peru. There, under the motto "Light and Virtue of America," he opened a model school, and in the same room operated a candle factory. Under this rubric Samuel Robinson, who had wanted to turn the world into a paradise for all and succeeded only in making it a hell for himself, dipped his wick — and in off moments taught the children.

So went Bolívar's world.

Time was working against Bolívar now. He could no longer delay, even though he believed that his presence in Lima was necessary as a unifying force to keep the Republic together. If he lingered here any longer, the whole of his life work, and his finest creation, the Republic of Gran Colombia, would fall apart.

His firm decision to leave threw Lima into great agitation. For as much as many feared his power, they feared his departing even more. They looked around at the thousands of Colombian troops, they thought of the brigands that haunted the hills about their city, they examined all the factions within the government, and, seeing the focal points of chaos, they grew apprehensive of the future. Delegations came out to visit him, they exhausted every form of flattery to urge him to remain. A committee of the most striking society women drove to his villa in open carriages, to entreat him to reconsider. And there, under the cold eye of

Manuela, one of the most luscious of them read aloud a poetic appeal.

Bolívar drank all this in, promised to reconsider.

"Ladies, dear ladies, silence is the only answer I can give to your enchanting words."

William Tudor, who stood on the fringe of the crowd, cocked his right eye and said, "They have influenced his ardent character almost to madness." But later, when the delegation had gone, Bolívar went to the door with Tudor and told him with firmness, "I shall go to Colombia."

Colonel Daniel O'Leary was the first of his aides to be dispatched. His mission was to ride the twenty-eight hundred miles to Venezuela, to survey conditions there, and to have a report ready for Bolívar on his arrival.

To Quito he sent a veteran of Napoleon, one who served the Emperor at Austerlitz: "Tomorrow, on August 8th," Bolívar informed the government in Bogotá, "my aide-de-camp Colonel Charles Demarquet is leaving for Quito to gather our men together and maintain peace."

Then he prepared for his own departure.

And for Manuela, this meant another leave-taking, another time of separation. Obviously she could not accompany him; the journey was hard and long, and it was to be made at what would be a killing pace for a woman. There were other considerations too, more forcible than these. His mission was now to mend the rifts between men, not exaggerate them, and the presence of La Sáenz, whose name and reputation was already talked about, would upset his plans. He did not know his future. If the governments could be unified, he envisioned himself retiring from office and living on his estates; there in the peace and ease of sanctuary, Manuela would be with him again. It was a golden dream.

Meanwhile, Bolívar felt very deeply the equivocal position in which he would leave Manuela. She would be, in effect, a discarded mistress. Without him, she would be put upon by the women of Lima. It was a terrible situation. In secrecy he drew together his most trusted friends, including the Minister of War and humpbacked Cayetano Freyre, and placed her well-being in their hands.

Manuela did not attend the great farewell banquet given in Bolívar's honor. Nor was she at the smaller one on September 2nd with his personal staff, but later that night they took supper in his bedroom. And in that room, with its secret door which led to her dressing room, Manuela gave her lover a farewell that only she knew how to give.

All the remaining days of September Simón Bolívar was on the move. His presence seemed to create harmony everywhere, but as soon as he disappeared the personal conflicts began all over again. In Quito they gave him a welcome such as he had when he first rode into it four years before. He found there some news of Lima — a note from faithful Cayetano Freyre, saying "Doña Manuelita is well," and some letters from Manuela. There was in Quito a new pledge of unity, and yet the hydra heads of disunity shot up again as he rode north.

Along the mountain trail over which he had once ridden in triumph, Bolívar picked his way. The treeless rolling Andes seemed at peace. The purple flowers of the potatos, planted and tended by the Indians, climbed the mountain shoulders seemingly to the level of the sky. Bolívar was filled with nostalgia for days of lost happiness, and his thoughts were torn from political realities to Manuela. On October 6, when he reached the little town of Ibarra where, years before, he had written to Manuela, he was overcome with the memory of her, and sat down to write a long-promised letter:

MY CHARMING MANUELA,
  Your letter delighted me. Everything in you is love. I, too, am suffering from this searing fever, which consumes us like two children. In my old age I suffer from a sickness I should have long since forgotten. Only you keep me in this condition. You beg me to tell you that I love *no one else but you*. No, *I do not love anyone*, nor shall I love anyone else. The shrine which is yours will

never be desecrated by another idol or image, unless it be God himself. Believe me — I love you, and shall love only you, and nobody else but you. Live for me and for yourself. Live to console the unfortunate ones, and your lover who longs for you.

I am so tired with all this travel and with all the troubles of your country that I shall not have time to write you long accounts as you wish me to do But if I do not pray, day and night in turn I think of your charms, and when we shall see each other, and what I shall do when I see you again. No more with my own hand! Do not write.

After this, Simón Bolívar was swallowed up in the Andean world.

10

THE RISE AND THE FALL

THE NEXT REVOLT came with the changing of the guard.

The moment, it is certainly true, had been cleverly selected by its leader, for he had consulted the almanac, and on the night of the 25th of January, 1827, there would be a total eclipse of the moon. Under the cover of a veiled sky, the revolting troops could be shuffled about without untoward suspicion. During the night, Colombian soldiers clad in their coarse green homespun sauntered in groups of twos and threes toward the center of Lima. There, in the dark shadows of projecting eaves, Colonel José Bustamente, muffling his voice behind a great black Spanish cloak, directed them to their prearranged places. All through the dark silent hours, the troops took their positions; the five gates were heavily guarded, the parapets were lined with soldiers. At the precise moment, every house in which there lived a general officer of the Colombian army was surrounded. Before the sun appeared over the Andes all Lima knew what had happened during the night — the Colombian troops had revolted against their generals.

William Tudor, awakened by his servant, slipped into clothes and made a tour of the city:

On the 26th [January] the people of Lima were surprised to find that the Colombian troops . . . occupied the great Square at daylight and sentinels at all corners prevented everyone from entering it. On that day shops were shut and business suspended.

It was soon known that a majority of the officers — the present commander of the troops is Lt. Colonel Bustamante — had arrested their two Generals, Jacinto Lara and Arthur Sandes and five Colonels; and, so completely was the business executed, that they were all arrested in their beds without opposition, and hitherto this revolution has not cost a drop of blood The Castles of Callao had been occupied the evening before. These officers and a few others of subaltern rank were sent prisoners to the Castles, and the troops were then marched to their respective quarters.

The Minister of War, Tomás de Heres, who was supposed to protect Manuela, was the only one who escaped. He had been outside the city, and when news of the revolt reached him he fled in a canoe and boarded a French warship lying in harbor. Cayetano Freyre, stripped to his underclothes, found himself clapped into jail, deprived of his office; and Pérez, the other protector of Manuela, was under house arrest. There was no one left of Bolívar's faction, no one at liberty — except Manuela.

Ten days later, at his headquarters, Colonel Bustamente looked over his reports with intense satisfaction He had carried out the conspiracy of Santander perfectly. There had been no bloodshed; all of Bolívar's principal officers, himself excepted, were incommunicado; and the Colombian troops had received their first arrears of back pay. As soon as Simón Bolívar left Lima, Santander had sent his agents down to lay the groundwork of this plot. He made contact with those Peruvians who, disliking Bolívar and his political ideas, would move when they had assurance that the Colombian army would be neutralized. Santander's agent found the ideal "neutralizer" in Colonel Bustamente. He was a "political" soldier, a friend of the Vice-President, and he moved through life like a bishop on a chessboard — obliquely. He gathered the sergeants of the Colombian battalions and told them that only the Vice-President of Gran Colombia, Santander, supported their liberties; that the constitution as drawn by General Bolívar marked a return to despotism. Besides, if they would take part in the conspiracy and arrest their officers, their back pay would be given

them, they would go home, and he, Bustamente, would be made
a general.

Bustamente had left nothing to chance. All outgoing mail from
Lima was being censored, all travelers were subject to the strictest
scrutiny; so that by the time Simón Bolívar learned of the revolt, it
would be too late for him to intervene Everything was proceeding
perfectly, and already some of the Colombian troops were on their
way home from Peru. Nothing to chance. . . . Then an orderly
burst in to tell him that Manuela, dressed in the uniform of a
colonel, was in the army barracks trying to bring about a counterrevolution.

Manuela was a favorite among the soldiers. They liked this
woman who could ride like a man, and who could yet be, when
the occasion demanded, so very feminine. She had gone out of her
way, many times, to see that they got things to relieve the eternal
monotony of the army. Moreover they were restless in their barracks while waiting repatriation, worried about their reception
in Colombia. Now she walked up and down among them, a heroic
little figure in her colonel's uniform, pleading, cajoling, threatening, and brandishing a drawn sword for emphasis. Manuela stood
alone against the revolt.

The Peruvian government too was taking no chances. At twelve
o'clock that night soldiers appeared at her house, seized her in
bed, and brought her protesting and fighting to the Convent of
the Nazarenas. Colonel Bustamente himself took charge of the
case. Through the iron grating of the cloistered nunnery, he advised the Abbess that Manuela was to be kept in seclusion, to be
allowed no communication with anyone, and above all not to
have pen or paper. The Abbess Agustina de San Joaquín did not
like the role thrust upon her, but the gentleman could be assured
that she would understand how to handle the señora, and that
from this cloistered nunnery she would communicate with no
one.

The next morning Manuela wrote a letter to Cristóbal Amuero
protesting her arrest:

Señor Consul of Gran Colombia:

To you as representative of the Republic to which I have the honor to belong, I wish to state that at twelve o'clock at night on the 7th of February, this present year of 1827, my house was entered. I was in the village of Magdalena, where I have always lived. They ordered me to surrender and to proceed under arrest to the capital. I was not able at once to do so because of my poor state of health, the result was that an officer was left in my room to keep me under observation all night; all the streets surrounding my house were full of troops. The following day I was taken to the Convent of the Nazarenas as a prisoner of war or as a criminal, as I am not truly the latter, I do not know for what reason I should be considered the former.

Up until now the reason for my imprisonment has not been made known to me, nor who is my accuser; and the process is entirely inquisitorial. I maintain that I am a Colombian and that there is lacking here the consideration and gratitude owed to this nation, and further I claim the privileges which the rights of men extend to those persons imprisoned, justly or unjustly.

I place my case in your very capable hands. I do not know if there is a reason or not that I should be judged as Peruvian, if so then let them punish me as a Peruvian. The Government has forgotten Article 117 of the Constitution of this country.

My vindication is absolutely necessary. Permit me to remind you that as a representative of the Republic of Colombia, it is your duty to demand it, and you should do so with all the energy befitting a representative. I insist that the justice of my case will find favor in the eyes of all thinking men, the only competent judges of one such as myself, whose only guilt is to belong to a Republic which has brought so much good to Peru.

Cristóbal Amuero tried to do something for Manuela, but he himself was in so much danger that he raised only feeble protest.

He was like all the late agents of General Bolívar [said William Tudor], some of whom have good reasons to fear the investigations which the Peruvian Congress will doubtlessly make. All of them have seen their hopes of fortunes and title destroyed, but have remained unmolested in this city. Some of them have unquestionably been engaged in secret intrigues of which Mr. Ármero [Amuero] a merchant and Colombia chargé d'affaires — a man like almost all of the agents of Bolívar of unprincipled character — was the ostensible mover.

The Ides of March were upon Manuela. She wrote letters to soldiers whom she knew in the battalions, she searched out her remaining friends by letter, hoping to get some news to Simón Bolívar. Her captors increased their precautions. The letters went out from the convent just the same. They caught Jonotás with some of the dispatches in her turban and hurried her off without trial to the women's prison at Casas Matas, notorious for its unsanitary conditions and the perversion of its inmates, but in it they threw Jonotás, nevertheless (for they thought her to be a hermaphrodite, something like a mollusc, the active and passive libidinal principles being united within her, so that her sexual state was in equilibrium). So Natan, dressed like a nun, became Manuela's courier.

The letters were taking effect. There were several outbreaks among the Colombian soldiers. The Peruvians lived in fear of them. Peruvian troops were brought down and "kept on the alert, with bayonets fixed and ready to be called out at any moment." But just at the time they were being raised to a fever pitch to declare for Bolívar the transports arrived, and on March 19th two thousand of them were marched aboard. A Peruvian official said to William Tudor: "We had never expected to get rid of them without a battle."

Manuela had ample time in the confines of the nunnery to go over her rise and her fall. It hardly seemed possible that so much had happened to her in five years. In 1822 the world, her world, had been full of promise. Later, as she moved with the army and with history, there had been moments of peril and days of despair, yet always her love for Simón Bolívar and for his ideals had sustained her. Even during the difficulties with her husband, there had always been the future. Her rise as the favorite of La Magdalena, with the social power of a vicereine, had been rapid and wonderful. Now in a few weeks it was all gone, position, property, future — and lost to her now when she needed him most was

Bolívar. At thirty years of age she had won and lost. The old uneasiness returned to her, that feeling of "unbelonging." It alternately upset her and exacerbated her, and she was shattered by the rapidity of her fall. Yet there was no dissolving into tears; the slightest feeling of coercion awakened in her an animal fury.

The Peruvian officials called her an ill-tongued harpy, and, in the words of the Foreign Secretary, she was "insulting the public honor and morals." He complained that even though "she was confined within a nunnery she ridiculed the order of Incommunicado imposed on her and she continued to receive visits from officials of the government." At last, in fear of a counterrevolution which her activities were promoting, he issued her an ultimatum, and on April 14 reported it to Santander:

> Cristóbal Amuero and Manuela Sáenz have never once ceased their efforts to seduce the loyalties of the people and expend their energies in the direction of counterrevolution. I have precise details, which is beyond one's imagining, of the scandalous correspondence between Consul Amuero — and his woman.
>
> Therefore I have sent an ultimatum at four this afternoon to Manuela Sáenz, which states that she must leave Peru within twenty-four hours. If her departure is not verified within this time, I shall imprison her in Casas Matas.

The brig *Bluecher* sailed north toward Ecuador, under lowering gray clouds. All around it the world was opaque with a thick mist, low-flying cormorants came by, skimming in tight formation, close to the white-capped sea. Then they too disappeared, and there was only the creaking of the plunging ship to remind the reluctant voyagers that they were living a real moment and not some foolish dream. So this was the end of the great battle of liberation. This was the final recompense for all the privations, the high hopes, the dream of peace and independence. The officers who led them to victory arrested by their own troops, imprisoned without trial, then shoved on board ship at night and sent off like criminals infected with a plague. General Lara, prison-pale, was uncommunicative. Arthur Sandes tried to make conversation with Manuela, and then let it go. Not so Córdoba. He was in a fury. Before boarding the ship he had made official report to Simón Bolívar:

> The Foreign Minister called the Consul of Colombia and told him to prepare me and the other officers and troops still in Lima so as to leave the following day The city was alarmed and now even more so from the provocations of Manuela Sáenz. . . . She embarked with me.

Manuela stung Córdoba with invective, she was incensed at him for not taking a firmer stand against the conspirators, and she accused him of disloyalty toward Simón Bolívar Now Córdoba made no concealment of his hatred for Manuela; he believed that her escapades had much to do with the resentment of the Peruvians against them. There was a bitter argument. A young lieutenant tried to intervene and was pushed aside.

> It was the impertinent manner of Manuela Sáenz, and the manner in which she treated Córdoba and the travesty she made of him in front of the other officers, that caused the general to treat her with *brusquerie;* this was the opening motif of their animosity.

The bitterness did not diminish as they came to Guayaquil. Córdoba was so enraged at one point that, had Manuela been a man, he would have put a pistol ball right between her eyes. It was unfortunate that they separated at Guayaquil in this mood, for one should not quarrel with one of the Furies.

Guayaquil was draped in misery. The split-bamboo houses, light and airy and thatched with palm, looked more like the huts of a run-down Indian village than the buildings of the first port of Ecuador. The streets were quagmires, gray-black buzzards fought in the mud over the offal no one thought to remove. The canteens were filled with undisciplined soldiers, and the whole place smelled with the sickly fumes of crude sugar-cane rum. There had been a revolt here too; the officers were confined to quarters. Manuela was not allowed to communicate with anyone. Jonotás came out of steerage as disarranged as a floor mop, and together they planned their trip to Quito. It was not to be in state, as she had traveled five years before. The whole journey was to be on foot:

So she left there with an escort of four Colombian soldiers whom she chose from among the handsomest men of the regiment. She walked in small journeys with no servant other than her mulattress — in ten days she arrived in Quito.

Autumn

The Years 1827–1830

PART THREE

Bogotá

11

BOGOTÁ, CITY OF HOLY FAITH

Doom hung about the houses, drifted like a miasma around the sullen people, sprang up at the whispered conversations of the soldiers, suspended its terror-pinioned wings over the land.

Manuela felt it as soon as she had crossed the invisible line that separated her native country from Colombia. There were no *vivas* here, no words of cheer for the mud-splattered soldiers who accompanied her. Once these Venezuelan lancers would have been received in every house as blood brothers, now the most wretched peasants turned their backs when they approached. The revolution had bled white every hope, every feeling. The land had passed in these three hundred years from savagery into feudalism, from monarchy to republic. Now it was passing from revolution into anarchy.

Manuela was unable to ignore it. At first she gave little heed to the scrawls *Down with Bolívar* freshly daubed on the white-washed houses; but when the complaints became vocal she unleashed her tongue, lashing the harbingers of discontent with a billingsgate she could use on occasions such as this. Everywhere throughout Colombia she met the familiar pattern. On her arrival in village or town, people would seek her out and pour upon her all their lamentations. They had been buoyed up by some dream of a social apocalypse which the wars for independence were to bring; now they were reaping the winter wheat of these lost

illusions. There were disease, poverty, want. Commerce was at a
standstill. Soldiers mustered out after long service walked the
land and showed their wounds stinking with gangrene. Times were
worse, they moaned, than when the Spaniards were in possession
of the land. Bolívar was a tyrant, just as unprincipled as the *godos*
who had fought for their King and Mother Spain.

So went the impressions from mountain to mountain, village to
village.

What was this *dies irae* that hovered over Colombia, what was
this dirge of chaos moaned by everyone? Was this the anarchy
which Simón Bolívar had so long feared — now misery, given
counterpoint by disaffection, had become dissonance? She could
understand now why Bolívar had need of her, and for him she was
taking this long journey by horse from Quito to Bogotá, through
mountains perched on end and over sky-high *paramos* scoured by
hail-laden winds.

It had been months before Manuela had heard from him. She
had rested in Quito, at her brother's home, nursing her bruised
soul. Still nothing came from him, no letter, no brief message to
assuage her feelings. To be exiled from Peru, to be treated like a
strumpet, to have lost in one moment a social position which she
had so long wanted, to be reduced to momentary indigence, to
"unbelong" again . . .

At first the ignominy of exile, the loss of everything which had
been something to her, had calmed to the stupor of shock; but
when this wore off and she surveyed her loss, she was overwhelmed
by its immensity. Her brother José María, now a general in the
army of the Republic, was immensely kind. He took her to his
home near the Plaza of San Francisco and there tried to shield
her from the barbs thrown at her by the women of Quito, who,
with venom undiminished by the years, gave the prostrated
Manuela a fine display of their animosities. This could have been
in a sense endured, had it not been for Simón's silence. Naturally
she knew that he was overburdened by events — that ever since
he had left Lima in the autumn of 1826, he had been in the saddle

riding across the serrated face of South America, passing from crisis into crisis. The revolt of his own regiments in Lima, the moment he left it, threw him into unbounded rage. But then, cut off by vast distances from all contact with Peru and forced into frustrated inaction, he sank for weeks into a lethargy of indecision, shivering in the night-agonies of ague and the day-agonies of melancholia.

Then one day there came a letter. It was dated September 11, 1827, and it had taken almost two months to reach her from Bogotá. General Arthur Sandes, whom she had not seen since the time they were exiled, personally delivered it into her hands. It was a beautiful letter:

> MANUELA:
>
> The memory of your enchantments dissolves the frost of my years . . . your love revives a life that is expiring. I cannot live without you. I can see you always even though I am far away from you. Come. Come to me. Come now.

She was wanted. Yet that one letter could not erase at once the neglect by which she felt he had denied her. She would go, of course, for she felt, she knew, she was needed. But she would first make her own position clear and unequivocal:

> I am very angry, and very ill. How true it is that long absences kill little loves and increase great passions. You had a little love for me, and the long separation killed it. But I, I who had a great passion for you, kept it to preserve my peace and happiness. And this love endures and will endure so long as Manuela lives. . . .
>
> I am leaving for Bogotá the first of December — and I come because you call me to you. However, once I am there, do not afterward suggest that I return to Quito; better that I should die than to be taken for some shameless trull.

So she left, as she had promised. And with a familiar retinue — a squadron of lancers to guard her, much of Bolívar's personal equipment that he had left behind in the rapidity of his movements, the strongboxes of his private archives which she still guarded like a Pandora's box, the mules loaded with the traveling trunks of her wardrobe, and the slaves and the servants.

Colonel Charles Demarquet was her escort. A self-possessed, much-traveled Frenchman doomed by his love of battle to be forever a soldier, he had fought with Napoleon at Austerlitz and there lost three fingers. He found himself at the age of forty still Mars's creature. He was now Bolívar's aide-de-camp, this interlude with Manuela was a welcome departure from the downing of rebellions. And if there were opportunities for conquest here, he made nothing of them; for "Manuela," said a friend of his, "went to New Granada under the guidance of my friend Colonel Demarquet. . . . He always affirmed that he had been a platonic guide."

It was a long and frightful journey. It would have been bad enough in its thousand miles when the roads had been the King's Highway, paved with stone, its bridges kept in repair, and its taverns operating under royal license Now it was a small hell-journey. There was little or no food; bridges destroyed during the war remained unrepaired; gangs of discharged soldiers infested the highways, waylaying any who did not take the precaution to go well armed. All along the way General Bolívar had alerted his officers to be on watch for the caravan of Manuela. More than that. for when she reached the verdant Cauca valley on her way to the small colonial city of Popayán, a letter of encouragement, in his own hand, awaited her.

So it went on day after day, through the verdant valleys, up the sides of the Andes, down again into the gorges of rushing rivers. Christmas of 1827 came and went. Nothing marked it but the steady fall of rain, a rain which had usurped the place of the sun. The climate and the sullenness of the people had a depressing effect on everyone. Manuela must have wondered about the strange alchemy of love. For love and love alone sustained her; the feeling of being wanted was an elixir in her that gave her courage to go on. Simón's letter, read and reread, lay under her military pelisse: ". . . your love revives a life that is expiring. I cannot live without you. Come. Come to me. Come now."

*   *   *

One month and nine days after leaving Quito — just a few days beyond the New Year of 1828 — the mule caravan came to the flat environs of Bogotá. The animals, mud-splattered and weary, galled by saddle sores from the long ride, seemed to sense the end of the journey. At Cuatro Esquinas — The Four Corners — the caravan came to the stone-paved road, here still called the King's Highway. A little settlement strung out along the road, thick mud walls and dun-colored, windowless houses thatched with straw, huddled among the agave plants.

The lancers unwound their legs from the saddle pommels, swung their feet into stirrups, straightened their jaguar-skin shakos and lifted up their steel-tipped bamboo shafts, on which hung limply the gonfalons of the Republic; they prepared for their entrance into the capital. Still the pattern of their reception did not change. People emerged briefly from their houses and looked at the squadron, then quickly, sullenly, went back inside and barricaded the doors.

The earth, too, was unsmiling. The light of a rainy sky trembled on the willows, shedding verdurous gloom over the green savannahs. Even the chattering Jonotás, who usually could extract humor from the most terrible of moments, had fallen silent.

To Manuela, there was a single reason for the discontent she had seen these thousand miles. The reason was contained in a word, in a name. It was . . . Santander. This "man of laws," with his stupid dithyrambs about liberty, his double-tongue and his double-dealing, had brought the country to the edge of civil war. Bolívar had come back to Colombia to end the disunity, but his policies of reconciliation had merely opened wider the wounds of perfidy. He knew well what was needed; how had he phrased it?

As long as the leaders congregate around me, Colombia will remain united; afterward there will be civil war.

Yes, Bolívar was the catalyst. The three divisions of the Republic — Venezuela, Colombia, and Ecuador — had little in common. In large measure their interests conflicted; there was no common economic policy; the distances were great — and un-bridged; the Andes, unyielding and monolithic, divided the land into spheres of particularism, where each section was ruled by its own self-centered leader. There was only a single element — an ideal, a name, a man — who held all these discordant elements to-gether. And that was Bolívar. Her poor Simón was prematurely wearing himself out by his constant riding back and forth between the contending parties, trying to hold them together in some semblance of unity until the Republic could climb out of the chaos that a war of fourteen years had created. And how was he treated? No sooner had he left Lima than Santander sent down agents and brought about a revolt in his regiments; his finest officers were arrested, sent out of the country they had freed. It was impossible for Santander to deny it; he had ordered the church bells of Bogotá rung as if for a great victory.

For Bolívar, it was the last straw, the one thing needed to con-vince him that, as Manuela had long known, Santander was indeed "the enemy." "I can no longer rely on him," the Liberator said, "I have no longer any confidence in his heart or his morals."

So Bolívar reassumed the duties of his office, and called for broader powers to meet the present emergencies and to crush rebellions wherever they reared themselves. Then he demanded a new constitution. "We must make a new social contract — the people must redeem their sovereignty."

Santander responded "Dictatorship," and came out openly against him with formidable opposition. Bolívar answered "Or chaos." And so they were joined in combat. Now, where once there were cheers, Manuela heard Bolívar's name hissed with execrations. The time of reckoning was at hand.

The narrow streets of Bogotá were empty as they entered. The sun, breaking through the heavy mist, glistened moistly on the wet cobblestones; for a moment it highlighted the squat color-splashed buildings; then it disappeared, and its place was usurped by the mist. Manuela, who had lived amidst the gay Sevillian architecture of Lima, was depressed by her first view of the capital

of Gran Colombia. She could hardly believe that it had a population of twenty thousand. The streets were so narrow that if one
were sufficiently long-armed he might meet the hand of his
neighbor stretched out from the other side. The buildings had
nothing of the airy gayness of Lima, they were box-like, heavy, of
thick-walled adobe construction — easily converted into massive
fortresses once the great doors were closed. The windows, heavily
barred or grilled, were without glass: the cold Bogotá air (as well
as the curiosity of the passers-by) was met by screens of thickly
starched muslin.

Bogotá lay at the foot of mountains that reared up behind the
city. Its principal street, the Calle de Comercio, ran with an un-
erring straightness through its heart; and along it was a monotonous line of buildings — the stores — all barred with grills as if they
were barracks. Of God, Bogotá had a divine sufficiency. The principal buildings were churches or convents — six for monks, four
for nuns, and two (the College of the Holy Rosary was the most
famed) for schools of higher learning. Bogotá, as Manuela was
soon to learn forcibly, was intensely religious, despite twenty years
of war, one third of the real estate in the capital was still in the
hands of the Church.

The squadron, with Colonel Demarquet in the lead position,
emerged from the winding Calle de Florian and clattered in the
great plaza, scattering on its way a few Indians who had braved
the sharp cold rain to draw water from the fountain in the center.
The plaza was the amphitheater of Bogotá, markets were held
there on Fridays, religious processions when the divine calendar
decreed it, and bullfights when bulls could be found. And now
as the reign of terror gripped the land, it was the arena for public
executions. The Cathedral, stately and massive, was at one end;
governmental buildings, not in the least different from any of
the other one-storied structures of the capital, flanked the other
sides.

Colonel Demarquet summoned with his mutilated left hand one
of the Indians. The man snatched the sodden hat from his head,

pulled at the rug-like *ruana* draped across his shoulders, and in proper humility listened to the questions. Did he know where the Liberator, General Bolívar, was staying at this moment? Was he at his manor house — the Quinta — or was he at the Palace of San Carlos? The Indian suggested he must be living at the Quinta, for the Colonel could see that Bogotá had been rocked only recently by a terrible earthquake, which had left many of the churches topless and the governmental palace in partial ruins.

Manuela would have preferred to go to the Palace, anywhere other than the Quinta. After the long journey, she had need of the ministry of Jonotás — to be bathed and perfumed with verbena water, to have her artful pastel make-up applied, to slip out of her riding clothes and be enfolded into some cashmere affair that would give her body grace and poise. It was — need the Colonel be reminded? — almost two years since she had been seen by the General.

Demarquet was a soldier. He had his orders; and the orders were to bring Manuela to his General at once on arrival. While he was, as a Frenchman, delighted to be taking some part in an *affaire de coeur*, he would in this instance follow exactly his commands from Bolívar. To the Quinta!

With night hanging its blue veils over the streets of Bogotá, the squadron went on its way. The stores were closed, the narrow sidewalks silent and deserted; only a few of the streets were pallidly lit by small candles which flickered behind glass globes. People who ventured abroad were accompanied by a servant, who led the way with a small light to break a darkness as black as a wolf's mouth.

The villa of Bolívar — the Quinta — lay north of the city. The squadron clattered along the cobblestones — the while raising a regiment of barking dogs — crossed the Carmen Bridge which spanned the San Agustín River, and made for the suburbs.

On a rise of ground partially enveloped in mist was the Quinta. It lay at the base of a gigantic mountain, at the mouth of the Boquerón. Through this gap in the mountains, heavy, moisture-

laden fog clouds drifted in to bank the city. Ribands of fog drifted
through the cedars, the oaks, and the stately cypresses. The trees
were covered with aerial parasites that verdured their host plants
in gray-green color; these gathered the mist and gave it off as
tinkling rain. Buried in the mass of foliage was the villa, brilliant
with lights. Sounds of laughter drifted across the night, joining
the croaking of the frogs.

"Halt!"

The voice of the sentry cut across the night like a whip slashing
the air.

"Halt!"

And soldiers, rifles at ready, poured out of the guardhouse near
the gate. They surrounded the squadron.

"Who lives?" queried a disembodied voice, as shadows became
men and men became bayonet-tipped guns.

"The Liberator."

The officer of the guard moved forward, waved his lamp in
Colonel Demarquet's face. There was instant recognition. And a
salute. He moved around to the others, examined their papers. He
then held his light up to Manuela.

The startled officer saw a self-possessed woman in her thirties
looking down on him with a strange, enigmatic smile. She was
dressed in a hussar's uniform, blood-red pants, skintight and
braided in black arabesques, a military pelisse, and black military
jackboots, whose golden spurs gave out, as the horse stirred rest-
lessly, a sound like the tinkling of a small golden bell. A brace of
brass Turkish pistols, cocked and ready for use, was at her knees.
And, as if her attractive face did not suggest that she was indeed
woman, coral earrings dropped from her ears. A woman, dressed
like a hussar, riding at night — the officer was almost ready to
begin a lengthy questioning when Colonel Demarquet, having
enjoyed the moment long enough, leaned from his horse and said
in a confidential tone, "This, Señor Capitán, is La Sáenz."

Lining the path to the villa, between the thick moss-covered
trees, were the mementos of battles. Cannons that had been

dragged by Bolívar's troops to the heights of Carabobo stood there in proud dignity, despite their broken caissons. There were bronze mortars, used at the siege of Pasto, captured Spanish pieces still bearing the arms of Fernando VII. Manuela walked by them, following the path to the villa, the tinkling of her golden spurs joining the trilling of the tree frogs.

Glass doors opened into the foyer where candles behind hurricane glass threw dancing shadows over the patterned red walls. In the soft light, Manuela could see mahogany furniture, Empire in style, upholstered in red damask; a sofa painted in golden lacquer; a chair heavily ornamented with gold leaf. On the right of the foyer was a small salon, also in red and gold, its walls hung with pictures of Bolívar's battles. A lone candle glowed in the massive glass candelabrum.

Manuela passed through the French doors that led to the library — a large room, papered in a warm red with a dark leaf pattern, and lit by a large cut-glass candelabrum, where a hundred tapers glowed like the Pleiades.

The day of the Congress of Ocaña was at hand, and all of Bolívar's warriors were there, the officers of his legions who had fought all the crucial battles of the war of independence. There was William Fergusson, lively and gay; serious little O'Leary, now a general; young Bedford Wilson, the son of Sir Robert Wilson; and, since the days in Peru attached in warm affection to the cause of Bolívar, Colonel Ibarra and Thomas Menby. And Dr. Moore, complaining without cease of the ague which the dampness of Bogotá brought on. All were there, all of Manuela's old friends, they whose lives had been bound together by his ideals.

There were, also, faces new to her. One of these was General Urdaneta, a handsome officer and now a member of Bolívar's military cabinet. Like his leader, he was a Venezuelan, a complete man, who under stress had serenity and exhibited personal bravery. In this political world, where the double tongue of the adder was in daily usage, he remained frank and firm, always assuming complete responsibility for his acts. His house in Bogotá, where his attractive wife Dolores held sway, was a center of refinement and noblesse. Urdaneta would have no difficulty in including Manuela in the affection that he held for Simón Bolívar.

Nor would José Paris. José — everyone called him Pepé — was the only one present in civilian dress, powder-blue broadcloth frock coat, white shirt with high collar. He was one of Bolívar's most self-effacing friends, a sensitive, well-traveled gentleman, whose father had held lucrative offices under the Spanish Crown. Pepé Paris had lived in Spain and France, and knew everyone of consequence. He had served in the revolution; then when actual combat had ceased, he had opened Colombia's famous emerald mines, and now was one of the wealthy men of Bogotá. He was personally close to Simón Bolívar, whom he helped in the management of his finances, but he at times entered the political scene. His equanimity was hated by the political enemy.

Everyone present — except General Córdoba, who could not dissemble his hatred for Manuela — greeted her with the same respect they would have shown Simón Bolívar's wife; for she was, beyond this, a companion-in-arms, one who had gone through the test of fire with them in defeat and triumph.

It was the eve of Ocaña — the seating of the Congress that was to decide the fate of Gran Colombia, and, in a more personal sense, to decide the glory of Simón Bolívar. This meeting of his principal advisers at the villa was less a conference to work out parliamentary stratagems than a council of war to prevent the disintegration of Colombia. But with Manuela here the council drifted into personalities, and in the warmth generated by Fergusson's generous pouring of Irish whisky the meeting evaporated into pandemonium.

This brought out Bolívar's secretary, José Santana. He had not seen Manuela since leaving Lima, and was delighted to have her again with them. It had been Don José who had kept up a continuous flow of correspondence with her, when Bolívar did not have time to write; it was José who had been the amanuensis of passion, quilling the love letters which Bolívar dictated to him.

He led her to Bolívar's study, and Manuela entered without knocking. She had ridden a thousand miles to answer his summons: "Come. Come to me. Come now."

Some time later, when José Palacios was closing the foyer door, he heard the wild laughter of Manuela and the sound of her golden spurs tinkling musically as they fell to the floor.

12

THE DIALECTICS OF LOVE AND HATE

THEY WALKED in the garden.

It was a beautiful day, still vibrant with the emotions of the night; about Manuela hung an aura of loveliness, and the musk of passion. Time had not stripped her of a particle of her mystery and fascination, and she still remembered — so few others had — how to give to Simón Bolívar's intense nature a new flow of energy. Hand in hand, she in a cashmere with ermine-lined hood, he in blue uniform with silver braid, they walked between the beds of primroses. A toothless gardener, showing his vacant gums, bowed before them and mumbled in good-natured raillery, "Your Excellency, the Queen of Sheba has come to admire the beauty of the flowers in the gardens of Solomon."

Between the century-old cedars, where bell-shaped fuchsias dropped red-flowering tear-petals, were massed honeysuckle and wild roses. In the center of the formal garden was a fountain carved from gray stone, whose gushing water filled the quiet days with eternal murmuring. The villa was a one-story colonial house, with red tiled roof and red brick floors; the ceilings were low, decorated in gold leaf. There were four rooms and a foyer — library, salon, dining room, and bedroom — warmed on cold Bogotá nights by a fireplace in the library, and by charcoal braziers in the other rooms. The villa had been built in the beginning of the century by José Antonio Portocarrero, under the shadows of the moun-

tains of Monserrate. The estate had passed on the death of Portocarrero to his daughter, who, being under suspicion as a royalist
sympathizer, was more than willing to sell it to the new Republic.
On July 16, 1820, the Quinta had been given to Simón Bolívar "as
a small demonstration of gratitude and recognition . . . for the
immense sacrifices that he had made in the restitution of liberty."

This villa was home to Simón Bolívar. Whenever he was not
campaigning and within Gran Colombia, he would ride there and
in the tranquil melancholy of the honeysuckle and the cedars he
would attempt to regain something of his lost self. And now with
Manuela here . . .

Manuela saw, in the cold morning light, the great change that
had come over him. His thin, weathered face told of the days he
had spent in the open under the pitiless burn of the tropical sun.
The very elements had etched their glyphs into his face. His hair,
the thick black mop which he had combed in the romantic
Byronic style, now almost ashen, swept forward in ordered dis-
array as if it were wind-tossed Manuela was shocked by his appearance. She had always thought of him as at their first meeting
in 1822, when in a gold-embroidered uniform of sanguine red he
rode the streets of Quito in triumph on a white horse.

Now the lithe, once tireless body was used up. It was 1828,
and he was forty-five years of age, a moment which in the tropics
signals the sapping of vitality. Bolívar was a tired man physically
and mentally, even though his pen had not yet lost its vigor of
expression, or his voice the timbre of excitement. Still there were
dangerous signposts, warning signals which Manuela could easily
read. Twenty years of riding back and forth across the mountains
had destroyed his prodigious vitality. Bolívar was suddenly, prematurely old.

His enemies, harvesting their planted hates, liked to put it all
on Manuela, saying that Samson succumbing to the wiles of a har-
ridan had at least regained enough of his strength to pull down
his own wretched world upon himself. But this Bolívar could not
do, he lacked the strength.

"He is bewitched by La Sáenz."

Time had multiplied Manuela's powers, and she was persuaded that if anything could save him, it was she. She made certain that he was not bothered with trivialities. Many details, since she had full knowledge of the politics, she handled herself. Visitors did not always get to Bolívar directly, and his secretaries and herself managed between them to save his strength — and his spleen. Although he was often outraged by Manuela's ascendancy over him, he allowed himself in these first weeks to be guided in many things by her. As a matter of fact, the villa was efficiently, if informally, operated. María Luisa, an Indian woman whose numerous skirts made her look like a tea cozy, was the cook. Petrona, as graceful as a two-wheeled oxcart, swept through the rooms. José Palacios, seemingly as indestructible as the Andes, served as always as the general's valet and major-domo. This left Manuela the time to act as mistress of the chalet. She was remembered in this role by a young Colombian:

> I was received by one of the most attractive women that I could remember; her complexion was pearl-white, the face oval; all her salient features were handsome; eyes that carried one away, dynamic and commanding. There was too a luscious moistness about her as if she just emerged from a bath spiced by fragrant verbena. With flattering suavity, thanks to her servant Petrona who arranged her dress, she invited me to walk in the garden of the Quinta. This grand lady was, in that gallant epoch, the animating spirit of the house and of the villa of Bolívar.

They were often in the garden, strolling together through the stands of Venezuelan pine which Bolívar had planted to remind him of his boyhood home. When the sun warmed the thin air, they would walk under a trellis enflowered with purple bougainvillea to the swimming pool. It was built like the baths of Caligula, walled by a high whitewashed barricade and filled with water, the color of lapis lazuli when it reflected the Bogotá sky. Above the pool was the naked rock escarpment of the mountain. A small room, its brick floor carpeted with woven rush, was Manuela's dressing room; beyond the French doors of purple glass, the pool danced invitingly. It became part of a sort of choreography of love — the walk, the confidences, the tingling sensation of the water, then again the walk in the sunlight. The regimen imposed by Manuela was having good effect; the chest-racking cough which Bolívar tried always to smother was now less violent, and there was a return of his good humor. As on the day when they brought him a new gardener.

"My General, here is the gardener you have asked for."

Bolívar dropped Manuela's arm and, with the good-natured bantering she had long remembered as a part of him, he turned to the old man. Recommended as a humble and honest man, he had been summoned to the villa without being told the nature of the audience. An old soldier, as anyone could see from the badly mended blue greatcoat and the saber scar across the mouth, his face was deeply lined and almost toothless — if one overlooked the two lonely incisors that pushed out his upper lip. He had fought for the last Spanish Viceroy, and had been in Bogotá the day the courier brought in the startling news of Bolívar's overwhelming victory at Boyacá. As much as he tried to disguise his speech, he could not hide the accents that proclaimed him a *godo*. He had done odd jobs about the city, keeping to himself, afraid that any ill wind might flush him out and blow him to the gibbet. When he heard that he had been summoned to Bolívar, he was certain that his luck had run out. He crossed himself three times and fell into step behind the guard. Certain of his fate, he trembled as if palsied before the Liberator and waited for what he thought would be the sentence of death.

"Your name."

"José María Alvarez, a creature of Your Excellency's."

"Where are you from?"

"Cartagena."

"You don't have the appearance of a Cartagenian," said Bolívar, remembering that most of that Caribbean city's inhabitants had Negro blood.

"I meant to say that I was born in Cartagena of Levant."

"So then you are a royalist."

"Señor," shouted the old soldier with concern and trembling, "I am Spanish and republican. You see, Your Excellency, you see, I was born in the valley of Andorra which is a republic, my mother was a Catalan who brought me —"

"Enough," said Bolívar, holding up his index finger and wagging it back and forth in front of the man's startled face. "Enough. Are you married?"

"Not exactly," he replied, happy over the change of subject. "That is, not exactly — still the same as being married."

"What is your occupation?"

"In my country, I was a farmer, a gardener."

"Very well. You will have charge of the gardens of this Quinta, that is, if you prove satisfactory."

"By the Good Mary," the Spaniard shouted, his eyes sparkling with delight, "if the earth is good and there is plenty of fertilizer, I will give you such cabbages and carrots as Your Excellency has never eaten in his life."

Bolívar threw back his head and laughed, putting his arm about Manuela, delighted at his mixture of candor and arrogance. "Go then, and you will be given all you need to produce this; and from this day forward twenty pesos a month!"

José María, who had never seen this amount at one time in his whole life, dropped his hat and would have fallen at Bolívar's feet to give him thanks. But Bolívar moved away, and Manuela turned to the old man and said, "*Vaya*, he is not the lion that he is painted."

Bogotá was not Lima. In this small city, wrapped in the folds of the Andes, a deep religious feeling held society in strict conformity to ancient mores. Here was none of Lima's gaiety, or its cosmopolitanism. Moreover, Bogotá was hostile to foreigners; its conventions were absolute; and while Eros quested afield, as elsewhere, his straying was covered by a thick veil of moral cant.

Bogotá society was depressing and dull — but it was the Bogotá way. And into its midst dropped Manuela.

Her reputation had preceded her — Santander saw to that — and everyone expected the worst. She did not disappoint them. She rode through the streets in her hussar's uniform, accompanied by her fantastic slaves; her manners, like her speech, were extravagant, imprudent, impetuous:

> One day [a friend later recalled] while riding through the streets of Bogotá, she noticed a soldier carrying orders in a billet placed, as it was customary, at the end of his rifle. Manuela galloped down upon the poor foot soldier, grabbed the billet while passing. The whole incident took only an instant. The soldier fired at her; she reined in her horse, came about and replaced the billet and rode off again, an act of folly

It shocked Bogotá society to see the Liberator-President riding in an open landau (the only one in the city) with his mistress. It angered many a woman in Bogotá, with whom he had once had casual affairs, that this Manuela should have triumphed over them all. It enraged his political enemies that this hetaira, as they called her, should have so great an ascendancy over him. Few knew — and few cared — that Manuela had become a vital necessity to him; that her passionate loyalty, her tenderness, her follies, her calculated imprudences were all part of the fabric of his love for her.

> Your love revives a life that is expiring. I cannot live without you. I cannot voluntarily renounce my Manuela.

She became the target for the barbs of his enemies; little scandalmongering broadsides, called *papeluchas*, pilloried her mercilessly under a thin guise of objectivity. "This Madame du Barry," they called her; and they spent bottles of printers' ink in classical allusions to the irreparable harm woman has done to man when she has entered the arena of politics. And — in their eyes most damning of all — they called her a foreigner.

"Why," Manuela asked, "do they call those to the south of us 'brothers,' and why do they yet call me a foreigner?"

This was the most polite of their epithets for her, but she flung back at them all of their slack-jawed gossip, and soon everyone who attacked her felt the nails of this amazon. It was only in the quiet of the villa that she could escape the attacks.

Yet if Manuela could escape the personal assaults on her in the isolation of the Quinta, she could not escape politics. No one could. Everyone's move in the city was dictated by politics. It appeared at every function. It was discussed in every home, in every street. One began the day with it, and with it ended the night. But politics no longer meant Bolívar's vision of a united South America: it was regional politics, petty, partisan, intensely personal. Its heart was the struggle between Bolívar and Santander. The whole of Gran Colombia was split into two violently opposed political factions. There was no compromise; no way to bridge the dichotomy.

The nation was bankrupt. The treasury was empty, and Gran Colombia was besieged by its creditors. Commerce was at a standstill. The plantations, which had flowered under Spanish rule, and declined as a natural consequence of war, had fallen into decay. Roads, which had once been maintained by the Crown, now were but quagmires. Old soldiers were everywhere, diseased, miserable, and penniless, with nothing more than unfilled promises of pay in their tattered uniforms. Bolívar threw himself into economic battle to relieve these strains. As in the old days, he was indefatigable. He preoccupied himself with customs duties, agriculture, education, hospitals, slavery, soldiers' welfare. But behind his back his opponents kept up a withering fire of invective. He wanted unity; his political enemies in reply shouted "Liberty." He wanted a new social contract; his adversaries, an implementing and perfecting of the old.

The first small victory was Bolívar's. His draft of a new constitution was ready and a constitutional convention was convoked in the little mountain town of Ocaña, miles from the poisonous atmosphere of Bogotá. The agenda called for order; actually, as everyone knew, it would be chaos. The situation demanded a strong hand. And so, in March 1828, off to the convention rode Bolívar, racked with coughing as he was. He never arrived there. On the way, things began to happen as he had feared. The disunity of Gran Colombia had reawakened Spain, and her fleet was cruising off the coast, seeking a place to land troops. Then, five hundred miles to the north, a section of the army in the fortress-city of Cartagena threatened revolt. Bolívar stopped at the little mountain town of Bucaramanga and surveyed his political dilemma: "If I go North, the South will disintegrate; if I go South, the North will revolt."

So Bolívar, puzzled into hesitation, went nowhere at all. He stayed in Bucaramanga, a strategic place from which to fly to any point of the compass. And there he sat in hectic impotence, giving over the direction of the Congress of Ocaña to General O'Leary. It was he who read Bolívar's message to the convention in the Church of St. Francis on April 2:

> Without force there is no virtue; without virtue the state dies. Anarchy destroys freedom, but unity preserves it. Give us, gentlemen, give us inexorable laws. . . . If the convention does not conduct itself with wisdom, and the people with prudence, there will begin a civil war, and God alone knows where it will end. . . .

The Convention began badly for Bolívar. His political enemies were able to outvote him on almost every issue, article by article. His new constitution was watered down until it began to lose all the executive powers he thought to gain. He rejected as beneath his dignity the idea of appearing himself at the convention to influence the delegates' opinion. Then when he suddenly decided to appear anyway, his delegates this time screamed in one voice: "Don't come, Your Excellency, your presence will be misunderstood."

Bolívar alternated between going and staying. "I can't improve things because I have no power to do so. I can't step over the barriers of a constitution which I must uphold. I cannot change the laws of our governmental system. I am not God, that I can change men and matters. . . ." And he threatened to resign, if the convention did not give up its chess-like intrigues

O'Leary, leading the fight, swore in good Irish when he read that letter, and his reply was forthright:

> For God's sake, don't say in your letters that you are leaving the country, even should that be your irrevocable decision, because it gives life and weapons to your enemies and works against your good friends.

So Bolívar stayed in the village of Bucaramanga for the sixty days of the convention, frustrated, angry, constantly bored. During the morning he would ride the countryside on his white horse, Paloma Blanca, in the dress of a country gentleman — white woolen trousers strapped beneath polished Cordovan boots, blue frock coat, and black stock, his tanned face hidden under a wide-brimmed sugar planter's Panama. In the afternoon he would rest in his hammock, or dictate to his secretaries. But when night closed in, his anger would return to gall him. Too often, in these days, his companions had to report, "The Liberator was in bad humor."

The sentence recurs in a diary of those sixty days. The present being out of joint, Simón Bolívar returned to his past, and in those periods of bad humor he reminisced with his French confidant, Colonel Louis Péroux de Lacroix. He spun out stories of his youth, his life in Paris when he had frequented the salons of the great, kept a ballet dancer for a mistress, had a box at the opera, and ridden the streets in an open gilt-painted landau, with lackeys in powdered periwigs. He spun back time to the moment that he possessed Fanny du Villars, replacing both her husband, a marshal of France, and her lover, King Louis XVIII himself. Only recently he had had a letter from this same Fanny: "After twenty-one years . . . my first love . . . your ring accompanies me. . . . Tell me (but in your own hand) that you still remember our love." And she had sent him a pastel portrait of herself.

Péroux de Lacroix was a picturesque *picaro*. A good officer and a loyal friend of Bolívar — fond of Manuela, too — his origins were so obscure that one could not extricate them from his own contrived legends. He had been born in France in 1781, and had served with Napoleon's staff in the invasion of Russia. Later he left for Stockholm with the Bernadottes, and was then sent to England, presumably to spy upon Louis XVIII, who was being kept there on diplomatic ice until he could be used against Napoleon. Lacroix had the chameleon quality of a Talleyrand; instead of spy, he became the monarch's confidant, so that when Napoleon sank in his own contradictions, his former officer saved something from the wreck. Soon he was operating a contraband fleet off the coast of Colombia. In 1823 he was given a place in Bolívar's army. Now he was part of the great cause, loyal and self-effacing.

But while Lacroix wrote down the rambling thoughts of his general, the world of Bolívar was coming apart at the seams. The convention continued badly. In the poisonous atmosphere of the Church of St. Francis, the brain was stupefied, the ears set hammering, the temples beat until all eyes were darkened with a veil of blood. The political battle had sunk from ideas to personalities; it had become a life-and-death struggle between Bolívar and Santander. They were not gods dwelling on Olympus, they were men of human appetites. The opposition suspected Bolívar of wishing to be a dictator, and in the midst of a debate on the language of the constitution, his name was hissed with execrations.

"Those wretched creatures," said Bolívar, "even the air they breathe, they owe to me . . . and they dare to suspect me."

Then Padilla revolted.

It had been in the Cartagena air for some time, and it was one of the principal reasons why Bolívar had not moved from the strategically placed village of Bucaramanga. Padilla was Santander's man; his action suggested that, if the convention went badly for the opposition, a military revolt would be the next step.

Padilla was a huge man; a mulatto, curly-pated and squint-eyed. In the revolutionary wars he had been a hero; he had once defeated a Spanish armada in a sea battle. Now he was confused and restless, and he remained, as always, fearless and violent. Sanguinary, too. Once he suspected a fellow officer of using loaded dice, but he said nothing — until the man reached out for the heap of silver pesos. Then Padilla whipped out a knife, drove it through the officer's hand into the table, and left him wriggling like a transfixed butterfly. Only recently he had publicly proclaimed his wife — who could stand no longer his amorous ferocity — a whore. Now he was in revolt. The United States Consul informed Henry Clay of the affair:

> This city has been for several days past in a state of alarm. The dwellings of all inhabitants have been closed apprehensive of a commencement of hostilities between the different factions. General Padilla, a man of colour, was the principle in the excitement. He fled at midnight and proceeded toward Ocaña . . . for the purpose of seeing Santander, who, it was said, was his adviser in this recent affair.

So, to plague Bolívar — when it was not Padilla, it was Páez, and when it was not that simple-headed theophagist, then it was Francisco de Paula Santander. All this provoked Manuela to write Bolívar:

> In the last mail, I said nothing about Cartagena so as not to speak of disagreeable things; now I congratulate you because the affair did not turn out as they had hoped. This is one thing Santander has done, not believing that he had done enough. *It is for this that we should kill him.* I wish to God that all these devils on two sticks, Paula [Santander], Padilla and Páez, would die. It will be a great day for Colombia when these vermin are exterminated, these and others who are sacrificing you with their foulness. It is a most humane thought. *That ten should die to save millions.*

And soon Bolívar was writing her from Bucaramanga:

April 3, 1828

GREETINGS:
I received, my dear Manuela, your three letters which have filled me with a thousand affections. Each letter had its merit, each its particular grace. One of your letters was very affection-

ate and filled me with tenderness, the other amused me very much by your sense of humor, and the third atoned for past and un-merited injuries. To all of them I reply with a word more eloquent than your model Éloise, *I am going to return to Bogotá*. We shall see each other soon. How does this strike you? Does it please you? Well, my love, thus am I, who loves you with all his soul.

BOLÍVAR

In Colombia, Bolívar was perhaps the only one who loved Manu-ela with all his soul. Her detractors now were legion. The first thing that women talked about when taking their morning choco-late was Manuela's latest escapade. On the street men exchanged pointed stories about her. Above all she was resented. The people did not like the way money from the depleted treasury was spent upon her. General Urdaneta often provided it:

> MY DEAR GENERAL BOLÍVAR:
> Enclosed another letter from Manuelita. Colonel Barriga, the paymaster, did not arrive with money for her, but she lacks not for it, I gave it to her.

At night there were parties at the Quinta, where Manuela dressed in the newest fashions. She had the latest magazines — the *London Mail, Variedades* — and from them copied dresses which were the envy of every woman of Bogotá. When she appeared in blue velvet, with gold-bordered short train, short sleeves, and long white kidskin gloves from Paris, she was lashed by the tongues of the ladies. To this Manuela reacted as always. With a flaunting dis-regard of their social prejudices, she flung their own loose morals back in their faces. At night, at the Quinta, in the company of the British Legion or others from Bogotá, she allowed her slave to make a charade of the women of the city. "Lolo" Boussingault, a French scientist living in Bogotá, wrote home about it:

> At night, Manuelita is metamorphosed; she feels, I believe, the effects of a few glasses of port, of which she is very fond. She cer-tainly wears rouge, her hair is artificially arranged and she has a lot of animation and is gay, but she uses risqué expressions.

And of Jonotás, her slave:

> It must be said that Manuelita is never separated from a young slave, a mulatress with woolly hair, a strong-faced woman always dressed as a soldier.
>
> This Jonotás is Manuelita's *alter ego*. A singular being, a comedian, a first-class mimic who would be successful in the theater anywhere. She has an amazing gift for imitation. She has an impassive face. As an actress she does the funniest things with imperturbable seriousness. I heard her mimic a monk preaching the Passion; nothing could be more laughable. For nearly an hour she held us under the spell of her eloquence, her gestures; the vocal intonations of the monks were exactly given.

No one was spared. Every woman who had criticized Manuela was mocked. Doña Teresa del Castillo y Rada, the wife of Bolívar's Secretary of the Treasury (who looked like a turtle), made ill-concealed reference to Manuela's sterility, was caricatured by the actress-slave. "Very unbecoming and very imprudent," said the Frenchman. And Ana, wife of a member of the famous Pombo family, was ridiculed as only Jonotás would vulgarly do it . . . for her inexhaustible fertility.

The talk got about. No walls could conceal it. It reached the ears of the Secretary of State, who was shocked at the slow disintegration of Bolívar's reputation. José María Restrepo was the patriarch of the Restrepos, a powerful and fecund tribe from the state of Antioquia. They were lawyers, traditionalists, and people of honor. Don José had a severe countenance, with the curved nose of a Sephardic Jew. He had guided Bolívar's foreign policy through all the vicissitudes of the past years; but now he was shaken by the accumulation of bitterness, and the extravagances of Manuela. He vowed to his wife that the history of Colombia which he was then writing would never mention the name of Manuela. . . .

Life was becoming difficult.

There was dangerous talk of assassination. Manuela had it from Colonel William Fergusson, who rode in from seeing the General:

His Excellency, separated from us, remained at a good distance
for more than an hour and a half, but we always kept him in our
sight, although he tried on more than one occasion to give us the
slip. When we returned he said:

"You are guarding me as much as though you suspected a plot
upon my life. Tell me frankly, has someone written you from the
convention?"

Seeing no one else answered, I took from under my military
coat a letter from O'Leary. He read it, raised his head and fixed
his eyes upon me:

"Do you all know about this letter?"

"Yes."

"Then," continued Bolívar, "read here what Briceño has sent
me," and he handed us a letter. "I did not show this to anyone or
speak about it, but as I know of the same incident, you all might
as well know that O'Leary's fears are justified."

Assassination! Then Simón Bolívar was really in danger of living
or dying his own Ides of March!

Manuela showed Fergusson some of the latest *papeluchas* that
circulated in the city and in the *Conductor*, calling Bolívar a "tyrant," among other things; they aroused her to fury. She knew the
author. It was fierce-tempered Vicente Azuero, who mixed vitriol
with his printer's ink. His gray hair had not given him the wisdom
of his years. Manuela decided to aid him in acquiring good judgment; she sent a huge dark lancer out on Bogotá's street to begin
his education. This soldier met the elderly Azuero walking the
Calle de Comercio, distributing the day's calumnies against Bolívar. The lancer knocked the old man spinning into the street, and
then with his high-heeled boots went to work on the pamphleteer's
face. Just then General Córdoba appeared. He was returning from
visiting his apple-cheeked fiancée, Fanny Henderson, when he saw
this Brobdingnagian creature in the act of kicking the old man
into insensibility. Córdoba drew his sword, backed the lancer to
the wall, and freed Azuero from death.

But before Córdoba could take action against Manuela, Fergusson was personally wrecking the office of another scandal
sheet, called the *Incombustible*. He caught young Florentino

González in the very act of committing to type an abusive and scathing attack on Bolívar, calling for "the death of the tyrant." There was more than politics here, for González had married a discarded mistress of Bolívar, the lovely Bernardina. A letter known to almost everyone had been written to her by the Liberator — "My adorable Bernardina . . . everything about you is love — you are everything in the world to me." González deeply resented Bolívar, but on the instant he transferred his hate to Fergusson. The furious Irishman pounded González until he was senseless, then set about to make a shambles out of that printing press that specialized in scandal.

The opposition, when they heard of it, thundered for Fergusson's head, and they demanded that Bolívar do something about it. Simón Bolívar was doing something, but not precisely what the opposition expected. He ordered his delegates, now in a political minority at Ocaña, to leave the convention; and thus, having no quorum, the whole Congress dissolved. The delegates found that their commissions had been retracted, and also that all the decisions of the Congress were disavowed. The army was called up, Bolívar changed from civilian attire into military uniform, and he ordered the office of Vice-President declared vacant. Then with his troops he moved on Bogotá.

"Now that the bull is out, we shall see who has the guts to take it by the tail."

On July 13, in the great plaza in front of the Cathedral, facing all of his generals bedizened with their medals, Bolívar took the oath of office and assumed full dictatorial power over the Republic:

> The good of the Republic does not consist in hateful dictatorship. Dictatorship is glorious only when it seals the abyss of revolution, but woe to a people that accustoms itself to live under dictatorial rule.

Now, seeking no refuge in dissimulation, he moved with determination. He meant to end chaos. He took up official residence at the Palace of San Carlos, and signed a series of decrees in an attempt to aid the economy of the country. He did not seek revenge; he merely wanted authority to bring an end to the political anarchy, to heal the wounds of factional strife Everything was to be done with *bienséance*. A good face was to be put on the whole procedure. So as to avoid public obloquy, Santander was selected as the first minister to the United States of America. The country's safety, its very existence, depended now on finesse, on how Bolívar could quiet the storm of this troubled time. Meanwhile, he had forgotten Manuela.

But she had not forgotten him. July 24 was his birthday, and Manuela as mistress of the Quinta prepared the manor for the celebrations. The outside of the building was festooned with flags, and in the gardens food-covered tables were arranged "with becoming elegance." Bolívar did not attend, but members of his Council did; and to give it official approval, a company of the Granadero Battalion were sent to drill in front of the villa for the guests. Manuela had her servants drag out barrels of *chicha* for the soldiers, while within the Quinta the persons of quality drank a heady port:

> When the wine had taken its effects [said a participant] one of the guests unfortunately mentioned the name of Santander. It had the effect of a spark dropping into an open gunpowder cask. With their tongues loosened, all guests let flow their invective upon the man whom they believed to be the principal enemy of Bolívar. In a still more unfortunate moment one of the guests proposed that, following an old Spanish custom, they shoot Santander in effigy.

Manuela took up the challenge. Jonotás dragged out a sack, they stuffed it with old clothes, dressed it in a castoff officer's uniform, put a bicornered hat on "Santander." Manuela herself drew the face of her enemy; somehow she got in the hauteur, the dark eyes, the long moustachios. And if there was any lingering doubt as to who it was, she painted a sign and hung it on the figure: *Francisco de Santander, killed for treason.*

A squad of soldiers, beginning to feel now the effect of the *chicha,* marched up and in mock heroics pulled "Santander" along to the gates, where he was propped up against the wall. The Dean of the Cathedral compromised the dignity of his cloth by giving the effigy the last rites of the Church. Then came the turn of Crofston.

Colonel Richard Crofston, of the British Legion, was as wild an Irishman as Fergusson, and as unpredictable as Manuela. It was said he was having an affair with Jonotás "who wore the uniform of a man with her hair cut short — but this did not stop Richard Crofston from loving her, which she returned."

Crofston ordered his adjutant to give the command to fire. In the day's first flash of reason, the Colombian officer sheathed his sword and said:

"I refuse, sir, to take part in this undignified farce."

Crofston swore at him, placed him under arrest, and then, taking his sword, drew up the soldiers and gave the order to fire.

"Santander" disintegrated before the volley.

It was a shot heard all around Bogotá.

In one burst of irresponsibility Manuela had destroyed the carefully laid plans of Bolívar's policy. It was her old enemy Córdoba who gave the details to the General. He wrote a bitterly frank letter to the Liberator.

Alone in the cold of his residence, Bolívar paced the floor. All through the afternoon his aides could hear the click-click of his military boots as they struck the floor with the crispness of castanets. Late in the afternoon of July 29, he called in his secretary and dictated part of a letter; then in disgust he rose, pulled the piece of paper away from the surprised man, curtly dismissed him, and sat down and wrote the message in his own hand:

My Dear General Córdoba:
    You know that I fully understand what you have told me. Obviously I see, more clearly than anyone else, the calculated stupidities made by my friends. I am thinking seriously of suspending Richard Crofston of the Granaderos and sending him away from

this command to serve elsewhere. He alone is guilty. But then he has a legal excuse, that it was not a public crime. Still it was an eminently despicable and a stupid one.

As for Manuela — the lovable fool — what would you want me to say to you? You well know from times past how often I have tried to separate myself from her. But this I have been unable to do, for she is so stubborn. However, since this has happened I shall have to use more determination and if need be force her to leave the country — or go where she will . . .

13

A NIGHT OF SEPTEMBER

THE PLAZUELA DE SAN CARLOS had been built in the times of
Carlos IV, when Spain was still mistress of her fate and had un-
challenged possession of her kingdoms beyond the seas. The imprint of the New World was upon it, even though its extended balconies suggested the buildings of Valencia and it followed the
unsocial tendency of Burgos by hiding its patios behind massive
doors. Thus only its ugly postern was to be seen from the street.
The Plazuela — the little plaza — had been built about a small
park, where there was a large gurgling fountain, here the people
drew their water, and horses slaked their thirst. Around the fountain, the two-storied buildings formed three parts of a square in
keeping with the spirit of the times and in obedience to good sense.
Below on the street, and around the square, rooms were rented
to merchants, where the more fortunate, those in possession of
the correct emoluments, might shop without fear of being knocked
down by horsemen or swept into the streets by pack-loaded
Indians.

To those who had lived through the revolution, the Plazuela
remained a symbol of the spirit of independence, for here on the
ground floor, in a secret room, the famous Antonio Nariño had
printed, in 1794, the first Spanish translation of *The Rights of Man*.
It was a publication which launched the revolution, and sent
Nariño off to ten horrible years in a stinking North African dungeon.

On the second floor, running about the whole building, were living quarters which shared the veranda and the balconies that projected over the Plazuela. One apartment here had great advantage; part of the balcony overhung the street, and from it one could see the Palace of San Carlos where Bolívar lived, and in the other direction the Calle de Comercio, the principal street of commerce and promenade. San Ignacio, the church of the Jesuits, was directly in front of it; from this balcony could be seen the elite of Bogotá as they attended their daily ministrations to God. Besides, here one could listen to the latest gossip and see the latest fashions. This was the heart of Bogotá, especially designed for someone who wanted to be in on the very genesis of things.

In the first week of August, 1828, despite the dictum of Bolívar that she be "removed from the public gaze," Manuela Sáenz tinkled thirty-two silver pesos into the hands of the patrician Señor Don Pedro Lasso de la Vega, and received in return two huge iron keys. She took possession of that apartment.

Bolívar received this news with icy disapprobation. Since the "shooting" of Santander a profound estrangement had grown between him and Manuela. At first there had been violent scenes between them — not followed, as in the past, by delicious reconciliations. Manuela remained splenetic and uncompromising. In answer to his demands that she quit the capital, she reminded him of what she had written when he had first asked her to come to him: ". . . once I am there, do not afterward suggest that I return to Quito."

Well then, could she not alter the pattern of her strange behavior, could she not control these contradictions in her character, these unbecoming gestures? Surely Manuela . . . but then, exactly, this *was* Manuela. He must by now know her for what she was — a formidable character, who loved her friends and hated her enemies.

And as to her political actions: one did not have to be a sibyl to know that, if Bolívar did not do away with Santander and those about him, they would kill him, in just the same manner as Caesar was killed. It was foolish to close one's eyes to it; what she said, what she did, was the only course of action in a country divided against itself. Half measures were always repugnant to her; only harm could be caused by things half said, things half done. And as for the chaos of the moment, those revolutionaries in France had had the right answer more than thirty years ago — the Anointed Terror. Thus Manuela.

And so, sweeping along the reluctant Pepé Paris, she began the acquisition of things for her apartment. There were gilded mirrors crowned with the fashionable Empire eagle; sofas covered with blood-red damask, recently imported from France; china from England and glassware from Philadelphia, very rare and exceedingly expensive. The wines, the brandies, the sherries, she got through her friendship with members of the British Legion. Thus equipped, Manuela settled down — that is, as much as she could ever settle down with her ménage of slaves and servants and hangers-on.

And her animals. She was fond of all animals, especially cats, who roamed the house in bewildering numbers. And to add to the confusion, someone brought her a spectacled bear cub, a black bear with eyes encircled by round patches of white fur, giving it its "spectacles." It soon became Manuela's favorite. Lolo Boussingault wrote home, explaining this strange world where he lived:

> Manuela adores animals. She has a bear cub which is impossible, it has the entire run of the house. The nasty beast likes to play with all the visitors, but if you pat him he will scratch at your hands terribly, or cling to your legs so firmly it is difficult to extricate yourself.
>
> One morning I paid Manuelita a call. As she wasn't yet up, I had to go into her bedroom. I saw a terrible scene. The little bear was stretched out on his mistress, his horrible claws resting on her breasts. Seeing me there, Manuelita spoke to me with great calm: "Don Juan, go to the kitchen and bring me a bowl of milk. This devilish bear will not let me go."
>
> I got the milk. The bear slowly let go of Manuela, crawled down to drink. After that, calling Coxe, an Englishman, we

chained the bear, whom we pulled down, growling, into the court-
yard. Coxe then executed him.

"But see," Manuelita said, showing me her throat and part of
her breasts, "I am not wounded."

In her own way Manuela was playing her role. She kept her
eyes and ears open, and with her sense of the drift of feelings and
opinions, she was once more an intelligence center. In the mornings, her slaves would go to the market, ostensibly to gather the
day's food; actually they were listening to the mood of the people.
Jonotás, with her experience in Lima and Quito, had no trouble in
ferreting out, from women, soldiers, and the lower echelons of
Bogotá society, all of the complaints and the rumors. Then, with
little dark Isabela balancing a vegetable-filled basket on her head,
she would come back to the Plazuela and bring to her mistress the
whole of the day's harvest. In the morning hours, Manuela could
be seen on the balcony that overhung the street in front of the
church of the Jesuits. From this vantage point she watched the
building where Simón Bolívar lived, and she could take in an edge
of the plaza. There were few movements that her fine brown eyes
did not see:

> Manuelita is always visible. In the morning she wears a negli-
> gee which is not without attraction; her arms are naked — she
> makes sure not to hide them, she embroiders while showing the
> prettiest fingers in the world. She talks a little and smokes *ciga-*
> *rillos* with lovely grace. Her behavior at this time of day is modest.
> She gives and welcomes news.

Then at night it was the *tertulias*. Manuela had altered this
ancient Spanish custom, an informal party for conversation. She
served spirits, strong and heady wines. There in her apartment,
beneath the dancing light of the cut-glass candelabra, she would
hold her salon. She was radiant in an off-shoulder white muslin
gown with the waistline tucked high under her breasts, and a scarf
about her shoulders, poppy-red with scalloped edgings. For night
also she brought a change of mood, to animation and gaiety.

These *tertulias* were in essence political rallies. The friends of

Bolívar came; so did the members of the British Legion — Fergusson, O'Leary, Sandes, Dr. Moore — and others of Bogotá's society who had cast their own lives in the crucible of Bolívar's destiny. Young Boussingault, who headed a mission of French scientists and was destined to be one day the president of the Académie des Sciences in Paris, witnessed all this with wondering eyes. Much of it he reported home in his letters:

> Like all favorites of powerful political men, Manuela attracts courtiers. Her courtesies and her generosities are, as a matter of fact, inexhaustible.

Manuela was developing her role. She was, at these *tertulias*, influencing the opinions of men who were important to Simón Bolívar. For beneath her "follies" there was something else. Bolívar might speak of her as his "lovable fool," and her enemies might call her many harsher names, but they realized, all too late, that they had misjudged her. The strange apparatus of her extravagant behavior was only an incredible façade to hide her real intentions, her political manipulations for Simón Bolívar's ideals. Although she was a handsome, self-possessed woman, still her charm was inferior to her talents; and the combination of the two was insurmountable. Manuela was very astute. Her notorious "follies" were only occasional, and beyond the gaudy display of her baroque personality she demonstrated her ability at political intrigue in a hundred ways.

There was a pattern in public behavior. Manuela could see it through all the news that poured in upon her. It was now an open secret: there was an organized conspiracy directed against Bolívar. It welled up from the lowest rungs of society, into the salons of the intellectuals. The unpaid, grumbling soldiers were being influenced. The women, complaining about the high cost of food, were being told that all the fault emanated from Bolívar and his policies. The merchants groaned over the decay of their business; the aristocracy over their loss of privilege; the intelligentsia over the restraints of the dictatorship. Out of these regiments of the discontented was developing the army of revolt; and with it, a shibboleth: "There is no liberty as long as Bolívar lives."

Manuela sensed it, and spilled out her warnings like a Cassandra. She begged Bolívar not to travel without an armed escort; he refused. His officers insisted that they be given authority to ferret out the conspirators; he denied them this. He wanted less dictatorial decrees, not more. He felt that he must concentrate on the economic rehabilitation of the country, since this, if accomplished, would put to rest most of the complaints. It was only when the voice of Pepé Paris joined the others in the Council, urging him for his safety to discontinue his daily horseback rides, that he felt the seriousness of the moment. He doubled the palace guard. José Palacios brought his two great mastiffs from the Quinta to reinforce the sentries. These were, however, the only precautions that Bolívar would allow.

The names of some of the conspirators were even known. As yet they had taken no steps beyond careless talk, the sort of grandiose talk which comes when *chicha* loosens the tongue, without revealing any definite form of action. One thing, however, was certain: General Santander was the nucleus of the conspiracy; it whirled around his arrogant personality. Although he had been appointed Minister to the United States in the beginning of the month, he had so far made no preparation to go. Now Bolívar ordered, in a tone which certainly did not belong to the language of diplomacy, "General Santander will leave the country by September 5th."

This decision hurried up the plans for revolt. Bolívar was to be murdered at the Masked Ball.

It was a normal August night in Bogotá. The rain fell lightly yet insistently. The cobblestone streets glistened pallidly from the small lights which people, by law, now placed in front of their houses. Across from the Palace of San Carlos was the Coloseo Theater, a three-storied building, simple and elegant. It was the one theater of Bogotá, copied after the Variété in Paris; but since there were no professionals, the actors were only amateurs drawn from those of talent within the city. The interior was candle-lit, the hall empty of seats — for everyone brought his own for a performance. On this night the large hall was lined with chairs brought by the servants, and an orchestra — a harp, two violins, a cello and a battered horn — was squeaking out the first strains of a Spanish *contredanse*. Soon, under the spell of wine and enlivening spirits, they would change to a local dance, the *cachucha*, danced like the minuet, but with the sinuous body movements of a bolero.

The masked ball was popular in Bogotá. In this city of few amusements, it furnished to the women, experts with the needle, an excuse to fashion costumes of considerable ingenuity. It also allowed them to carry on, under the disguise, the love affairs which they could not have openly in the small, circumscribed society of the town. The hall was already filled when Manuela arrived. She had suggested that Bolívar should not come, for she had had it from a servant, who had it from someone else, that an attempt would be made on his life that night. Unmasked and still wearing her hussar's uniform, she had gone to the hall without calling at the Palace. In the blaze of costumes about the entrance, and in the dimly lighted foyer, she passed unnoticed, since it was presumed she was in costume. She mounted the stairs behind Marcelo Tenorio, a man of some distinction. Then she saw him accosted on the stairway by another man, costumed as a Spanish conquistador, in a simulated coat of mail. When Tenorio was beside him, the man lifted his visor and said:

"Do you know me?"

Tenorio kept silent.

"Within a half hour, when the clock strikes twelve — death to the tyrant."

And the man opened his doublet, on which was painted the rising sun, and showed a knife stuck in his belt.

"We are twelve," he said enigmatically. "The result: silence "

Manuela, unaware if Bolívar had arrived yet or not, made her way to the entrance of the theater, within which the masked dancers were going through the first steps of the *cachucha*. The Mayor of the city, Don Ventura, dressed in short satin knee breeches, stood by the door. He saw a woman dressed as a hussar about to pass, her eyes searching beyond him for the figure of Bolívar. He barred the way.

"But I am Manuela Sáenz," she said.

"I don't care," he replied, "if you are Saint Manuela. You can't enter here in men's clothing."

No one spoke quite that way to Manuela, and she began at once to raise a disturbance. At that very moment Bolívar had arrived with Colonel Fergusson and General Córdoba; they were at the outer door speaking with some of the officials. Near them, waiting as usual for her mistress, was Jonotás, disheveled and dirty. The combination of Manuela arguing with the Mayor of the city, and the filthily disarranged Jonotás, was too much for the frayed nerves of Bolívar.

"Is this really the slave of Manuela?"

"Yes, my General," answered Fergusson.

"This is insufferable." And, pushing Jonotás aside, he moved toward the street.

General Córdoba, wrapped in a blue Spanish cape, made after him.

"You are going, my General?"

"Yes, and I go away very disgusted. Accompany me."

Later and alone in the falling rain, Manuela made her way back to her apartment.

The nadir of their relationship had now been reached. Bolívar made no attempt at communication, so that she was certain he misunderstood her presence that night at the Masked Ball. He was not convinced that the people would attempt his life; he considered himself invulnerable to such attacks; therefore Manuela's vulgar display was inexplicable. She remained in torment at their estrangement, and from the depths of that misery she wrote him a short note:

Sir:

I know you are vexed with me, but it was not my fault. With the pain of this displeasure upon me, I can scarcely sleep. However this much remains certain. I will not come to your house, until you ask for me, or want to see me.

Even the arrival of Fernando Bolívar failed to break down the wall between them. Manuela had hurried over to the Palace of San Carlos as soon as she heard he had come in order to be of aid, for she knew the great affection in which Bolívar held this favorite nephew.

Fernando Bolívar had arrived unexpectedly. He had ridden in from Caracas, twenty-four days in the saddle, crossing the anemic llanos, climbing over the Andes, to reach Bogotá. He had been briefed on his long ride by José Ravenga, one of the Ministers of Council, but he did not expect to see what he did see. He had come at once from the United States when he received the message from Simón Bolívar: he was needed. Although he was young, his education in North America, his knowledge of events, were important now to Gran Colombia. What his Uncle Simón did not mention was that, in this crescendo of hate and terror, he had desperate need of people who because of blood ties would give him unquestioned loyalty.

And who better than Fernando? The son of his favorite sister, María Antonia, born in Caracas in 1810, Bolívar had sent him to Philadelphia for his education. He was studying at Germantown Academy when the Marquis de La Fayette made his much-heralded return to the United States, and the old General made the journey out to Germantown just to be presented to the nephew of Simón Bolívar. So great was the prestige of his uncle that on his graduation he was offered an appointment to West Point. This he refused, wishing to attend Jefferson's college in Virginia. It was the year 1826, the year that Thomas Jefferson would die, yet the venerable statesman came out personally to install the nephew of Bolívar in his own college. In North America, as throughout Europe, Simón Bolívar was respected as one of the great men of the century; everywhere, it seemed, the name of Bolívar was held in great esteem.

But on his homecoming Fernando Bolívar was shocked by the reality. In Venezuela the name of Bolívar was hissed. All along the two thousand miles that separated Caracas from Bogotá, the young Bolívar could see the elements of chaos. Bogotá itself was an armed camp; he could not escape the feeling of tension that gripped the city. Fernando tried not to show his reactions to the situation, but his face was too open to dissemble the things he felt. It was a handsome face, with sharp, clean-cut features; his hair, slightly curly, was parted on one side in a sort of *coup de vent;* his body, something like that of Simón Bolívar, was delicate, lithe, almost epicene.

Installed in the Palace of San Carlos, he was writing by September 17 to friends in Philadelphia, describing his new home:

> It is a house, two stories high, built with good taste and luxuriously furnished. In the patio is a beautiful fountain, surrounded by a garden filled with flowers, abundant with roses and above all with carnations which grow superbly in this climate. The principal patio is enclosed with an iron railing; the arrangement on the second floc · is different in that it has only a corridor which leads to the dining room and the interior room occupied by my uncle. On the street side (bounded by the Jesuit church) there are five rooms of varying size, the first one being where the Council of Ministers meets. The last one, a luxuriously papered room, serves as a dormitory. Here there is a superbly fashioned matrimonial bed; I sleep here with my friend Lieutenant Andrés Ibarra, who is an aide to my uncle.

Fernando Bolívar met Fergusson and Wilson, with whom he could converse in English; Juan Santana, also American-educated, "who could speak various languages"; and, of course, Manuela Sáenz — whose special relationship with his uncle, as well as with the state, he soon knew and accepted. "I encountered here," he said, "something resembling the air of a family."

The Palace had also the air of war. Anyone approaching the building was given a scrutiny unknown in the past, and José

Palacios's two animals, "beautiful dogs, one bay-colored, the other ruddy," roamed about the gardens alert to all sounds. There was added tension, for word had just come from Bolivia (it took over five months to arrive) that there had been a revolution there. General Sucre had been wounded in the face and arm, and had resigned under pressure. He was now riding back to Quito. This intelligence only exacerbated the nerves of those who stayed about Bolívar's person; for rumors that the conspiracy against the government was set, even to the time and place, grew with each succeeding day. Santander, who had been ordered to leave Bogotá by September 5 "one way or another," was still there, outwardly preserving complete ignorance. But he was well informed. . . .

The basic plan — to assassinate Simón Bolívar, to seize the government — had been well worked out. Yet it was like all conspiracies formed by a motley group of plotters; all had different ideas of what they wanted. Still, for the moment, they could agree. The first step was obvious — to kill.

Lolo Boussingault observed it all, and understood it, for as a Frenchman he had been nurtured on violence, and knew something of revolution's characteristics. He wrote home:

> The royalist party is conspiring actively; nocturnal reunions take place regularly at the homes of well-placed people; no one seeks to conceal anything. The police have been instructed to arrest the conspirators, but they do nothing. They are conspiring for liberty. This is their excuse — as well as their strength, although in fact with many of them there is more ambition involved than patriotism. The most active group are young students, who meet on the pretense of studying with several of the professors of the college of San Bartolomeo, who are also involved. Its secret aim is to overthrow Bolívar's government. I know this since it is directed by a very old Frenchman, Dr. Arganil, one of the *sans-culottes* of Marseilles and the French Revolution, and by another intelligent Frenchman, Auguste Hormet, and too, by an officer of Venezuela named Pedro Carujo.

The conspiracy was conceived in the romantic tradition. Like Charlotte Corday, who knifed Marat in his bath "for liberty," most of the conspirators were young, scarcely twenty. Among them were Vargas Tejada, an idealist incapable of killing even a cockroach; Florentino González, a literary figure; Ospina, a student of philosophy. Yet it derived something of a classical touch from its leader, old Dr. Arganil, a mysterious figure who had been swept up to America's shores by the spindrift of the revolution in which he had lent a hand. They had no idea how they would proceed to bind the outlying provinces to their government; that rested presumably with Santander, it was talked of in romantic terms. Yet they had to have military men to swing the army, they found them in the turncoat Colonel Ramón Guerrera of Bolívar's staff, and in another traitor, Major Pedro Carujo. A bellicose soldier five feet tall, red-headed, he was Spanish-born. In the wars, he had fought at first with fanatic loyalty for the Spaniard, then he went over to Bolívar after the republican victory.

The uprising was planned for October 28, the day of St. Simon. Bolívar's patron saint. In the midst of the celebrations they would strike: Bolívar, Urdaneta, Manuela, and others were marked for death. All was in readiness. Instead of which . . .

Instead of which, it all happened unexpectedly. On the afternoon of September 25, a Captain Triana stumbled into his barracks, as drunk as Bacchus. He bumped into another officer. They quarreled. Then Triana drew his sword, mounted a table and shouted at the top of his lungs, "The time has come to drown the tyranny of Bolívar in oceans of blood."

The incident was reported, the Captain jailed, and the information brought to Bolívar. Colonel Ramón Guerrera, knowing that this drunken talk had opened the secret of the conspiracy, immediately made contact with Major Carujo; they had to act with great speed. The conspirators were summoned to meet at once at the home of Luis Vargas Tejada, in the parish of Santa Barbara. It was no small gathering on that night of infamy, with a member of the general staff plotting Bolívar's death with others. They knew not what they were planning and had no idea beyond the murder, apart from asking Santander to aid them in the formation of a new government. And Bolívar thought that the revolt was insignificant and that they would fall like rats into a trap.

Santander, although he was not physically present at the meeting, did not reject the idea of conspiracy or of murder; neither did he inform the authorities. Perhaps, as he sat alone in his dimly lighted house, conspicuous so that he would be seen by the two soldiers who watched the door, he thought of himself as some demiurge who would descend from a new Olympus when the conspiracy had dispatched Bolívar, to respond to the call of the people, to rule them, despite the blood on his hands, under the cold beauty of the Law. . . .

The conspirators were now thirty. It was agreed that they must strike that night. All other plans must go into discard. They were to be formed into three groups. Those led by the little gamecock Pedro Carujo would assault the palace and kill Bolívar. Colonel Guerrera, aided by other military men, would reduce the Vargas Battalion to impotency and release Padilla, who languished in a cell close by. The third group would hold itself in readiness to come to the aid of either of the other two.

A night of September.

It had rained all the afternoon of the 25th, it was almost freezing; the cold penetrated the unheated houses, leaving a bone-shaking chill over everything. The rain had stopped in the evening, the clouds broke and streamed away, and at nightfall the full moon rose; it was almost as bright as day.

José Palacios, his massive body silhouetted against the shadows, came to Manuela's apartment accompanied by his two monstrous dogs. He carried a message from his master: "I am suffering with a terrible headache, please come to me now."

Manuela, in a pique over the long neglect, answered, "Tell His Excellency that I am more ill than he is, and I should not come."

José Palacios left, yet was back at once. The request was urgent. "Please come."

As the street was still damp with rain, Manuela put a pair of double-soled rubber boots over her satin slippers, wrapped a warm cashmere scarf about her neck, and crossed the street to the Palace, with Jonotás in attendance as always. She entered the door between the guards, climbed the stairs and went into Bolívar's room without knocking. He was sitting in a warm bath. After greeting her and telling her how delighted he was that she came, he said, "There is to be a revolution."

"I know it. I am glad that you had notice of it in good time. You never believe my information and you always received my suggestions unfavorably."

Still, he had not taken too many precautions. The guard had been doubled, the officers in the barracks altered, and by his bed Bolívar had his sword and pistols.

He asked Manuela to read to him, and soon he grew sleepy. Tenderly she helped him to bed. Then, candle in hand, she went to the room that was hers when she visited him.

The silence of Bogotá was like a stagnant pool. In the distance came the cry of the *sereno*, "Ave Maria. Twelve o'clock and all is well . . ."

And now at midnight, going in twos and threes so as not to arouse suspicion, the first group of conspirators gathered at the Bridge of San Agustín. Then, through the silent streets, light-slashed only here and there as the moon cut through the ink-black shadows, they approached their goal. In the Plazuela de San Carlos, below Manuela's apartment, they paused to arm themselves with sabers and pistols, thoughtfully taken from the barracks by Major Carujo. Then they moved on the Palace of San Carlos.

But at that moment, seeing the dark forms come out of the night, one of the sentries half raised his rifle and challenged:

"Who lives?"

He had expected the usual response, "The Liberator." Instead, Major Carujo shouted "Liberty." His followers seized the sentries, bent back their necks; knives flashed in the moonlight, and in a moment the guards lay drowning in their own blood. Now the killers forced open the large doors and debouched through the hallways to search out Bolívar. Their clatter waked the dogs, who set up a barking; the household was aroused. Young Andrés Ibarra was the first to oppose them. He had hastily slipped into his military jacket and seized a weapon; he met some of the conspirators coming up the stairs. Struck from behind, he dropped his saber and slowly sank to the floor, trying in his few moments of consciousness to stanch the flow of his blood.

Manuela, too, hearing the dogs and the commotion, ran to Bolívar's room and awakened him. He was up in a moment. His pistol in one hand, his sword in the other, he moved toward the door. Manuela burst out laughing.

"Can you imagine wanting to defend yourself in that attire! In your nightshirt, with a rapier in hand? Don Quixote in person. Put on your uniform."

Bolívar was dressed in a moment.

"Bravo, I am dressed, what do we do now?"

They could hear the commotion throughout the Palace, the barking of the dogs, the sound of firing, confused shouts: "Where is the tyrant?" "Death to Bolívar!" "Long live Liberty!"

Manuela made Bolívar put on her double-soled rubber boots, and flung a cape over him; then, picking up his sword, she looked out the door, tiptoed back to him, and whispered, "Don't you remember telling me that Pepé Paris said that this window which opens on the street might be a good place to escape from?"

With that she quietly raised the window. There was no one to be seen. It was a short nine-foot drop to the street.

"Jump."

He leaped to the window, turned to embrace Manuela, and let himself down. She waited, her heart beating louder than the sound of his footsteps as he ran toward the bridge over the river. Then, sword in hand, she turned to the door. The conspirators burst into the room.

"Where is Bolívar?"

"In the council room."

"And the open window, why is the window opened? Has he escaped?"

"No. He is in the council room. I opened the window only to see what the commotion was about."

They seized her, knocked the saber from her hand, and pushed her before them to the council room. It was empty. The conspirators began to grow desperate. They searched the council room, Bolívar's bedroom, the kitchen, the salon; the Liberator was not to be found. Manuela, smiling coldly as she watched them, had just time to whisper to José Palacios. In a moment he was lost in the shadows; then he sped after his master.

Soon the killers returned to Manuela. They marched her before them, a saber at her back, while she counted the minutes. Each moment that passed without their discovering Simón Bolívar made more certain the failure of the plot; and by now, she knew he had gained the bridge. There were shots at the barracks, the sound of a cannon being fired at close range, and small arms too. Candle lights were flickering up all over the city; the surprise element of the conspiracy, at least, had failed.

As Manuela was swept across the crimson-stained floor, she saw Ibarra lying in an ever-widening circle of blood. Pushing aside her guards, she knelt down beside him, ripped off her petticoat, bandaged the wound, and put a tourniquet about his arm. Ibarra opened his eyes and asked weakly, "Is the Liberator dead?"

"No, Ibarra, he is alive."

Manuela was overheard Now she got off the floor and flung at them defiantly, "Yes, Bolívar is alive."

One of her captors struck at her. His fist slashed her in the ear and she fell forward. Everyone crowded about her with knives raised, while from the floor she screamed defiance

"Go on, kill me, kill me, you miserable cowards."

Auguste Hormet, the Frenchman, jumped between the knives and threw up his arms.

"Stop it, we are not here to murder women."

But Major Carujo, full of resentment toward anyone that

towered over his five feet, aimed a kick at the prostrate Manuela, it grazed her shoulder and struck her head. Then they picked her up, shoved her into Bolívar's room, locked the door and placed a guard before it. No one paid attention to her head wound.

"Long, long afterward," wrote Boussingault, "you could see the imprint of the blow on Manuelita's forehead."

The sound of someone running brought Manuela to the window, the same window from which, only moments before, Simón Bolívar had slipped out to escape the trap. It was Colonel Fergusson. Half dressed, with drawn saber, he was running toward the entrance of the Palace. Manuela shouted to him. He stopped.

"Where is the Liberator?"

But Manuela could not answer because of the guard at her door. She put her finger to her lips, nodding and trying to indicate without saying it that Simón Bolívar had escaped. Fergusson moved toward the entrance.

"Don't," Manuela shouted to him. "Don't come in. They will kill you."

Caution was not one of William Fergusson's virtues. He rushed to the door — and ran right into the man he had once chastised. Major Carujo raised his pistol, and fired at point-blank range right into the Irishman's face. Fergusson dropped his saber and threw up his hands over a geyser of blood. His knees buckled. Even then Carujo picked up the saber and slashed him with it. But there was no need. Fergusson was dead before he fell to the floor.

Bogotá was now aroused. All that had occurred took precisely ten minutes. In the rapidly moving drama, the plotters were unable to communicate with each other; they were blinded now by the terror of having failed. One party of them had seized some artillery pieces, trained them on the barracks, and started firing into the headquarters of the Vargas Battalion. Colonel Charles Whittle, commander of the battalion, who had seen service at Waterloo, stood in full view of the firing. He held a brace of pistols, and he promised to blow out the brains of any of his soldiers who surrendered. Then he directed his snipers to pick off those who

were firing the cannon The marksmen did their work well. Soon
the dead lay in strange postures around the piece, the others fled.
Boussingault, an eyewitness to it, said, "It was due to the Vargas
Battalion, and especially to Colonel Whittle, its commander, that
the plot failed, a brave and excellent officer."

By now, fearing the worst, all of Bolívar's officers were converging on the Palace. Dr. Moore helped Manuela, and Jonotás
dragged the body of Fergusson inside. Fernando Bolívar was
covered with blood from trying to stanch Fergusson's wounds.
He was shaken terribly by these events, he seemed paler and more
fragile than ever.

Soon General Urdaneta arrived with a body of troops. They
found Fergusson dead, the sentries with their throats cut. Ibarra
was as pale as death, but, thanks to Manuela's timely aid, alive.
Manuela leaned against the side of the door, her head bruised, a
hand bleeding, her dress ripped . . .

The first question everyone asked was, "Where is Bolívar?"

Where was he? At the moment he was hiding under a bridge, his
legs sunk in the stinking *cloacina exuviae* of the river. After he had
jumped from the window, he ran past the theater, the Coloseo,
keeping to the shadows. Hearing footsteps, he crouched down,
pistol in hand; but he soon made out the huge frame of José
Palacios. They both ran for the Carmen Viaduct that bridged the
San Agustín River, hoping to escape into the suburbs; but hearing
voices in the night coming from the other side, they slid down
under the bridge, and there crouched knee-deep in the water that
contained the sewage of Bogotá.

Together they sat and waited — the unquestioning, devoted
José, the freed slave, who could neither read nor write — and
Simón Bolívar, who had liberated half a continent. He had given
his fortune, his energies and his health for the cause of liberty. He
had been, only a few years back, the idol of the continent, the toast
of Europe, the spiritual successor of George Washington. Poets
had sung his praises, and men had cast aside all their private hopes
to follow his bright star. Now the wheel of his fate had made the

full circle. He sat there in torment, trembling with ague, in the cold of the night. The terrible events on that night of September had struck him a fearful blow.

"I am mortally wounded," he said, "their daggers have penetrated my heart."

It was a wound for which there was no sovereign balm. Something in him died that night; his prodigious vanity was shattered, his enemies had planted their flags in the ruins of his hopes. Even now, with all the sounds of firing, he had no idea of what was occurring. Perhaps the conspirators had been successful.

Then they heard more shouting. His soldiers were looking for him with the welcome rallying cry of "Long live the Liberator!"

Simón Bolívar crawled out of the flowing cesspool, embraced the men, commanded a horse, and quickly went to the barracks where he changed into a clean uniform. Then he rode out to the plaza

The efficient General Urdaneta had things in hand. Hundreds of suspects had already been arrested; they stood to one side, manacled and dispirited. The entire Bogotá garrison was drawn up in the square and they spontaneously broke into a cheer when they saw him ride up.

Everyone could see how these events had affected Bolívar; those hours under the bridge had corroded his soul. He spoke in a hoarse voice, as hollow as if he spoke from the tomb. Simply, eloquently, he thanked them for their loyalty. Then, one by one, all his generals rode up to offer congratulations. When Santander offered his hand, Bolívar cut him down in brittle contempt.

"As usually happens in unsuccessful revolts," observed Boussingault from his fine observation seat, "the undecided — and there were many — pronounced themselves for the victor. I have known several who behaved this way, among others the Vice-President of the Republic — General Santander."

Now Bolívar made his way back to the residence. The sky was beginning to lighten and sweep away the darkness. The streets were lined with people with candle lamps, cheering their Libera-

tor-President All his intimates were waiting for him. Fernando
Bolívar, still smeared with blood, always remembered that hour:

> It was five in the morning, perhaps it was four; however, as
> much as I would forget the impressions of that unfortunate night,
> I remember them as if they were yesterday.

Then Bolívar saw Manuela. He was too dazed by events to see
her injuries, the bruised head, the cut hand. In the sight of everyone, he embraced her, and profoundly moved, said:

"Manuela, my Manuela, you are the liberatress of the Liberator."

Manuela had kept herself well under control. There could be
no letting go now, for she could see the terrible agitation in Simón
Bolívar. She followed him to his room, helped him to undress.
He tried to lie down and rest. He could not. He sprang up, began
to pace the room.

"Tell me what happened, yes, all, everything."

But before she could start the narrative, he interrupted, "Don't
tell me more."

Then almost in the same breath, he asked again for the fearful
details.

Thus in the morning of September 26 did the day of wrath break
across the horizon.

14

DANSE MACABRE

A SIMPLE GALLOWS was being raised in the great square directly
in front of the Cathedral, for the time had not been allowed the
public hangman to prepare an elaborate gibbet. It worried him a
good deal, and he complained loudly about it when the crossbar
was put into place. Next he hung several stout ropes from which,
if God willed it, would soon dangle the bodies of those who had
the misfortune to fail. The first hangings had been routine — simple
soldiers who had taken part in the uprising, witless knuckleheads
who died with the same stoic indifference with which they had
lived their lives. These events, much to the chagrin of the execu-
tioner, lacked the finesse that public affairs of this sort ought to
have had; for these should be performances with a long series of
ornate and pious accompaniments. Still it would be different with
those now being tried. . . .

The examinations had been going on for days. At first Bolívar
could not rest until he had a deposition from everyone who had
taken active part in the conspiracy. One by one, those implicated
were brought before him. Colonel Crofston dragged in the young
Frenchman Auguste Hornet. The would-be assassin shook off his
captor's arm, and spoke to Bolívar with cold insolence; whereupon
the legionnaire, angered at this hauteur, fell upon him and began
to choke him. But Bolívar sprang up, pulled them apart, and curtly
ordered Crofston to fall back.

"And this is the man you would kill," said Pepé Paris, alluding
to Bolívar who had just saved him.

"Not the man," responded Hormet, "but the symbol of his power."

As the depositions were taken, first from one, then from the other, Bolívar, who was familiar with the stratagems of plotters, grew visibly shocked at the depth of the conspiracy. He had first thought it involved only an isolated group of malcontents, used by the *Santanderistas* to gain political control. But these were young students, people of good family, university professors, and even a member of his own general staff

So then it was the *people* who misunderstood him, who did not know or care about his personal sacrifices or his efforts to hold Gran Colombia together. In short, as he now understood from this précis of revolt, it was the people who had planned his death. Then there was only one decision left him — he would grant a general amnesty and resign his offices.

General Urdaneta vehemently protested against such a procedure. They were dealing here with a conspiracy which, if allowed to develop, would be the death of the Republic. Bolívar by resigning would condone the revolt; he would repay the loyalty of his officers and his soldiers by abandoning them; and he would bring chaos down upon the land. At first even the other voices of his Council, speaking in similar vein, failed to move Bolívar from his firm resolve. Then it was Manuela. She had warned Bolívar years ago about Santander — even then she could see the patterns of his perfidy — but Bolívar would not listen. Everyone knew that Santander's ambition had no scruples. Did Bolívar think that this failure would not be followed by another attempt on his life? At this moment, the Republic must hold mercy to be patricide. The only way out was the anointed terror. And she repeated what she had written to him earlier: "Better that ten should die, in order that millions be saved."

Bolívar yielded. He signed a decree appointing Rafael Urdaneta, with four other officers and four judges, as a trial court. From its judgments there would be no appeal save to himself, Simón Bolívar. Then five days after the 25th of September Santander was arrested, placed in close confinement, and held for trial. After that — the dance of death.

By the morning of October 2 the hangman had worked out the choreography. A bugler sounded the prelude at eleven o'clock. and the bells of the cathedral answered in subdued antiphony. The plaza slowly filled with people to witness the executions, for this was a public spectacle. A fair had been installed around the edges of the square, where hucksters in their best woolen *ruanas* sold cakes and bread, and urged the bystanders to buy for their hats the blue, gold, and red cockades of the Republic Into the press of people burst a file of soldiers, marching to drums and tambourines. In their center, hands tied in front of him, was Colonel Ramón Guerrera, in the uniform of a colonel of the Vargas Battalion. He had been condemned to death. His eyes were cast downward to a large crucifix held in his hands, he looked at no one as he marched to death.

Not so Padilla. In full regalia of a general of the armies, bedizened with medals, Padilla, bellicose to the end, walked with head erect. He gave no ear to the exhortations of the priests beside him and he looked across the vast crowd with an insolent stare of contempt. Padilla was a huge man, curly-pated and dark-skinned, standing head and shoulders above everyone, his fierce dignity made somewhat grotesque by his squint eyes.

The death line halted in front of the improvised gallows, where six wrist-thick ropes hung down, the nooses open and ready for the dreadful business. General Urdaneta, in a gold-embroidered red uniform, stood in front of the condemned men and read the sentences of the court. Then, to the sound of muffled drums, the soldiers began to strip rank and medals from the doomed men. Colonel Guerrera submitted mildly to the last humiliations. But Padilla's black face was wreathed in fury, as he strained at his bonds and shouted, "These medals were given to me not by Bolívar, but by the Republic."

The voice became muted as the soldiers slipped the loose gray cassock of the condemned over his head and shoved him to the gibbet stool. As the hangman adjusted the noose about his neck, Padilla burst out again in final protest; in a voice like an avenging angel he bellowed, "Long live the Republic! Long live liberty!"

At that moment the soldiers kicked the stools from under the condemned men; their bodies dropped a few feet and were left dangling in space. Colonel Guerrera did a brief *entrechat* for his *danse macabre*, and with proper respect for the amenities of the moment died quickly. But not Padilla. His huge bull neck took the shock of the plunge, and in his struggles he broke the cords that bound his arms. Then he seized the noose and began to wrestle with it. The hangman, who had never seen this done before, stood wide-mouthed with astonishment; and through the crowd ran a murmur of admiration. Urdaneta wanted no heroics. He signaled the officer of the guard; a squad of soldiers rushed forward, and at point-blank range fired into Padilla's writhing body.

The gallows was kept busy for weeks. And, in addition to executions, there were imprisonments and exilings. Personable young Florentino González escaped to the jungles and was condemned to death *in absentia*. Manuela's old enemy, Vicente Azuero, was taken into custody, and even though he could not be connected directly with the conspiracy he was thrown into prison. But that "miserable Pedro Carujo," that diminutive bundle of terror, one of the leaders of the conspiracy and the assassin of William Fergusson, escaped the fate of Padilla. He struck a bargain with his captors. He would be sentenced to perpetual exile; and in return for this clemency he would incriminate another. He would turn state's evidence against General Santander.

The trial of Santander was elaborate and detailed, and its unraveling was followed with the greatest interest by the foreign consuls, now much in evidence in Bogotá. He was, after all, one of the cofounders of the Republic. He had labored tirelessly to give Bolívar the elements of his victories. His opposition to Bolívar was as natural as it was understandable; he objected to the *personalismo* of the other's government, he wanted more liberty for

the individual than was then envisioned by his rival. Santander
wanted liberty, Bolívar wanted unity. Inevitably, one of them had
to lose.

Now, at this moment, the wounds were too fresh for the operation of pure reason. This much was certain about Santander's
guilt: he had known, despite his dignified asseveration of ignorance, of the conspiracy against Bolívar and against the government. He had condoned it, he had given the plotters advice, and
he was an officer in the army and a member of the government.
These facts were quite enough. It was ridiculous to speak of justice. The evidence against him was strained and in some cases im-
probable; but this was a matter of treason. The government's position was too untenable to let it become involved in a protracted
trial; so Santander was condemned to death. The Council suggested leniency; Manuela was vehemently against it. Padilla, one
of her three "P's," had died on the gallows; why not Santander,
the spiritual leader of the revolt? No argument could change her;
Santander should die How the quondam Vice-President, resting
uneasily in his cell and waiting the outcome of his plea for clemency, must have wished that he had not aroused the fury in that
woman! He knew now that she was no fool, she was a force; and
he regretted that, in his life of vertiginous intrigue, he had not
known it.

This time, however, Manuela did not prevail. There had been
enough bloodletting for Simón Bolívar. He said, "I believe it was
our ruin not to have come to terms with Santander." And he
changed the sentence to perpetual banishment from the realm.

All during these trials, Bolívar kept to his villa; he remained
in the privacy of his bedroom, tormented by fever and tortured
by doubts. Had his procedures been correct? Was he right in
abandoning peaceful political methods for the terror? The constant questioning made inroads on his health, there was the
return of his cough, and he had now constantly to bury his face
in his handkerchief. His face had a lean, dry look; and his thin,

vivid lips were flecked ofttimes with blood-stained saliva; his dark
eyes, bright with fever, glittered like jewels.

The illness was visibly consuming Bolívar, he was wasting away
with every day. Manuela brought in a doctor, who diagnosed a
return of the tuberculosis and prescribed rest and nourishment.
Bolívar was to avoid all excitement, and desist entirely from par-
ticipating in the affairs of the state. And if he did not? The question
was rhetorical; for if he did not, there was only one prognosis
that the Scot could give — an early death. Dr. Richard Cheyne
called often at the Quinta and soon he supplanted the older Dr.
Moore. Cheyne was young, scarcely twenty-five; he had been
educated at the University of Edinburgh, and had come, one
knows not for what reason, to Bogotá to set up practice. Bolívar
liked his modern medical ideas, for the big Scot was earnest without the desiccating touch of the professional. He became very
much attached to Manuela too, and it was hinted, strongly hinted,
that there was more between them than a passing flirtation.

"I have only known Manuela," said Boussingault, "to have two
ostensible lovers in Bogotá. One was Doctor Cheyne . . ."

Whatever the relationship between them, Cheyne aided Manuela in every way possible to help the Liberator recover something of his health. Manuela was persuaded that if anything could
bring about his recovery, it would be her watchful and devoted
care.

No attempt now was made to maintain the fiction; Manuela
lived openly at the villa with Simón Bolívar. Since the night she
saved his life, a new dignity had come to her. Those who at first
were put off by her — for the pattern of her strange behavior was
irritating to many — now realized the depths of her loyalty to
Bolívar, and could understand something of his deep affection
for her. They could see that she had a fidelity which nothing
altered, and that she was ready to give her life for the ideal that
she professed. Those who had criticized her most were now most
noticeably drawn to her; they called her "The Liberatress." And
in this new role she spent all her time at the Quinta with Bolívar.

For weeks he remained inconsolable, his letters were full of despair. For he could not escape the fact that the people, who constituted his "glory," had attempted his death, and thereby the ruin of the Republic which he had created.

"My heart is broken," he cried, "and the prestige of my name is gone." Such was the state of Bolívar's mind when young August Le Moyne, an agent of the French Government, called on him in company with the French Consul:

> We arrived at the Quinta and were received in the salon by a lady named Manuela Sáenz, the same lady who on the night of the 25th of September exhibited so much valor in saving the life of the Liberator; she told us he was not in good health, he having taken a purgative just that morning and feeling unwell. She asked us the nature of our visit, and left to see if we could be received. In a few minutes, there appeared a man with a large jaundiced face, sickly in aspect, wrapped up in a dressing gown, with a nightcap and slippers; his emaciated legs were stuck into ill-fitting flannel pants; in a word it was the same costume as worn by the miserable Argan as described by Molière in *Le Malade Imaginaire*. He looked more like a man going to the dressing room than one about to receive visitors. This was Bolívar, the Colombian hero. Once I was presented, he insisted that we sit down, then he began to speak to us in French.
>
> The first words we expressed were in respect to his health. he responded: "Oh my," and he showed us his emaciated arms. "It is not natural laws that have reduced me to the state which you now see, but the bitterness which surrounds my heart. The people, who were unable to kill me with knives, have morally assassinated me with their ingratitude and their calumnies, in other times they praised me as if I were a god, now they wish to soil me with their spittle, when I am not here to crush all those demagogues, they tear each other apart as if they were wolves, and the edifice that I have built with so much work, they destroy with the fangs of revolution."

Everyone had hoped and believed that, with October's end and the end of the bloodletting, the aura of dissolution and fear that hung over Bogotá would be lifted. The gibbet had done its work, and had been taken down. The residue of common soldiers, upon whom sentence had not been meted out — there were a hundred of them — were granted a general amnesty and sent into the provinces, away from the capital city. Only the principal enemy, Santander, remained, but soon he too was sent away from Bogotá. Manuela had a letter from a friend who escorted him to the fortress of Cartagena, the first stage of his journey into exile:

MY DEAR LADY,
  We arrived yesterday at Guaduas — the only novelty was that "the Man" Santander became a little ill. I can assure you he is very humble, he does not wish to see anyone and said that he never wants to return to Colombia.

Manuela would have liked to see him exiled to hell; still it was good that he was gone. The feeling that they had broken the ring of conspiracy gave Bolívar a certain sense of ease.

Moreover, he was able to rely on Urdaneta, the only real victor of the conspiracy of the 25th of September. Bolívar gave over to him the administration of the government, and he emerged as *the* power behind the throne. He was a complete gentleman, who maintained a calm indifference in face of crises, and always preserved his serenity in emergencies. He never lost anything, forgot anything. He refused to fill his life, as did others, with exclamations of *mea culpa*, or of melancholy. His every act was done with firmness and frankness. There was no problem with Urdaneta. Bolívar's loyalties were his loyalties; besides, between him and Manuela there was complete understanding

In those days the Republic seemed to be making rapid economic recovery and some European capital was coming into the country. A Herr Elbers of Hamburg received a franchise to operate steam side-wheelers on the Magdalena River and this gave great impetus to the moving of freight. An Englishman arrived to put up a small mill. Gran Colombia's exports had risen, and, with the fear of chaos abated, businessmen were releasing more and yet more of their hoarded silver pesos. The United States was sending a minister, the renowned General William Henry Harrison. Yet under the thin earthcrust Gran Colombia writhed and turned from the inner pressure of events Once more it burst its seams and sent forth new flows of blood-red revolt.

Again it was the *caudillos,* the leaders of isolated regions, who wished to rule, not to be ruled. On the distant llanos of Venezuela it was General Páez, in Ecuador it was General Flores; in southern Colombia there was a whole list of dissidents. In Peru it was something else — for Bolívar had never been reconciled to the rebellion of his troops in Lima, or the insult that had been offered to him and Gran Colombia — and there was talk of war.

But on Simón Bolívar's saint's day, the 28th of October, the General gave a grand ball at the Palace of San Carlos.

For Bogotá, which had not the traditional opulence of Lima, it was a very brilliant affair, principally because the capital was now filled with the representatives of foreign governments. It had all the glamour of an international event. England was represented by Mr. Henderson, whose daughter, the apple-cheeked Fanny, was engaged to youthful General Córdoba. The French had sent their Baron Gros, a strange character, a master of intrigue, who was in Bogotá to lay the groundwork for a monarchy under the protection of France. He was being watched very assiduously by Colonel Johnson, the military attaché from Washington, who had come there in anticipation of the arrival of the first American minister. Yet the gaiety of the party seemed forced, though the little orchestra in the green uniform of the Granaderos played some popular boleros.

Simón Bolívar attended, entering with Manuela on his arm. He came *en frac,* in white woolen smallclothes, silk stockings, buckled shoes, and a long black tail coat. He wore only a single decoration, the medallion of George Washington, which hung about his emaciated neck on a blue *moiré* silk ribbon. Manuela, too, was strangely subdued. Since that September night her one care, her one thought was Bolívar, and she entered the room on his arm with a dignity that gave, it seemed, a greater sensuality to her lithe body. Her *décolletage* was emphasized by a diamond and emerald necklace. Bolívar now tired very easily and they stayed only long enough to satisfy protocol.

And it was well, perhaps, that they did leave, for they too might have fallen victims to the contagion so general in Bogotá. Tempers were short. Some nameless, some unidentifiable rancor still gripped the capital, even though the terror had gone with the last executions. But violence remained in the very air, and it now reached the high levels of diplomacy.

The Consul of the Low Countries, Stewart by name, had just arrived in Bogotá. He was a gay companion, but as proud and sensitive as a Spanish grandee. And he loved to gamble. "There was a game one night," remembered Boussingault "The table was covered with the stakes. At eleven o'clock there was an earthquake. Everyone ran out into the street — the Consul from Holland fled with the others — but he was the only one who picked up his gold before dashing out of the gaming room." A deliberate sort of man.

No one remembered how it started. The diplomats were drinking brandy; they were joined by Colonel Miranda, the son of the famous General Miranda. The conversation turned on politics, the recent uprising was discussed; then the Consul of Holland made an unfortunate remark of which Manuela was the target. Miranda flushed angry at the inference; there was a venomous exchange of words, and the officer, expressing the general mood and completely forgetting himself, slapped the diplomat. A duel was the only solution. Colonel Johnson, acting as Miranda's second, suggested sabers — for he was a good swordsman. But Monsieur Stewart, the offended party, demanded pistols.

A cloud of gloom seemed to drop on the grand ball that had been designed as a love feast. The news traveled quickly. Manuela, feeling herself involved, tried to get in touch with Consul Stewart, but was rebuffed. All through the night she could hear Miranda, who lived close by, practicing with his pistols.

They met the next morning, on the hills above the Fucha River, overlooking Bogotá. It was cold. A light rain fell like a Scotch mist, giving the look of cat's fur to the heavy cloaks of the dueling party. Richard Cheyne was present as doctor and stood with his black case under his arm, wondering to which of the two he would be required to give medical aid.

Stewart arrived in semimilitary dress; on his head, completely unsuitable to the event, he wore a wide-brimmed Panama. Colonel Miranda came in full uniform, wearing a hussar's bearskin shako at a jaunty angle. They took their positions. After the usual attempt at reconciliation had been put forward and refused by both parties, Stewart raised his pistol, took deliberate aim, and fired. The bullet came so close to Miranda's head that it tore a strip from his furred busby. Miranda then put his pistol under his arm and, with a humanity all out of step with the times, saluted his adversary and gave him the opportunity to apologize. The Consul was livid.

"Shoot, for if you do not, I will kill you as I would a dog."

Miranda slowly brought down his pistol, aimed at the black ribbon about the crown of his adversary's hat, and pulled the trigger.

There was no need for the presence of Dr. Cheyne. Stewart had been shot right through the head.

The military police were on Miranda's trail at once. With the help of his brother officers, he contrived to escape the city and join his corps of lancers. It did him no good, however. A few weeks later his soldiers revolted and hacked him to pieces with their sabers.

Such happenings were symptomatic of the times, and they affected Bolívar as if he himself had experienced every death. He was supposed to rest, but could not. Things were going badly all over the country, and the relations between Peru and Gran Colombia had deteriorated so much in the last weeks that people talked openly of hostile actions. A Peruvian fleet had sailed to blockade the coast, and intelligence reports slowly drifted up to tell of Peruvian troops marching into Ecuador. There was only one possible course now. Bolívar must ride southward to defend the bastions of Gran Colombia. But how could he, in his state of health, ride a thousand miles to do battle — he who could hardly stay in the saddle more than two hours at a time? Certainly it was no love of power that sent this tragic half-man, the creator of the Republic, again into battle.

On January 1, 1829, the heart of the Andes trembled. Peru had invaded Ecuador. Bolívar hurriedly called General Sucre out of retirement in Quito, assembled his armies, placed Manuela under the protection of a triad of his trusted advisers. Then, in obvious pain, he mounted his horse and set forth into the chaos . . . a modern Don Quixote riding off to tilt with the windmills of perfidy.

15

AND SO—MANUELA

Manuela is always visible."

And it was now impossible to conceive Bogotá without her. In the morning she was on her balcony overlooking the narrow street, eying the well-dressed people entering San Ignacio for early mass. Later, dressed in her hussar's garb, she rode abroad, with the usual whispered comments floating behind her. And in the evenings, her *tertulias*.

She did not involve herself directly in politics — Bolívar insisted at least on that. The loom of Bogotá's political life was in the capable hands of General Urdaneta, and she allowed him the weaving. Her mission now, as she saw it, beyond the routine gathering of the Liberator's personal correspondence, was that of political catalyst. She would further bind Bolívar's personal and political friends to him by constant reminders of him, even though at the moment he was on his way to Ecuador to repel the invasion from Peru. Letters from him, dispatches from his aides, rumors, scandal, dire warnings, were given out at the *tertulias*. Usually they were followed by drinking, sometimes a dance, and often a performance by Jonotás, whose mimicking black face was the joy and horror of all Bogotá.

Bolívar's concern over Manuela, even though he was miles from the font and source of his passion, was very touching. He had put her well-being in the hands of three of his most trusted friends: the self-effacing Pepé Paris, who was devoted to albeit bewildered by Manuela; John Illingsworth — whom everyone called "Illingsrot" — the English sea captain, an old friend of hers and a passionate partisan of his; and General Urdaneta, who had in recent months become virtually the Liberator's *alter ego.*

This last of the triad controlled the purse strings. "I gave five hundred pesos to Manuela," he said, writing to Bolívar; and later, "I delivered another five hundred pesos to M. — keeping in my possession the other thousand." She seemed to consume more money than the mint possessed, for again and again Urdaneta was writing about it: "Manuela received the five hundred pesos you left for her after you departed the first of January, she asked me for another four hundred and yesterday another four hundred, which she said she needed urgently . . . so I sent it over."

To which solicitude Bolívar answered, "Thank you for informing me about the four hundred pesos you gave Manuelita . . ." And again, when nearing the Ecuadorian frontier, "I was very ill, but now I have improved; please tell this to Manuelita."

John Illingsworth was detailed to give her sober English counsel, but he might as well have given advice to a volcano. Manuela was guided mostly by Manuela. The good-looking young medico, Dr. Cheyne, called often at her house — too often, thought John Illingsworth. And another young man, William Wills, who loved to play the violin for her, was at the apartment so constantly that someone said he might as well occupy one of the guest rooms. "And to think," wrote a Frenchman, "that the dear Liberator wrote his friend Illingsworth to watch over her well and give her advice."

Pepé Paris looked in on her whenever he was in the vicinity. Tall, graced with good manners, an engagingly easy person to know, Don Pepé was the most constant of her friends. His normality was refreshing in contrast to the equatorially lush attitudes of the others that surrounded her. One could always rely on Pepé. He never contended that he *knew* Manuela — some of the things that she did he could never understand — but he realized that people often hide their true natures under an elaborate façade of unrelated behavior. He knew that under the baroque aspects of Manuela lay a true and loyal person, and he liked her. He often brought his wife Juana María on his visits to Manuela, so that a show of propriety would be preserved and the gossips would not link his name in intimacy with hers. At the moment Paris was engaged, in the black hole of the jungle, in operating the famous emerald mine at Muzo, a mine which yielded the finest stones in the world. For this reason he was often absent from the capital, and writing to Bolívar he had to say, "I have not seen Manuelita for some days."

And later, when he had presented her with some emeralds to which she seemed for some unfathomable reason indifferent, "I have not seen Manuela for I feel put out that she did not like the emeralds. But today I shall see her."

And on that day he brought his own Manuelita, his charming diminutive daughter, to meet the other Manuelita. At this *tertulia*, the unpredictable Sáenz "arranged" a marriage between Señorita Paris and the personable Lolo Boussingault. The young French scientist had been attracted to her — everyone knew that — but still, marriage . . . It was days later that he could write home about it:

> Now this Manuela Sáenz abhors marriage. Yet despite this she is always taken with the notion of arranging marriages between other people, seeming to tell them: "Marriage pledges one to nothing, it is a passion of pleasure."
>
> Well, it was me, that night, that she designated as her victim. It must be known that here in South America marriage is purely a religious act — never civil. It suffices only that in the presence of a priest you declare that you desire to be united. You receive the benediction and that is all. People are married everywhere. In the street, at a ball; several of my comrades have been married in the interval between two glasses of punch — among others Colonel Demarquet (who is married to one of Manuela's family). He regretted it, even though his wife is beautiful, charming, and from a very honorable family.
>
> Well, that night at a *tertulia*, Pepé Paris (the one who has become so rich exploiting the emerald mines) was there with his daughter, a delightful person, very small, only four feet eight

inches tall. That there is a certain feeling between us is true. Manuela Sáenz knew of this; at about the time midnight was to strike, there seemed to go through the company a feeling of excitement A friend, an Englishman, came and whispered to me, "Jean, look out, a priest is about to appear."

Manuela Sáenz had brought him there without my knowing it and would have seen us married; but then, being warned and without anyone noticing it, I made a prudent retreat.

Several days after this, I found myself with my "fiancée." I put to her this time the question of marriage, on condition that she decide to live in Europe. She consented to make a trip to France, but she declared to me frankly that she did not want to stay there.

So I left. I kissed her miniature hand, jumped on my horse, and rode away. I never saw the small and graceful Señorita Paris again.

"But let me tell you about Manuela Sáenz."

And thus many people in Paris began to learn about this extraordinary woman, from the pen of Jean-Baptiste Boussingault. He was a handsome young man. Thirty-three years old (a year older than Manuela), he was born in Paris of a German-speaking Alsatian mother (who called him Lolo) and a French father, a minor official in the city government. He was studying chemistry at the Sorbonne when a letter arrived from Simón Bolívar, addressed to the savants of France. Gran Colombia had been ruined by the revolution, her intellectuals had been deported or shot; her educational institutions, particularly the technical ones, were now non-existent. The Liberator-President asked the French savants to choose five young scientists and send them to Gran Colombia to survey the material wealth of the state and to re-establish its cultural life. The chosen ones were Désiré Roulin, physician and artist; Jacques Bourdon, topographer; Goudot; Ribera; and Boussingault. When Jean-Baptiste arrived in America he carried a letter of introduction from the great Alexander von Humboldt to Bolívar. The Liberator instantly liked this young man of the generous nose, the wide, expressive brown eyes, the high forehead dominated by an ample mop of rumpled hair.

Bolívar made him a colonel, attached him to his staff, and placed him in charge of assessing the natural resources of Gran Colombia. No one believed, at that time, that this young and personable Lolo Boussingault would some day become a famed scientist, or that he kept a journal of events and people, and constantly wrote home — he was in fact a weekly courier of the news from the New World:

> But, dear Mamá, let me tell you about Manuela Sáenz —
> Although Manuelita does not admit her age, she seems to be about twenty-nine or thirty years of age; she is, in all the burst of her irregular beauty, a handsome woman, light figure, brown eyes, an indecisive look, pink complexion on a white background; she has black hair . . .

And so he ran on, telling his "dear Mamá" of Manuela's manners and caprices, of her household and history, of her affairs with Bolívar, with James Thorne, with Fausto d'Elhuyar in Quito long ago. . . . But some of the details were not fit for the eyes of his proper *Hausfrau* mother; and these he narrated instead to his brother:

> And then there is Jonotás, the mulatress-slave of Manuela from whom she is never separated; she is a young slave Negress with woolly hair, a striking woman, always dressed as a soldier except in the circumstances of which I will tell you. She is really the shadow of her mistress — but this is just gossip here — also supposed to be her mistress's lover, conforming to a vice common in Peru. I have been witness with my own eyes to this vice, with a few of my comrades. We formed a group to attend this impure but very diverting ceremony at a *tertulia* . . .
> But of this Jonotás — she is a singular being, a comedian, a mime, with an amazing gift for imitation. Her face is impassive and she discusses the funniest things with an outward seriousness. Now one night . . .
> The mulatress changed into the clothes of her sex, the costume for dancing the *ñapangas* of Quito. She performed, to our great satisfaction, the most lascivious dance. She pivoted first with great rapidity, then, stopping and lowering herself, her petticoat inflated with air, did what the children at home call a *fromage;* then

with great writhing and lascivious movements she lowered herself
to the floor for a moment, then getting up, she went off, pirouet-
ting out of sight. But where she had squatted, one could see where
her naked cleft had contact with the floor. Loud applause, but it
was a revolting obscenity. Soon Jonotás returned, dressed once
again in military attire, as serious as if she had not just given this
scandalous exhibition.

He added a little, too, about his own encounters with the
amazing La Sáenz:

> One night I went to her apartment to get a letter of recommen-
> dation, which had been promised me. The letter was addressed to
> her brother, General José María Sáenz, living in Quito, where I
> was going, as you know. She had just left the dinner table and
> received me in a small drawing room. During our conversation,
> she praised the skill of her countrywomen at embroidery, and as
> proof she wanted to show me an artistically worked petticoat.
> Then without embarrassment — and in the most natural way in
> the world — she took the bottom of her petticoat and lifted it in
> such a way that I could see the really remarkable work of the
> women of Quito.
> But I was constrained to see something *else* other than the
> embroidered petticoat.
> "Look now, *mon cher Jean*, how this is done."
> "But done to a turn, madame," said I, making an allusion to her
> legs.
> The situation was becoming really embarrassing to my modesty,
> when I was removed from this position by the entrance of the
> Englishman, William Wills, who came in unannounced. Without
> being the least disconcerted, Manuela said, "I was just showing
> Don Juan the embroideries of Quito."

Then from the south came news more disturbing than the lace
on Manuela's petticoat. The Peruvian army had penetrated into
the Ecuadorian highlands and was pushing on to Quito. Of more
immediate danger — some of the officers in Bolívar's southern
Colombian armies were said to be in contact with the Peruvians,
and hoping to join forces with them over the prostrate body of
Ecuador. The dashing General Córdoba was called away from the
arms of his Fanny, and in his fashion he quickly subdued the

would-be rebels. Then, to secure the dissidents to the army for the impending war with Peru, Bolívar granted a general amnesty. Córdoba ranted and fumed at these palliative measures, but Bolívar remained adamant. Then he sent orders to General Sucre to take to the field and defeat the enemy. At first Sucre refused. He was living in despair. In Bolivia he had put down a revolt, and had been wounded in the head and arm; political events since then had killed the last of his enthusiasm.

Sucre was without ambitions or passions, except that for his girl wife. He had been married to his Mariana, heiress to the title and property of the Marquis de Solanda, and during the intervals following his return his dainty Marquesa had given him a daughter, Teresa. He soon saw that his marriage was a mistake. He transformed his passion for his wife into a fervent love for his child.

But even though his right arm was paralyzed from a bullet wound, and his heart saddened by his failure in love, Sucre could not forget his old companion-in-arms. He knew that Bolívar was too ill to lead troops into battle. He therefore massed his forces, and in the last weeks of February, 1829, moved down to meet the Peruvians. Here was the tragedy of disunity; the opposing generals, Sucre and La Mar, had fought together on the plains of Ayacucho as blood brothers, but now they were enemies. Sucre, although outnumbered, knew the land; besides, the new sighting devices on his rifles played havoc in the Peruvian ranks. Before that time, bullets went where the devil sent them but now:

> Today it is a joy; the coward and the brave man are felled on the battlefield with the simplicity of solving the equation in the third degree. One dies mathematically, by the rule, without mistakes in addition or a slip of the pen, and in the end this must be a consolation to the one who is shuffling off this mortal coil. No question about it, today a cannon ball is something almost scientific, born with an education and knowing exactly where it is going. This is progress, and all the rest is folderol.

Thanks to this device the Battle of Tarqui, fought on February 27, 1829, was an overwhelming victory for Sucre and Gran Co-

lombia. It took a month for the news of the fight to reach Bogotá;
and by that time a new character had joined the *dramatis personae*
on the confused political stage of the Republic. Already he had
a speaking part of importance:

To Martin Van Buren   *March 28, 1829*
Secretary of State

Sir:

  I have the honor to inform you that an officer from the headquarters of General Bolívar has just arrived bringing information
of the complete defeat of the Peruvian army and the conclusion
of peace. . . . Nothing can exceed the joy with which this news
has been received here.

                                    William H. Harrison

The hero of Tippecanoe, General William Henry Harrison, arrived in Bogotá under trying conditions. The long horseback journey from the Magdalena River had irritated his old battle wounds,
the dampness of Bogotá inflamed his gout, and the country to
which the pathos of distance had once lent enchantment upset
him at every turn. A veteran of wars against Indian and Briton,
well-meaning albeit bungling (and just twelve years away from
the presidency of his country), he was an opinionated old soldier,
out of step the moment he arrived.

  "An old servant of the United States," Boussingault described
him in these days, "angular movements, education not very high,
affecting extreme demagogic opinions. Because of what he considered to be the requirements of his official position, he invited to his evening gatherings Americans of the working class,
honest fellows, as a matter of fact with much better public manners than their Ambassador."

  When, for example, at a large banquet in Bogotá given on the
anniversary of the Battle of Boyacá, the Yorktown of Colombia, a
gentleman proposed a toast to the two illustrious liberators of
America, Bolívar and Washington — it was the thing to associate
these two names even though there was very little resemblance

between their characters — old General Harrison got angry, and waving his glass with undiplomatic insistence declared, "Washington dead is worth more than Bolívar alive."

Now anyone, most of all an ambassador, should have known that this was not the thing to say while the memory of the attempt on Bolívar's life was still fresh; and especially not when one of the dinner guests was Manuela Sáenz, who had saved him. From that day forward, Harrison was marked by Manuela as an enemy.

And there were other enemies too. "The English-American colony," observed Boussingault, "was very hostile to the Liberator." And there were suggestions of another conspiracy forming against Bolívar. This time it seemed to emanate from sources around General Córdoba. He was close to the British, and his love for Fanny Henderson brought him to the homes of many who were openly opposed to Simón Bolívar; what he already did bordered on sedition. Córdoba was a romantic, passionate, restless, and confused. When Manuela heard of his cabal she shifted her rumor-gathering in that direction.

Still, when the news of the victory of Tarqui came to Bogotá, Manuela could no longer restrain herself, the weeks of anxiety, the waiting, the wondering came to an end with the news of the complete victory of General Sucre. She organized a picnic in honor of the event. Boussingault, like others of Manuela's intimate circle, was a guest:

> We were in the midst of the dry season. Our rendezvous was at eight o'clock in the morning on Carrera Street, in front of the house of John Illingsworth.
>
> Well, at that hour, when we started, much to my surprise I noted, far off in front, a corps of cavalrymen who had preceded me, and amazingly enough among them there was a superior officer. Strange, too, for we were all supposed to go on the picnic in civilian clothes. The presence of an officer surprised me.
>
> When I approached to salute the colonel, he maneuvered in such a fashion as to hide his face. The result was, for the moment, a rather bizarre episode of horsemanship. Then suddenly "he" looked at me and burst out in a roar of feminine laughter. I saw

that the "officer" was a woman, very pretty, and in spite of the
enormous mustache she had put on her lip, I recognized her as
Manuelita.

We now directed ourselves toward the plains of Soacha, accompanied by a mule packed with food and wines. The weather was
splendid, one of those stirring mornings one sees only on the
temperate plateaus of the Cordilleras. The horses pawed the
ground, champed at the bit, until they were allowed to gallop.
Then there was a satanical race and we were approaching the hill
of Canoas, when suddenly "Colonel" Manuela tumbled off her
horse, and in such a manner as to frighten us out of our wits. She
was thrown out of the saddle, falling six feet from horse to
ground. Stunned by the blow, she lay there unmoving.

Fortunately, Dr. Richard Ninian Cheyne, a handsome Scots-
man, was with us. He unbuttoned the "Colonel's" uniform and I
said to him, "Make an examination of her, Doctor, you are familiar with the human body." As a matter of fact he had before;
he said "She's a woman of singular conformation." I never could
make him explain how she was conformed. All I know is that he
said she possessed a secret charm to make herself adored.

Manuela gained consciousness, heard my remarks about exam-
ining her; she fixed me with one eye and said lightly, "Don Juan,
you have a filthy mind."

The injuries proving to be slight, the examination was termi-
nated quickly and there was nothing serious, a very light sprain of
the left shoulder. The "Colonel's" mustaches (which had been cut
from fallen Spanish officers at Ayacucho, and made into a simulated mustache and presented to Manuela by the victors of the
battle) I had removed, then we got back into the saddle without
difficulty and, keeping our horses to a canter, we arrived at
Canoas. Here we left our horses to take the narrow path which
ended at the place where one could see the cascade.

The Falls of Tequendama drain the savannahs of Bogotá and
tumble in a violent roar of water to rocks three hundred fifty feet
below. The beautiful painting that I have seen, owned by Baron
Gros, the French Consul, while excellent, does not give the whole
idea of the mass of water; the painting lacks emotion, vitality,
movement, the water there is motionless and silent, in nature the
Falls go over in a yellow watery mass of vapor and sound.

I proposed that we admire the Falls of Tequendama first, then
have lunch. Illingsworth seconded this thought, but Colonel

Manuelita announced that we should have lunch immediately and threw a tablecloth on the ground. At once the spread was covered with the most delicious of edibles and the most delectable of wines; champagne dominated the spirits. The ride had stimulated our appetites. We devoured the food, we drank too much, and Manuelita was of a wild and contagious gaiety. As we were eight, an unlucky number, I said it was to be feared that there would be at least one of us who would be precipitated into that whirlpool of the tumbling cascade.

An English missionary who was there began to improvise some mad verses on hell and heaven, and the end of the world, two Irishmen, stuffed and overstuffed, went to sleep and started to snore, as if in insult to beautiful nature. As I contemplated them, I suddenly was drawn to Manuelita, standing on the edge of a rock overhanging the falls, making wild gestures. The din of the roaring Tequendama kept us from hearing what she was shouting. I immediately leaped toward her and, grabbing her by the collar, sought to pull her back to safety Impossible; and the struggle on the edge of the abyss was becoming steadily dangerous, I was sliding into the slippery rock-cavity, and so I increased my hold on her thighs. Dr. Cheyne, now seeing the danger in which this madly gay and tipsy maenad placed us, ran up, attached himself to a stout tree, then he grabbed with his left hand the long and magnificent tresses of this imprudent Manuela just at the moment when she seemed decided to jump into space.

Thus we spent, Cheyne and I, a terrible quarter of an hour, until our calls brought others and Manuelita was put into a place of safety.

Once we were safe, we decided to return to Bogotá; the two Irishmen were still snoring; I poured some water on their backs, and they woke up spluttering, thinking themselves under the water-cascade. Before leaving we threw the empty bottles into the maelstrom; one of them stuck there and eventually, covered with moss, fell the entire drop of the falls without breaking. Thus the legend of the bottle of the Commander Don Juan was born.

We trotted back to Bogotá, calmly although very tired; at sundown we entered the city. At night, we were united again in Manuelita's salon; she looked fresh as morning, with natural flowers woven into her black hair She was charming, nice to everyone, speaking of the waterfall with high enthusiasm:

"We will return there," she was saying, " — and soon."

What an amazing person Manuelita is! Such weaknesses, such light-heartedness, such courage, such devotion. . . .

General Harrison to himself: "April, 1829. The personal envoys of Charles X of France were received with marked distinction. . . ."

The French delegation was a large entourage, and its members had been chosen for their titles or for the prestige of their names — the Duc de Montebello, the son of the great soldier Marshal Lannes, Charles de Bresson, the confidential agent of the King of France. They were received with a deference that made plain old General Harrison writhe with anger, a sentiment which was echoed by the British Consul. The memory of France and her aggressions was still fresh in English minds, and his government was uneasy about Gallic intervention in the political arena of South America, a region which, since the defeat of Spain, had been Great Britain's exclusive hunting ground.

As if natural, the agents of the King of France called upon Manuela. Lolo Boussingault was there at the reception:

> I met at the Duc de Montebello's one of my old schoolmates of the Imperial Academy; we were in the sixth grade then, in the class of Professor Couanne, an old dragoon of Napoleon, who had had part of his right buttock shot off by a shell, and so he wore a satin pad to fill up the cavity, a sort of pincushion. Remember — and wasn't it humiliating — the way we had to kneel at the master's chair for the slightest blunder? Well, while the professor held forth, we used to amuse ourselves, sitting at his feet, by sticking pins in that part of his pincushion buttock. It happened one day that my friend, whom I met at Manuela's, was put on the other side of him and mistaking the side, stuck his long pin in the wrong buttock.

The French had come to Bogotá for serious purposes. In the Liberator's absence in the south, discontent had again seized the country, and this time from a new direction. The party of Santander, to be sure, was scattered and ineffective; but now there was dissension in Bolívar's own group of supporters. Some of them wanted a return of monarchy to give continuity to Gran Colombia; general elections, in their minds, would only open again the wounds of anarchy. Who would succeed Bolívar? No one else had the talisman of his glory, no one else in the public eye could bind together all the dissentient people, conquer distance and geography. Who else then but a king, some prince who would assume power under a constitutional monarchy?

What did Bolívar himself think of the plan? His sister María Antonia could have answered for him, just as she did when the crown was offered to him in Lima in 1826: "The title of Liberator is your real one; it has extolled your name among the great of the earth. You should repudiate anyone who offers you a crown."

Bolívar was aware of the negotiations, but he did nothing to encourage or discourage them. Yet it was General Rafael Urdaneta — the chief of government during Bolívar's absence — who advanced the plan. If Gran Colombia could not survive under the present republican form, then it should have its permanence under the aegis of monarchy. Colombia had seemingly gone the full circle. The new dissidents, in view of their professed love of Bolívar, were terribly cold-blooded. They knew that the Liberator was an ill man. Not a *moribundus* perhaps; but the doctor had said that tuberculosis was upon him, and that it would consume him if he did not soon rest from his labors. They also knew that Bolívar, despite his asseverations to the contrary, was sterile.

No, at the rate he was consuming himself, Bolívar could not be expected to live long. Therefore, he would be offered the crown of Gran Colombia under the protection of the King of France; and on his demise, the throne would pass to Louis Philippe, Duc d'Orléans.

The return to the monarchical idea had, no doubt, much support among the upper classes and the higher clergy. The glamour that these French envoys brought in their train — the latest styles, the most fashionable scents of Paris, the prestige of their titles, the feeling of protection that came with being under the aegis of the King of France — struck those living in the austere simplicity of

Bogotá as a beautiful chimera, a fascinating escape from republican chaos

The one disturbing element in the plan was Manuela. She could not now be separated from Bolívar, especially after the night when she saved his life. They belonged to one another. So if Simón Bolívar became King of Gran Colombia — then what of Manuela? Would she become Queen? Over this, the council for the establishment of a constitutional monarchy spent more argument than over all the other technicalities; they gave to it fuller attention than the other problems that these decisions would awake. Let her be then a mistress-consort, a sort of Colombian Madame du Barry. . . .

General Harrison again to himself: "July 23, 1829. Affairs of the country fast reaching a crisis."

And they were. Moreover, Harrison had knowledge of them, for he had in some sense given implied support to a movement against Bolívar; he was privy to the uprising planned by General Córdoba.

The Council was still divided on the question of Manuela; but the Secretary of State was not divided in his opinion about the whole speculation. José Manuel Restrepo, proud and honorable, shook with wrath at such political metaphysics. His handsome head with its generous nose took on more dignity than those about him had ever seen. He brought against these plans thundering arguments and venerable aphorisms, and when he saw that he would be outvoted, after ten years' service in his present office, he resigned.

Further, the French delegation was not in good humor now. They had been in the country for months and had not yet seen Bolívar. It was as Boussingault said:

> They arrived when Bolívar was in the south, in Quito I believe. M. de Bresson wrote him asking his permission to go there and present his letters to him. There was no answer. . . . One could easily see that he did not care to receive the visit of the French delegation. The diplomats were piqued at the lack of enthusiasm shown by the Liberator in his relationship with them; they could

not understand it. The Ministers had received them with the
greatest deference, and the Chief of State seemed hardly interested in receiving them.

I got the key to the enigma from Pepé Paris (who never having accepted any official position was his intimate friend, the confidant of Bolívar). He told him how difficult it would be for him
to receive, in his sad and shabby quarters, the French envoys,
one of whom was the son of Marshal Lannes, of the great empire.
When he looked about him, he saw the lack of resources, even
poverty, his palace was a hovel, his soldiers in rags. His vanity
suffered from it. Looked at from a distance, he appeared surrounded by an aura of glory, which gradually vanished as one
approached his person. He knew it, that is why he eluded the
French delegates. As much as he depended on contact with the
diplomatic world, he preferred, whenever possible, to remain
invisible. . . .

The government of the Bourbons have constantly showed themselves hostile to the insurrection of the Spanish colonies; however,
when the Republic was recognized by the United States, England and Holland, France determined to send its royal commis-
sion to Colombia. But they never obtained their audience with
the Liberator. . . . It was, as one can see, a question of pride.

It was a question of pride too with Córdoba. No place had been
found for him in the interim administration, and for years he had
been drifting away from the Liberator's government; he was a
man of war. And Bolívar knew the fundamental weaknesses of his
character:

General Córdoba has rare military valor but also a hard and
unbending character, a ridiculous arrogance and an excessive
vanity, which are only virtues for the battlefield, beyond that
they are dangerous.

What was the drift of Córdoba's ideas? Manuela had tried to
determine it for some time, but her hatred for him colored much
that she could discover. There was certainly some connection between the talk of revolt and Córdoba's connection with the thinking in the English-American colony. Manuela knew, everyone
knew, that the English disliked the monarchical plan as given out
by Bolívar's inner councils; and Córdoba was decidedly influenced

by the British Consul. After all, he was engaged to the Consul's daughter; and it could be that, while ostensibly visiting her, he was actually holding treasonable discussions with her father.

Córdoba was a popular hero. Next to Simón Bolívar himself, no other person in all of Gran Colombia inspired so much public enthusiasm. A boy soldier at fourteen, he had fought through all of the battles of the revolution. It was his charge that won the battle for Quito. It was his valor in face of the enemy at the final engagement in Peru which was the turning point of that battle of decision. He was a handsome warrior, with a fine-looking head, sloe eyes, and a military bearing. At first, the people rallied to him in the Cauca Valley, where he was exceedingly popular. He had delegates sworn personally to him rather than to the government; and the battalions he commanded under the colors of Gran Colombia took their oath to move with him against the troops of Simón Bolívar. All this soon became known, but in writing of the matter to Bolívar, General Urdaneta suggested compromise: "I will try to draw him into the Cabinet."

But Córdoba could not be so easily appeased. His revolt was spreading all down the valley. Thus far he had taken no military steps, yet the disaffection was growing. It was as dangerous to Córdoba as it was to Bolívar — for the young firebrand operated under a fatal delusion. He mistook popular acclaim for popular will. Furthermore, the defects of his personality began to show themselves. First he was enthusiastic, then he drifted into a defeatist melancholia. He was flattered by the attentions of General Harrison, who breathed fire every time the word "monarchy" was mentioned, and he naturally assumed that when he wed the daughter of the British Consul, he was making a military alliance with Great Britain. Córdoba knew little about the cerebral processes.

Manuela was dining on the night of September 8th with Urdaneta when a courier, wet with mud and rain, came in to report that General Córdoba had started his revolt. He had seized the barracks at Medellín, and a large body of troops was rallying to his standard. It seemed that the disaffection was greater than they had suspected. Unless the government moved quickly, the revolt would gain headway. Things had happened just as Manuela told Bolívar they would. She had suspected Córdoba for years. Besides he had incurred her implacable hatred, her fixed unalterable resentment. Yet Urdaneta thought lightly of the revolt: "I think I can handle the Córdoba affair quietly."

Still he sent for his best officer, General Daniel O'Leary; he was to take nine hundred of his picked troops, drawn mostly from the Albion Battalion, and liquidate the revolt. Fanny Henderson, through her tears, wrote to Córdoba, asking him to be careful, telling him in the time-worn phrases of love that she would die if anything happened to him.

But Córdoba, again having mistaken popular acclaim for popular will, found that his army melted away at the first suggestion of opposition. Outnumbered by O'Leary's soldiers, cut off from reinforcements by the cavalry, he lay entrenched in a strong position, selling each one of the lives of his men dearly, until O'Leary used an ancient stratagem; he feigned retreat to draw out the enemy. The hero of Ayacucho tried to keep his raw soldiers from the trap. It was in vain. They rushed right into a counterattack that cut them down in droves. Córdoba himself, severely wounded, crawled off into a house. There he lay in his own blood, sword in hand, waiting to fight off whoever should appear. Led by informers, O'Leary soon appeared with his legions. To a young, sandy-haired legionnaire, Irish-born Rupert Hand, O'Leary said, "Sir, that is the way to the house. If Córdoba is there, kill him."

The nation was shocked by the death of their young hero. It seemed a great waste, for such as Córdoba were needed in building up the Republic. All blame fell on Bolívar, and overnight, it seemed, his popularity reached its nadir. Once more, on the walls of Bogotá, abusive scrawls shouted, *Down with Bolívar! Down with the dictator!*

As for Bolívar, painfully riding through the provinces, he was unaware of the death of Córdoba, or even of the battle that had taken place. One month after the tragic incident, he was given intelligence of it. He was terribly agitated over Córdoba's "pitiful and tragic terminus," although he had been estranged from him. He was plunged to the depths of despair by these deaths of the Republic's leaders, and by the perfidy that surrounded him:

> My grief knows no bounds Slander strangles me as the serpents strangled Laocoön. I cannot stand it any longer; I am tired, I have had enough. . . . During twenty years of work, I have done what I could Who has the right to demand more of me? I have passed forty-six years; and the worst of it is that I have spent these years without being a god, who is above suffering. I cannot bear more. I cannot bear more. A hundred times a day my heart tells me so.

The cheers were now hollow echoes. When he at last returned to the capital on January 15, 1830, he rode through silent rows of people. The bunting overhead, in the colors of the Republic, said *Long Live Bolívar!* The streets had been decorated with arches laced with laurel, the generals, bemedaled and jackbooted, accompanied him to the sound of cannon and the ringing of bells. Urdaneta had outdone himself. The school children had been given a holiday. Money, swept up from the all but empty treasury, had been spent for fireworks, streamers, arches, flags, to create the illusion of delirium at the return of the Liberator. But he could see, on the walls of the houses, freshly posted handbills still dripping wet with calumny:

> It was a never ending line of demonstrators [remembered Boussingault]. The long street was lined with hordes of people.
> "Don Francisco," I said to a schoolmaster who was in the procession, "your pupils are warm patriots."
> "They," said he, indicating the freshly washed brown faces. "They — not at all. You have noticed the man placed behind them to administer whippings when they don't shout loudly enough! These means are infallible."

So the people cheered, to order. Yet Bolívar was unmoved by them. He was ill, his cheeks hollow, his lips livid, and his eyes too bright in the fevered, tanned face. The people were shocked by his appearance; they seemed to feel that they were attending, if not the obsequies of the Republic, at least the *Götterdammerung* of their hero.

Bolívar was furious over the conditions that he found there in Bogotá. He blamed his ministers for everything, not only for bungling in local affairs, but for needless insults to foreign powers. For, when the Cabinet had found that General Harrison had been one of the instigators of Córdoba's revolt, they demanded that he be withdrawn as minister. But — "I will leave my post only by force," said the crusty General, standing, arms akimbo, in front of the courier. Then he was withdrawn under orders from Washington. And away, too, went the British Consul Henderson, with his high-colored little Fanny, who soon forgot her grief over Córdoba in marrying a London lawyer.

But Bolívar was still angry over the Cabinet's stupidities. They had killed Córdoba when he could have been placated; they caused bad relations with the United States and Great Britain when their friendship was needed most; they had brought the idea of monarchy into the plans of Gran Colombia, when they knew he would not accept it. He tongue-lashed his ministers until they resigned in a body. Then, shaken with coughing and illness, he retired to his villa, and to the care of his Manuela.

She had never seen him as he was now. He was not only ill, he remained outwardly indifferent to everything. His physicians came with increased frequency, yet they were at a loss to prevent the deep, body-convulsing cough which wracked him. After a fit of coughing, he would lie back as pallid as death while Manuela wiped from his lips the blood-tinted foam. She spent much of her time reading to him, when the weather permitted, under the moss-covered cypress trees. Whether through Manuela's care or through love, in those weeks he did improve, regaining enough of himself to welcome General Sucre when he arrived.

Sucre had ridden the thousand miles from Quito to respond to the last request of his friend. He had come to preside over the new Congress that had been called into action, so that a duly elected body might decide the destinies of the nation. Sucre! He was the one complete friend Bolívar had among the military. He was without personal ambition, and despite his passion for the cause of liberty he never presumed on his titles, which alone would have made him unusual in the period. Yet the pace and pattern of chaos had left their marks on him, his body, never robust, now seemed emaciated, and his simple, strong face seemed almost buried in the black hair and side whiskers that cascaded over his olive-skinned head. But more than fatigue appeared in his great large eyes, as Manuela noticed at once. What troubled Sucre? What caused his expressive brown eyes to fill with pensiveness whenever the conversation lagged?

It was his marriage. He had won every military battle — the four great victories of the wars for independence — but he was losing the battle with himself. The young Marquesa, his wife, had a lover, a general on his own staff, named Barriga. Sucre only suspected it — there was no proof — but the thought unnerved him. He did not speak of this: honor would not permit it But he gave all his love and his passion to his little daughter, Teresa, whom he idolized. When he had left Quito to ride to Bogotá, he had made out a curious last will and testament, beginning.

> At this moment my wife, Mariana, is not pregnant. If I should die, my daughter Teresa will acquire all of my estate, only if she predeceases me will my wife retain my estates.

With Sucre here to take charge of the Congress, Simón Bolívar did what it had been in his mind to do for some time. On March 1, he proclaimed his resignation from the Presidency:

> Today I have ceased to rule Listen to my last words. At the moment when my political career comes to an end, I implore, I demand in the name of Gran Colombia, that you remain united.

Having dedicated the Republic to anarchy by this action, Bolívar remained outwardly indifferent. But in his heart he wanted the people to come to him, to beg him again to take up the office of

President. Then, as the illness consumed him, he allowed himself to be swept hither and thither by the gusts of his passions He would return to France, where he and Manuela could spin out the remaining years of his life. No! — he would be the unifying principal of Gran Colombia, without holding public office; he would use his glory to knit the nation together. Again, overcome with melancholy, he would stuff his ears and refuse to listen to the narrations of chaos, as the reports poured in and Gran Colombia disintegrated.

Then like a thunderbolt it came — Venezuela had broken away from Gran Colombia. It had declared itself independent. It denied Simón Bolívar the right to cross its frontiers, and expunged his name from its list of heroes. That awakened him out of his lethargy. He put on his blue and gold uniform and summoned the still-functioning Cabinet of Ministers out to his villa. No sooner had all of his old colleagues taken their seats than he launched forth into a fevered address. He denounced José Antonio Páez, that simple-headed demagogue, for pulling Venezuela from the union. He demanded that the Cabinet restore him to office and that he be given power to make war on Venezuela.

There was an embarrassed silence. Bolívar had only to look at their faces to know what thoughts crossed their minds. They had lost confidence in him and in his infallible touch of victory. Another war, and with Venezuela, would be unpopular. Bolívar was shaken with anger, and strained by the inroads of fever. The Cabinet retired to deliberate. Then, unable to face him with their decision, they sent him a letter instead. It was from Castillo y Rada, a small man with a small soul, who had served him for years as Secretary of the Treasury. Bolívar dissolved into fury when he read it, for its purport could be read only too clearly behind the polite phrasing. The realities of the moment were obvious. Gran Colombia was breaking up. All the other states of the Republic would break away, leaving only the territory of Colombia. All else was lost. After this painful exordium, the letter went on that a new government based on this new reality should be formed. It should be a strong and representative government — but it should not contain Bolívar.

This was the first hint. Bolívar must have understood it; he exploded in a paroxysm of rage. Then, supported on Manuela's arm, he went out into the garden, coughing heavily in his cambric handkerchief.

It fell to his old friends to bring him, a few days later, the fateful message: his continued presence in Bogotá, in Colombia, was a threat to the tranquillity of the nation. Before a new government could be formed, he must leave.

Bolívar was to be exiled.

It was a few days before he was to go. He walked in his villa beside Manuela. There was so much to say, yet he could say little. The night before, he had given this house to his dear friend Pepé Paris, who in turn had reassigned it to his daughter, the same diminutive daughter who almost married Jean-Baptiste Boussingault. He gave his pictures and mementos of battle to other friends. He did not know where he was going, and possessions would only burden him. José Palacios, his blue eyes reddened by his tears, brought out the silver and gold plate which had been given to Bolívar at the height of his fame, and catalogued it for sale. Could it be possible? All it realized was seventeen thousand pesos — and that was all the money that Bolívar possessed in the world. He had once been the richest man in South America; now all he possessed in money was this paltry sum from the sale of his silver plate.

"Yet," said Boussingault, "he had fifteen years of illusions, fifteen years — it is a great deal during the course of one's brief existence."

Bolívar's old friends were now calling on him to make their farewell. Colonel Posada Gutiérrez found him in his garden walking across the beautiful meadow of the Quinta:

Bolívar's gait was slow and weary, his voice scarcely audible. We walked along the banks of the brook that wound through the silent landscape. Bolívar, with folded arms, contemplated the current — the image of human life.

"How much time," he said, "it takes for this water to mix with the infiniteness of the ocean, even as man in the decomposition of the grave mixes with the earth from which he comes. . . . Some parts evaporate like human glory . . ."

Then he threw his hands to his head, pressing his temples, and cried out in a trembling voice, "My glory, my glory! Why do they destroy it? Why do they calumniate me?"

The night before the day of his exile had been sleepless for everyone. All were on the alert. Manuela, a light blanket thrown over her clothed body, dozed near Bolívar's door. The guard was doubled. There had been rumors that Bolívar would not depart alive. And some of his loyal regiments, hearing of his impending eclipse, had revolted. Officials feared that there might be bloodletting. All through the night, Manuela could hear the subdued voices of the troops outside the villa as they exchanged signs of recognition. It mattered little. For her there was no sleep. The future was bare and forbidding. She was unable to accept the decision of his exile; she had fought against it as long as one can fight against overwhelming odds. The strain had, in these last days, exacted its toll: Manuela was as close to prostration as she ever allowed herself to come. The future — was there one? She had insisted that, this time, she accompany Bolívar, and not be left behind as in the past. All that she wanted, all that she had, was irrevocably tied to the fortunes of Simón Bolívar.

He refused to allow her this. He did not know where he was going. Perhaps he would sail for France, or Jamaica; his course was not clear. But the moment he knew, he would send for her. There was, too, the question of money. All he had was the seventeen thousand pesos. True, he had been voted thirty thousand pesos annually for life from the government; but it was obvious, from his past actions, that he would refuse it. It had been a dreadful day for him too. He knew that now his name meant nothing; the moment he left, the wolves would be upon Manuela. They made their farewells that night of the 7th of May, in the intimacy of the villa. She would not accompany him on this last ride,

In the morning, clear light bathed the hills. The night had brought a storm to clear the air and give Bogotá a fresh, delicious smell of earth. Then came the sun. A file of horsemen rode up to the Quinta to wait upon Bolívar. All the leading citizens of Bogotá were there, including many of the diplomats of foreign countries. They sat silently on their horses, the only sound the occasional trampling of hoofs. When Bolívar appeared there were subdued cheers, but he scarcely noticed them as José Palacios helped him mount. With his gnarled hand, the old servant flipped away the tears that coursed his cheeks, gave a last look at the Quinta, then followed his master on the road through the city.

The narrow cobbled streets were lined with silent people. Rumor, carried as it were on the breeze, traveled from house to house until everyone, without any other notice, knew: their Liberator was being exiled. Their grief now needed no claque; they sensed what they were losing. Tears fell on many cheeks that day, and no attempt was made to conceal them. At one corner a little child ran out in front of Bolívar's horse, stood on tiptoe to give him a nosegay of flowers. Then she ran quickly back to her mother's skirts, and with great dark eyes watched the cavalcade disappear into the distance.

All along the route horsemen mounted, one by one, and joined the silent procession, until they numbered almost a hundred. Everyone who shared Bolívar's victories and defeats was there — everyone except General Sucre. Bolívar had deliberately given him an incorrect hour of departure, so that they both would be spared the moment of last farewells. Bolívar was well out of the city when a courier rode up with a letter. The cavalcade stopped while he read it:

> When I came to your house to accompany you, you had already departed. Perhaps this is just as well, since I was spared the pain of a bitter farewell. In this hour, my heart oppressed, I do not know what to say to you. Words cannot express the feelings of my soul, but you know my emotions, for you have known that it was not your power that inspired the warmest feelings in me,

but your friendship. I shall always preserve that friendship whatever destiny awaits us, and I flatter myself that you will keep the opinion you had of me. Adieu, my General, receive as a token of friendship these tears shed for your absence. Be happy, wherever you may be, and, wherever you are, you may count on
Your faithful and devoted
SUCRE

Some miles farther on, where the savannahs came to an end and thick fog enveloped the land, Bolívar raised his emaciated hand to bring them all to a halt. Jean-Baptiste Boussingault, wearing the blue uniform of a colonel, was among the group:

> The cavalcade stopped between Chipalo and Piedras. It was the moment for final farewells. When I respectfully approached Bolívar, to give him a military salute, he stayed my hand; instead, his arms encircled me in an *abrazo*. He said, "I shall see you soon."
>
> I knew differently. His face carried the imprint of death, I knew that I would never see him again.

One by one, Bolívar embraced all who had come out with him. He was dry-eyed, as if the poignant moments had drained him. Here and there, with his scented handkerchief, he wiped the tears of an old comrade. Then, as if he could stand it no longer, he hoarsely commanded his entourage to mount, and those who were going with him into exile went ahead into the rolling white blanket of fog.

He put his foot in the stirrup, but failed at first to pull himself up. A friend rushed out to aid him, but he petulantly flung off the proffered hand and with great effort mounted his white horse. Without turning around, he slowly rode off into the mist. All of the silent figures uncovered and watched until Bolívar was swallowed up in the void. Then Colonel Patrick Campbell, once a British Legionnaire, broke the silence. He raised his black busby and spoke in a voice of deep emotion.

"He is gone, he is gone — the *gentleman* of Colombia."

16

"YOUR IMMENSE LOSS"

Guaduas
May 11, 1830

MY LOVE,

I am glad to tell you that I feel well, but I am filled with your grief and my own over our separation. *Mi amor,* I love you very much and I shall love you much more, if you will now be more reasonable than ever before. Be careful what you do, or you may ruin yourself, and that means ruin to both of us.

I am always your devoted lover,

BOLÍVAR

"Be careful what you do." Bolívar might just as well have asked the tributaries of the Amazon to be careful. The attacks against Manuela started even before the sound of his horse's hoofs died among the treeless hills. At first there were murmurs, then the members of the opposition, freed from prison, released their poisoned darts. Since there was no Bolívar on whom to lavish their hate, they fulminated against Manuela Sáenz. On the blank walls of convents billstickers put up their vilifications, and along the narrow streets of Bogotá a barefooted rabble distributed the little *papeluchas* which coarsely caricatured her. No one had to be told that this was the work of her old enemy Vicente Azuero, for no one in the Republic could match him in the art of vituperation. He had been released from prison the day that Bolívar departed, and had received a place in the Cabinet of the coalition government.

They should have known that Manuela would not take this supinely She slipped into her uniform, took up her lance, and rode

out into the street. Soon she found an Indian selling the offending
papeluchas. Whereupon she lowered her point, drove it into his
exposed rump, and sent him screaming down the Calle de Comercio. That night her servants ripped down the broadsides as fast as
they were put up on the walls.

Vicente Azuero, growling into his chocolate cup, directed all
his animadversions against Manuela. He was now, after all, Secretary of the Interior, and he decided to stop the grotesque activity
of Manuela's tongue. In the first salvo of the campaign, he demanded that Manuela turn over to the government all the papers
in Bolívar's private archives, which she had guarded these many
years. There was no equivocation in her answer.

> To your demands . . . may I say that I have nothing, abso-
> lutely nothing, in my possession that belongs to the government.
> . . . These private papers belong to His Excellency, the Lib-
> erator. I will surrender neither these papers nor these books.
> And can you show me the law which has outlawed General
> Bolívar and sent him into exile?

More than that: in the stillness of the Bogotá night, after the
watch had passed, Manuela sent out her servants with handbills,
which they scattered all around the city — broadsides urging the
return of Bolívar. In the morning, when Vicente Azuero walked
to his office, he saw along the buildings, like the erratic footprints
of a wall-walking monster of sedition, notices which proclaimed
in crude type: *Long Live Bolívar, Founder of the Republic!*

In an awesome rage, Azuero personally directed the removal of
the offending bills. Then he stormed into the Lord Mayor's office,
to demand that something be done about this Manuela Sáenz:

"There is known evidence that a Negress, dressed in a white
shortcoat and broad hat, affixed these subversive pasquinades on
the buildings alongside of the Cathedral, and on the walls of the
Church of San Francisco — and that the Negress responsible for
this act belongs to Manuela Sáenz."

No one believed that Manuela was a mere "lovable fool"; there
was obviously more behind these acts than the childish joy of caus-

ing discomfort. She was purposely undermining public confidence
in the coalition government. With General Urdaneta, who remained in the shadows, she was trying to effect its fall and to bring
about a recall of Simón Bolívar to the Presidency. She did not
have to create a new chaos; it was developing by itself, for without the guiding light of Bolívar's name the country was lost in
the trough of particularism. No one paid much attention to the
central authorities; each province was going its own way. In the
meanwhile Manuela was paying court to the soldiers of the El
Callao Regiment, composed of veterans of the battles of Peru. Her
aim was to keep fresh in their minds the victories in which Simón
Bolívar had led them; for they would be needed when he returned
from exile.

If any in Bogotá believed that the sacred festival of Corpus
Christi would bring an armistice in the battle of words, it was only
because they did not know the depth of the passions involved, or
the settled malignity of Vicente Azuero's nature. To most of the
folk, the festival of God transcended politics. The city was full of
people — mainly simple half-Indian peasants, barefooted and
wearing their *ruanas* — who had come in to see the parade of the
Saints, and to take part in the holy rituals. On the last day of the
festival the Saints had been carried into the Cathedral, and the
great square in front of it was cleared for a fireworks exhibition.

Manuela had spent that morning composing her next diatribe
against the government, and she had gone to the printing plant of
Bruno Espinosa to see it through the press. Jonotás, dressed for
once as a woman, was out circulating in the plaza, drinking *chicha*
and enjoying, with the rest of the bumpkins, the free-and-easies of
the fair. Near the fountain Indian workmen were erecting a bamboo platform; here the pyrotechnics would be displayed. Under
what appeared to simulate a fort they were making two crude figures, also of bamboo. Later fireworks would be attached to these,
and lighted for one corruscating moment. One figure was a man;
he was to be in uniform, a general. There was no doubt — it was

Bolívar. The other, in terrible caricature, with a face like a harpy eagle, was developing into a woman. There was no question who *she* was to be. The people massed about the platform, warmed by the *chicha*, were roaring their approval. Jonotás moved through the crowd, hurried the short distance to Manuela's apartment, and told her what she had seen.

"They are going to caricature the Liberator and you in the plaza."

By midafternoon the plaza was almost deserted, except for Indians who, like a file of harvester ants, moved back and forth from the fountain with their sienna-colored water jugs. A squad of soldiers in green uniforms of the Republic stood about the pyrotechnic platform, resting on their bayoneted rifles. The bamboo dummies were completed; the fireworks, tied with crude twine, were attached and ready for the spark that would ignite the flaming calumny. Under the man was a huge sign: DESPOTISM AND BOLÍVAR And under the female: TYRANNY AND MANUELA SÁENZ.

At first the soldiers paid no attention to the three mounted figures bearing down on them, they were hussars, armed as usual with iron-tipped lances. Only when the leading rider was before them, and they were looking into the black tunnels of a brace of pistols, did they know it was Manuela Sáenz. She directed the slaves to destroy the figures. A rope tied to the fragile bamboo pulled them out of place, and then Manuela took aim and discharged a pistol into the mass of fireworks. There was a roar like a cannonade, the horses reared back, a soldier slashed at the mount of Jonotás with his bayonet. Manuela put spurs to her steed, and in a hail of badly fired bullets sped away across the plaza.

The next morning Manuela was singled out for denunciation. Vicente Azuero spent the night preparing an early edition of his *papelucha*, the *Conductor*, where in the boldest type he demanded the guillotine for Manuela Sáenz:

> We understand that the Municipal Corporation prepared a castle of fireworks ornamented with figures . . . which were created to excite patriotism in the hearts of the people and persuade

them to hatred of tyranny. But a petulant woman, who was always in the van of General Bolívar and who goes about dressed in the daytime in male clothing, came out with her creatures, similarly clothed in a style which insulted all moral laws. This woman . . . extended her insolence toward the whole city. Dressed as a hussar she went to the plaza with two or three of her servants, whom she keeps in her house with money given her by the state, assaulted the guards, set off the fireworks with a pistol she carried, and then declaimed against the government, against liberty and against the people For attacking the guard she should be punished under a military ordinance and suffer the penalty of death. Instead the Vice-President called on her. Nothing produced so strange and lamentable a reaction as when the Vice-President personally went to the house of this foreigner to appease her . . .

The paper war was becoming more bitter. Manuela was creating just the confusion that was necessary to show the impotence of this interim government. But the attacks were too personal now not to answer in kind. She put up her lance and composed a stirring appeal:

Bogotá, 20th of June, 1830

To the Public:
    Because of the opinions held by those who attack me, I am obliged to speak out to the people, lest my silence would make me a criminal.
    I have offended no one in high office. What I have done is not dishonorable. Those who calumniate me do so because they are unable to persecute me legally; this is my vindication, since everyone knows how I have been insulted, slandered, vilified . . .
    I confess that I am not tolerant . . . but my serenity rests on the knowledge of the rightness of the cause of His Excellency, the Liberator. I shall never, never retreat a single step in that respect, from the friendship and gratitude I hold toward General Bolívar; and if anyone believes that to be a crime — it demonstrates the poverty of his soul.
    To the author of the piece in *La Aurora*, who should know that freedom of the press does not necessarily mean freedom to attack personalities — to him I answer in these words: He has vituperated me in the vilest of forms, I forgive him, but may I

be allowed a small observation? Why do they call those to the south "brother," and me a foreigner? Such as he can write all they want to — *my country is the whole of the American continent;* I was born under the equatorial line.

The dead are very readily open to reconciliation — not so the living. Manuela was surrounded by hate which bordered on the pathological. Her detractors seemed to distill scandal from every pore. Handbills vilifying her floated around the city like confetti, they were stuffed into the hands of people emerging from church; soldiers carried the *papeluchas* at the ends of their bayonets like billets; they were everywhere, pillorying Manuela with vitriol and printer's ink. But in her there was no retreat; she stood her ground and struck back. The spectacle of Manuela Sáenz standing off the pack, a woman fighting for the man she loved, now made an impression on many in Bogotá. Manuela had aid from an unexpected quarter, from those who were once her greatest detractors, the women of the city:

> It is urged by many that Señora Manuela Sáenz should be sent to prison or into exile . . . but the government should remember that when she had, as is well known, a tremendous influence — she used it for the public good, before and after that famous night of the 25th of September. We, the women of Bogotá, protest against the inflammatory libels which appear against this lady on the walls of all the streets.

This touch of reason did not end it Every day the crisis grew as the government found itself unable to cope with public unrest. The hurricane of handbills and inflammatory *papeluchas* still whirled about the city, with Manuela the target. Every night some billsticker plastered new attacks on her on the walls of Bogotá — and every morning they were torn down. The women of Bogotá, this time under the title of "Liberal Women," tried again:

> We honor, although we may disagree with, the sentiments that have been manifested by one of our sex. . . .
> Señora Sáenz, of whom we wrote, is certainly no delinquent. Insulted and provoked in various ways by people she has not

offended — these insults have caused great irritation . . . she has been exasperated into imprudence. But imprudence is not a crime. Manuela Sáenz has violated no laws, she has attacked the rights of no citizen.

And if Señora Sáenz has written or shouted "Long live Bolívar," where is the law which prohibits this?

The persecution of this lady has its origin in base and ignoble passions. Alone, without family in this city, she should be an object of commiseration and esteem rather than the victim of persecution. What heroism she has shown! What magnanimity! We hope that the heavens will treasure sentiments as noble as those which have been uttered by Manuela Sáenz, and that they will serve as an example for all of us.

The government was almost ready to consider the validity of these sentiments, the President prepared to take action, when a scurrilous pamphlet descended upon them. It was called *The Tower of Babel*, and it was a frontal attack on the government, striking at its ineffectiveness and its anarchy. It revealed secrets that only someone who had access to high sources could know. The writer was anonymous, the signature merely "A Friend of Bolívar." But the printer's name was on the paper, and soon Bruno Espinosa was dragged in by his black neckstock. The threat of the bastinado, a twist of the thumbscrew, and Espinosa screamed out the name of the author of the pamphlet. Then he collapsed.

> To the Alderman of the Cathedral District, Señor Domingo Duran:
>
> In virtue of the aforesaid legal authority invested in me, you will proceed to arrest and bring to prison Manuela Sáenz, the authoress of the imprint entitled *The Tower of Babel*, who is accused of inflammatory and seditious acts. You will proceed immediately to reduce to prison the said Manuela Sáenz and the moment this is done you will verify this with the undersigned
>
> Isidoro Carrizozo, Judge
>
> *Bogotá, July 19, 1830*

Domingo Duran set off bravely for the Plazuela de San Carlos. He armed the largest of his bailiffs with pikes, and as a special precaution strapped around his own potbelly a saber so large that it dragged the ground behind him. He lined up his men at the bottom of the apartments facing the Jesuit church, then alone he mounted the stairs to Manuela's door, holding in front of him the warrant for her arrest. Where he had expected resistance, he met none at all. The door was opened and he was courteously invited into the lady's bedroom. There she lay in charming *déshabillé*, a moistened cloth across her forehead, while her one free hand was massaged by Jonotás. Domingo Duran presented the warrant, but she did not even read it, instead she asked him if, gentleman that he was, he would be so ungallant as to expose to public gaze a woman so ill that she lay near death's door. Domingo Duran had not expected this. He had no instructions for it. And as Manuela in a low voice pleaded her illness, the confused man backed out the door, went down the stairs, and returned to his office, never realizing that he had failed to execute his orders. He reported to the judge what he had seen, the woman was ill, certainly His Excellency would not expect . . .

The judge was beside himself.

"The reason you gave me — that Manuela Sáenz was ill and that you were therefore unable to complete your orders to bring her to prison — has no validity at all. There are hospitals in our prisons. Therefore, in virtue of this, you are ordered to bring to the prison-hospital at once the said Manuela."

Once more Domingo Duran, fortified by a heavy draught of rum and looking like a rotund Silenus, pulled himself up the stairs to Manuela's apartment. He would not again be orally seduced.

This time he ran into a different Manuela. She stood at the top of the stairs in her hussar's uniform. The collar of the pelisse was open, revealing, had he had time to see it, her panting bosom. In her right hand was a naked saber.

"Señor Alderman, if you set one more foot above the other, I will run you through and make a widow of your fat Señora Duran."

Don Domingo fell backward down the stairs, almost taking with him some of his wooden-headed bailiffs in the process. He beat a hurried retreat, looking over his shoulder to see if that amazon still stood guard. In a half hour he was back. This time he brought the Lord Mayor, the judge, ten soldiers, and eight convicts who were granted leave from prison for the capture of the redoubtable Manuela.

Of course the commotion attracted a crowd This was precisely what the government did not want. The arrest was to have been made quietly, effectively, without publicity; but now it had developed into some sort of *opéra bouffe* Half of the police force, and the Lord Mayor himself, to arrest a single woman! The curious crowd blocked the street and flowed over into the Plazuela; some even stood on the fountain, braving the cool stream of water, to have a better place for the show.

The balcony was gained. There was no Manuela. They tried the doors, and found them locked. So Don Domingo applied his fat belly to them, others pushed from behind, and they flung at the doors. The portals gave way, half of the attackers fell into the room; when they recovered, they were looking into the barrels of two brass Turkish pistols. Manuela stood motionless. No one essayed a move toward her; there was a look on her face that suggested no compromise on her part. ("Be careful what you do," her lover had written, "or you may ruin yourself, and that means ruin to both of us.") It was a tense moment. Then Pepé Paris, warned of the imbroglio, arrived, wriggling his way through the press of soldiers and people. She liked Pepé Paris; he was properly punctilious. So, without once lowering her pistols, she talked over a compromise. Manuela Sáenz would surrender to save the face of the government, which already had lost more prestige by this affair than it could gain. She would submit to arrest, and accompany the bailiffs to prison. The arraignment would be merely formal. She would be released immediately. In this fashion, on her own terms, Manuela again went to jail.

Disintegration had come, as Simón Bolívar had said it would come. The province of Venezuela, which had broken away from the union, was involved in civil war. Ecuador, which also had withdrawn from Gran Colombia, was having its troubles. All over the land the *caudillos* were at work, breaking the union into small segments which they ruled with the methods of Janizaries. Bogotá now had no more power over its citizens than it had over the moon solstices. Soldiers murdered their officers, officers executed orders without consulting their superiors. Everyone seemed to carry a shibboleth on his person which read, "This citizen can do whatever he damn well pleases."

Somehow the government survived. True, it lacked identity; for the idea of continuity demanded identity, and the composition of the cabinet changed with each crisis. With Bolívar gone they lacked the ideal, there was no one strong enough to weld all the discordant parts together. Each day Manuela thought would be the government's last, but somehow it staggered along. And when it finally toppled, the push came from an unexpected source. A single pistol shot brought down the whole structure.

"General Sucre, on his way back to Quito, has been assassinated in the Berruecos Mountains."

Sucre had been warned, "Do not return to Quito without an escort." He had, it was true, no known personal enemies. Yet he was generally believed to be Bolívar's heir apparent, even though he deprecated public office.

"I do not refuse to serve the State," he had said, "but I wish to know the system and the aim. For a long time we have been without both, and I am too tired and too ill to work at hazard."

Still Sucre was regarded as the embodiment of the Bolivarian ideal, and for that reason, if not for others more obscure, he was a marked man. Before his decision to leave without guard, Manuela had shown him a cryptic bit in one of the scandal sheets of Bogotá. It read, "Perhaps Colonel Obando in Southern Colombia will do to Sucre what we have done to Bolívar."

Yet he did not believe himself threatened. He smiled at Manuela's warning, forgetting that she was, in her own way, something of a Cassandra. The assassins knew his route, it was the shortest way to Quito. In the Berruecos Mountains a road, cut deep by the plowing footsteps of time, snaked through the scrub forest. There, on a fog-filled morning, a single shot rang out, and Sucre dropped from his horse. The hole in his head was as large as a fist. He was dead before his body reached the ground. His Indian servant took one look at the cadaver, put spurs to his mount and disappeared.

The news, relayed to Bolívar on the coast, broke his silence.

"My God," he cried out, "they have shed the blood of Abel. It is impossible to live in a country where the most famous generals are cruelly and barbarously murdered, the very men to whom America owes its freedom. . . . I believe the purpose of the crime was to deprive the fatherland of my successor. I can no longer serve such a country."

Did Bolívar really mean what he said? Or was his expression, "I can no longer serve such a country," only an exclamation of grief and anger? For now the nation had need of him. The interim government had fallen and General Urdaneta had taken over, holding his power in trust for the return of Simón Bolívar. Throughout the autumn they waited in Bogotá for an answer to their pleas. They begged him to make a public statement, anything that might give them some hope of his early return and his resumption of the Presidency. Time was pitiless, and time too was important; then why did he not answer? And as the rain-filled November days came upon them, Manuela's worry became personal. It had been weeks since she had had a letter from him, and rumors floated up from the coast that he was very ill. But she had dismissed them:

> The Santanderistas may as well give up hope — because the Liberator is immortal He will never die, even if they should burn him. And at that, aren't they really lucky? But just think if he should die. The wretched opposition! Everyone would choose the Liberator as his saint. Even I, if I were to be so remiss as to survive him, even I would make him my saint, and despair over his death would perhaps drive me to do all manner of rash things.
>
> But just think if he should die . . .

She did not know, no one in Bogotá knew, that all they were doing was in vain. The neo-Bolivarian government would somehow have to move along without its symbol. The Liberator *was* dying.

And now it was hard upon him. He resisted at first with unfathomable strength, believing that his will, that will which had conquered the space and men of South America, could win out in this last struggle. He refused all medical aid, and sat in the heat of the coast wrapped in blankets, with his teeth chattering as if he were crossing the frozen *paramos* of the Andes. He maintained this fiction with approaching death. Between spasms of pain he dictated letters, a continuous flow of correspondence, until his strength was sapped, then he sank his livid face into the pillow and coughed blood-stained sputum into the cloth held by his nephew, Fernando Bolívar. Now he knew he must place himself under a physician's care; he thought of Jamaica, and dispatched a letter to an old friend, Maxwell Hyslop, who had helped him there during his exile in 1814. Then, to be ready for the voyage, he was taken aboard a brig to Santa Marta. In this Colombian harbor, in the encircling blue of the Caribbean, Simón Bolívar was examined by a Dr. Night, from an American ship, as well as by a French medico miraculously present in the little port. Dr. Night, whose name was its own augury, agreed with the Frenchman: the Liberator was moribund, he could not survive a long voyage. On December 1, 1830, he was carried ashore.

Santa Marta lies in a small crescent-shaped bay, framed by swishing coconut fronds. Two moldering Spanish forts, which played their part in the growth of empire, stand guard. The pellucid Caribbean Sea reflects the lapis lazuli of the sky. Its single row of buildings bends to the shape of the bay and follows the Malecón, the waterfront drive, until progress is stopped by the tumbling hills of the Andes. In the hinterland rise the verdurous mountains of Santa Marta, culminating in the snow-covered Sierra

Nevada. At the foot of the rise is fertile land, transformed by the hand of man into fields of sugar cane

For a week Simón Bolívar lay there in torment. His eyes were glassy, his skin dry and parched, and his voice sometimes so hoarse and feeble that he could barely whisper. Then a moment of irony. An old royalist, Don Joaquín de Mier, who once could have been his enemy, heard of the plight of the great Bolívar, and rode in person to offer the use of his own hacienda a few miles distant from the town. Tenderly, as if he were carrying a child, José Palacios gathered up his master in his arms and bore him out to a straw-lined oxcart. An oxcart! It was to be Simón Bolívar's last living ride.

San Pedro Alejandrino was a sugar hacienda. The one-storied house, red-tiled as was the custom, with cool ceramic floors, nestled among wide-buttressed trees. The scent of tamarinds was about it, and the pungent odor of sugar-cane juice being made into brown sugar. The furniture of the house expressed the tasteful opulence of its Spanish owner; large ornate commodes, richly carved rosewood refectory tables, massive pieces of solid mahogany, and beds whose elaborate posts were covered with mosquito netting as delicate as gossamer. In one of these beds, in the master's bedroom, they placed what was left of the body of Simón Bolívar.

The young French doctor was summoned, made his examination, and called Bolívar's staff into the salon. Dr. Alexandre Révérend, tall, serious, and restrained, came quickly to the point. The Liberator was in the last stages of tuberculosis, there was no doubt about his diagnosis — and the prognosis was death. He, Dr. Révérend, would issue daily bulletins, but in the meantime those who surrounded the Liberator were not to allow their faces or manner to reveal what they knew.

For a moment there seemed a dim hope. In the new atmosphere there was a return of strength. Bolívar was able to prop himself up, and began to take again an interest in all matters. Once more there were letters. He called in his secretary, dictated several documents on the politics of the country, on the people, on his destiny. Only once in a while did he allow himself to betray his weakness by saying, "I am very ill." Then the cardiac debility set in; he grew confused, then optimistic in his self-deception. He believed that a long sea voyage would effect a cure, and he thought of the West Indies.

"I shall go to Jamaica to cure myself."

Then he curtly ordered José Palacios to prepare for the trip.

"Well, let us go. What are we waiting for? Bring my luggage on board. They do not want us in this country."

So it went on for a week.

On December 11, his mind suddenly became normal again. Now he *knew*. Although keeping up the fiction and preserving his *bienséance* to the end, he now accepted his condition, and approached death in full consciousness. But he made no one aware of his knowledge until he called in his amanuensis to take a last letter to a friend:

> I write these lines in the last moments of my life to ask you for the only proof of friendship that you can still give me.

Then, as the doctor suggested, he put his affairs in order. He allowed the Bishop to speak to him of the state of his soul, he dictated his last will and testament. Then, and only then, did his thoughts turn in upon himself. Dr. Révérend did all he could to make these last moments free of pain; and to him, as he hovered near, Bolívar spoke.

"Why did you come to America?"

"For the sake of liberty, Your Excellency."

"And you found it here, Monsieur le Docteur?"

"Certainly, Your Excellency."

"Oh, then you have been more fortunate than I."

Then again the cardiac weakness; his mind wandered, and he talked of going to France with his doctor, to live under the tricolor. Next a return of reason, and then petulance. Smoking irritated him. In the last years he had allowed some of his companions to smoke in his presence, as he had never done before. Now the old irritations returned in force. When his dear friend General Sarda sat beside him during his last moments, he smoked a pipe. Bolívar opened his eyes and hoarsely barked in a commanding voice,

"Sarda, move your seat a bit farther away. No . . . more, more."

Sarda, hurt by the brittle tone, said with a touch of irritation, "My General, the odor of tobacco never bothered you when it came from Manuela . . ."

A look of infinite sadness came over Bolívar and his eyes brimmed with tears.

"Manuela! Ah, then . . ."

And Manuela — she was now distraught, for there had been no letters for weeks. She knew how long it took a letter to go — down the entire length of the Magdalena River by canoe, and then across to where Simón Bolívar was; yet there had been no answers to the letters of General Urdaneta either. Rumors kept reaching the city that Bolívar was very ill, near death — suppose they were true, and not inventions of his political enemies? He had asked her not to come to him, but she now felt that she must go. But she agreed with General Urdaneta that they would make one last attempt to get an answer before she made the trip. This time they summoned no ordinary courier. Manuela prevailed on Péroux de Lacroix to undertake the journey. He was Bolívar's confidant; his secret *Diary of Bucaramanga* detailed the frank discussions he had had with Bolívar of all these eventful years. Still Péroux de Lacroix had revealed nothing. He could be trusted. He was also a friend of Manuela, and he wished to relieve her of consuming anxiety. He left Bogotá at a gallop on November 29, and within the second week of his ride he arrived at the coast. There he learned that Bolívar was dying in Santa Marta. Taking a small coastal boat, he arrived at the port with the dawn, just as the church bells were plangently tolling in the day. As he picked his way through the small groups standing mutely about, he heard Bolívar's last proclamation being read aloud in front of the printer's office:

COLOMBIANS:

You have witnessed my efforts to establish liberty where formerly tyranny prevailed. I have labored unselfishly, sacrificing both my fortune and my tranquillity. When I became convinced that you mistrusted the integrity of my intentions, I renounced my power. My enemies have abused your credulity and have trampled on what I have held so sacred — my reputation and my love of liberty. I have been sacrificed to my persecutors; they have brought me to the brink of the grave; I forgive them.

At this moment of my departure from among you, my heart tells me that I should express my last wishes. I aspire to no other glory than the consolidation of Gran Colombia.

Colombians: My last wishes are for the happiness of my country. If my death can contribute anything toward the reconciliation of the conflicting parties for the unification of the country, I shall go to my grave in peace.

Now even Manuela heard it. The word came on the panting breath of Indians as they climbed the Andes, it filtered up with people arriving in canoes along the Magdalena River. Bolívar was ill and perhaps dying. For two weeks she awaited a reply, knowing that it could not come that quickly, hoping that it would; then she moved down from Bogotá, two days' horseback ride, to the river port of Honda. There she made ready for the long journey down to the coast. A large dugout canoe, covered with a *tolla* of banana leaves, was prepared; eight Indian paddlers were found; Jonotás moved about getting food for the trip. All was ready now for the descent. Manuela was about to step into the pirogue when a soldier rode up on a mud-splattered horse. He saluted, dug into his soiled jacket, and pulled out a letter. It was from Péroux de Lacroix, and dated from Cartagena, December 18, 1830.

Her eyes fell on the last sentence:

"Allow me, gracious lady, to mingle my tears with yours over your immense loss."

Manuela sank slowly to the ground, looked out on the flowing muddy river; then, through her tears, she read the whole letter:

My Respected and Sorrowful Lady.

I promised to write you and speak only the truth. Now I have finished your charge, and I shall now bring you the most fated of notices.

I arrived at Santa Marta on December 12 and left at once for the hacienda where I saw the Liberator. His Excellency was already then in a terrible state and fatally ill. I stayed in San Pedro until the 16th, and when I left, His Excellency was then in the last state of agony — all his friends surrounding him, including myself, were reduced to tears. About him were Generals Montilla, Silva, Portocarrero, Infante; Colonels Oruz, Paredes, Wilson; Captain Ibarra, Lieutenant Fernando Bolívar and some other friends.

Yes, my sorrowful lady; when I left, this great man was ready to quit this ungrateful earth and pass on to the mansions of the dead, there to take his seat in posterity and immortality, side by side with the heroes who have figured most on this miserable earth. I repeat to you, with a sentiment made more deep by my enlivening pain and with a heart filled with wounded bitterness, that I left the Liberator, on the 16th, in tranquil agony, but in which he cannot long endure. I am waiting any moment now for the fated notice. Meanwhile I am filled with agitation, with sadness, with tears for the father of our country, the unhappy and great Bolívar, killed by the perversity, the ingratitude of all of those who were his debtors and who received from him so many proofs of generosity. This then is the sad and dire notice of what I myself saw, and it is now my duty to send it to you. I hope that the heavens, which contain more justice than displayed by men, will look down on poor Colombia. . . .

Allow me, gracious lady, to mingle my tears with yours over your immense loss.

The letter dropped from Manuela's hand. A gust picked it up and whirled it tumbling along the banks of the silted river. Jonotás ran after it, reached it before it fell into the stream. But when she turned to give the letter back to her mistress, Manuela had already mounted and was slowly making her way back into the hills.

Winter

The Years 1830–1856

PART FOUR
Paita

17

THE GRAY CLIFFS
OF PAITA

THE SEAPORT of Paita, anchored in the wasteland of the Peruvian desert, faced the Pacific. Before it was a half-moon-shaped bay and the limitless expanse of the blue sea and the blue sky. The very existence of the town made jest of man's expedient nature; it was waterless, treeless, and desolate — worse than the desolation above Idumea. At its back, at its postern that fronted the desert, were high gray cliffs of bare rocks, frayed and crumbling — and beyond that the great Peruvian desert, a rainless land withering under a pitiless sun. On the downslope of the gray cliffs were the dwellings of the poor, a step in living not much higher than the shelters of troglodytes. Constructed of adobe and arranged in no special order, the huts looked like the mud nests of barn swallows.

Paita itself — the "Payta-town" of the American whalers — was a single street and a wharf. Quaint shops and dwellings lined both sides of the only road, buildings one- and two-storied, constructed like wicker baskets of woven cane withes, thinly plastered with mud and pastelled in chromatic hues. The walls of the houses were paper-thin, so fragile that one could push one's hand through them. The single thoroughfare was gray dust; thrown up by every passing foot to form a powdery, pumice-gray cloud overhead, it left a film over everything living and dead. Even the souls of the people seemed dust-colored. The only other living things in Payta-town (if one excepted the meager population and a few misshapen little trees, kept alive by drops of sacrificed water) were the legions of repulsive black buzzards and myriads of white-bellied termites.

Yet Paita was in fact something of a nirvana. It knew neither spring nor autumn, offering only winter to the spirit. There was an eternal sameness that gave to those who knew nothing else something of the relaxation of a soporific; and to those who came from outside, agitated in body or soul, it provided a merciful narcosis. Beyond the reach of time, it had nothing of time's ameliorating influence.

Paita had been founded in the springtime of the New World by Francisco Pizarro, as a port in which to unload the weapons of war for the conquest of the Inca. But time's passing had left no impress on it — the periodic conflagrations and the termites saw to that. The northernmost port in Peru, it had been in the eventful past the place where each newly arriving viceroy debarked with his retinue; for the coastal currents were strong, and the journey south by road saved an interminable voyage. Later Paita became the port for the cities that lay beyond the desert, and by 1835, in one of its periodic upthrusts, it was the last port of call for whaling ships. Whalers out of New Bedford victualed here; water, brought sixty miles in casks, was put on shipboard for the long Pacific haul.

The limbo for expatriates was also in Paita. The spate of revolutions and counterrevolutions that convulsed the new republics brought many a politician here in banishment. Its isolation and its desolation made it an ideal Elba; it was six hundred miles from Lima, so that the government had only nominal control over it, and it was hardly more than one hundred miles to the ports of Ecuador. Such contact as it had with the outside world was provided by the whaling ships, and by smaller coastal vessels that brought the merchandise to sell to the whalers. There was nothing here to arouse the ogre of politics; Paita was as near to death as one could get on this living earth.

Where the shaky wharf entered the one street of Payta-town stood a building well known to American whalers. It leaned crazily to one side, and its wickerwork showed through the cracked and broken plaster like the ribs of a stripped whale. Its ground floor was a small store, where garlands of garlic hung from the ceiling, and cakes of brown sugar drew a veritable hive of buzzing bees All sorts of oddments beloved by sailors were offered for sale, but the main bait was tobacco in dried leathery leaf, *cigarillos*, and long death-dealing cigars. Above the entrance was a sign as crazily angled as the leaning buildings of Paita:

Tobacco
English Spoken
Manuela Sáenz

She sat in the doorway crocheting. The well-modeled fingers, still pretty though not so well kept as in the past, flew in and out among the threads forming a beautiful pattern. Her coiffure had not altered either; the two strands of the lustrous hair were woven across the top of her head like a tiara, and in it, as always, was one small pink rose, which an aged gallant, one knew not how, managed to bring her every other day.

Her face still remained arresting, despite the slight heaviness which passing time had brought around the chin. Her dark eyes were bright, but they had lost their mischievous gleam. There was a placidity about her that transformed her entire being. She seemed utterly at peace. The wheel of Manuela's fate had now come full circle. On this October day in 1837 she had made an irrevocable decision; she would remain in exile. She had refused a safe conduct to return to Ecuador:

> What terrible anathema of hell had been communicated to me when the government ordered me from my country. . . .
> But my decision now is definite; I will not return to the soil of my country. It is, as you well understand, my friend, *easier to destroy than to make anew*. This order for my repatriation cannot now revive my deep affection for my country and for my friends. Now it is no longer possible.
> But one thing is certain. Paita or Lima, Manuela will always

be to you the Manuela whom you knew in 1822. Nothing gives
me greater peace than the tranquillity of my country, and nothing
gives me greater joy than tranquillity.

The joy of tranquillity . . . Now she had reached it through the
fire, and with that came an alteration in character. She sat alone
in her emptiness, in the ashes of her life, bereft of the one thing in
the whole world that to her was worth having. What had brought
about this transformation? It had been the experience of the
flames, for she had been burnt at the stake of human opinion. Now,
with Simón Bolívar dead, his name execrated in all the places over
the land, she could only say, "When he lived, I loved Bolívar.
Dead, I venerate him."

For it was not only Simón Bolívar she had lost, when he died in
1830, but a way of life, direction, an objective. Her world seemed
to fall apart on the day she received that letter telling of his death.
She had her servants catch and bring to her the most lethal of
serpents, the death-dealing fer-de-lance; and she provoked it to
bite her, as she desired it should, on the right shoulder:

> I arrived at Guaduas at night [wrote Boussingault], and
> Colonel Acosta, at whose house I alighted, came out to me cry-
> ing aloud that Manuelita was dying, that she had been bitten by
> one of the most venomous of snakes.
> Was it an attempt at suicide, did she want to die like Cleo-
> patra?
> I went to her house, where I found her stretched out on a sofa,
> her right arm hanging down swollen to the shoulder. How beau-
> tiful Manuelita was. . . .
> Immediately after the bite she was made to take some warm
> rum beverage. It is the remedy employed by the people of this
> country, for it is believed that inebriation stops the action of the
> poison. I applied a cataplasm to the arm . . . Manuelita went to
> sleep, and the next day she was well. I left her with the belief
> that she had made a deliberate attempt on her life.

Bogotá was a purgatory for her. With the Liberator gone, without the fear of reprisals from his avenging spirit, attacks against
her came from all sides. Within a few months after Bolívar had

been buried in the vaults of the Cathedral at Santa Marta, his old
enemy Santander returned — to Bogotá, and to power It was at
this point that Manuela's friends advised her to leave the city.
She sold her jewels for a mere thousand pesos, and moved her
entire retinue bag and baggage to Guanacas del Arroyo. Still the
removal of her inflammable personality did not alter their sus-
picions toward her; Santander suspected her of being the rallying
point of his opposition. The bloodletting did not stop. All those
who were suspected of plotting against the new government were
summarily tried — and shot. Nor could Manuela escape. She was
openly accused:

> They say that my house, where I live on the Sabana, is a ren-
> dezvous of all the malcontents. When my friends visit me, must
> I first ask them if they are content or discontent?
> Santander gives me an unimaginable valor, saying that I have
> the capacity for the most monstrous of deceptions.
> What I really am is a formidable character, friend of my
> friends, enemy of my enemies; I have nothing in common with
> this miserable Santander.

All this was very clever, but it would have been cleverer still if
Manuela had not said it. On January 1, 1834, Santander signed the
decree that sent her into exile. He gave her three days to leave
Bogotá. Manuela against the gods! It could not last long. She resisted, but a small army of bailiffs, soldiers, and ex-convicts seized
her, trussed her up, and in a brief time she and her slaves — still
in hussar's uniform — were conducted under guard down the
Magdalena River.

It was the long days in the dungeon at Cartagena, during the
early months of 1834, that brought about the first metamorphosis
in Manuela. Walls, cells, thick-barred windows, had heretofore
meant nothing to her; she could always get around them, even
through them. There had been something to fight for; outside,
somewhere, there had been Simón Bolívar. Now the bars were
impregnable. The fortress, built in the sixteenth century, was on a
spit of land which it was beyond the stratagems of Manuela to

bridge. She was isolated, alone, abandoned beyond aid or hope. When an English vessel arrived and brought her off, under guard, she found herself on the way to the island of Jamaica – to perpetual exile from her native land. On that green isle she was met by Maxwell Hyslop, Bolívar's old friend, who had helped the Liberator in his days of exile twenty years earlier. Now he aided Manuela. But there was no happiness here for her, no associations – and she longed for her native land. On May 6, 1835, she addressed herself to her old friend General Flores, President of Ecuador:

> I wait for this to arrive in your hands from this island. I wrote you often from Bogotá, yet without the smallest of answers. As you know, my bad script is famous. . . .
>
> But now times are hard. There exists in my hands your intimate correspondence with the Liberator, and I am going to make full use of it. Much effort did it cost me to save these papers in the year 1830 – and these papers remain my property – very much mine. . . . You know my rules of conduct. You know the rules by which I govern my life, and this is the way I shall go until I leave for the grave. *Time will justify me.*
>
> No one writes me now. And you see me alone on this island, abandoned by my family. I always remember with pleasure our old friendship, and in its name I beg that you aid me. . . .

There was a more than implied threat in this letter, and Flores knew precisely what she was intimating. She had his damaging correspondence with Bolívar. Manuela's was a pleading letter, but at the same time she was leveling a loaded gun at the man who, by force, had gained control of Ecuador. Even then her brother, General José María Sáenz, was his enemy. He opposed the secession of Ecuador from the union of Gran Colombia, raised the standard of revolt, and became an open, avowed opponent of General Flores. Even as Manuela was writing her letter, her brother was being executed before a firing squad.

A letter of invitation to return to her native land, a passport, and a safe-conduct signed by General Flores, were sent to her in

Jamaica; and weary of her Homeric travels, Manuela appeared once again, in October 1835, at the tropical port of Guayaquil. How many times she had made that trip from the humid seacoast to the Andes, and under so many varying conditions! It seemed that every important episode of her life involved these same mountain trails. Here, over this footworn path, she had come at the age of seventeen, escorted by monks, when she was expelled from the Convent of Santa Catalina. Here she had come in state in 1822, to return to Quito — and to meet Bolívar. Here in 1827 she had walked up, after her exile from Lima. And now once more the trail. There were familiar wayposts.

So she reached the mountain-bound village of Guaranda, under the shadows of a snow-encrusted glacier, but she got no farther. On the night of October 9 — she remembered the date well — there was a fearful pounding at the door of the house where she was staying, a knocking loud enough to awaken the night watch and raise all the dogs. In the glare of torches, soldiers with fixed bayonets stood by the door. A gentleman in a heavy Spanish cloak and a wide-brimmed Panama presented himself:

"Antonio Robelli, at your service. . . . I am ordered by the central government to arrest your journey to Quito. And I am further ordered to force your return to the point whence you came. By virtue of this order you will be pleased to return at once to Guayaquil . . ."

And with that — the official decree of her exile. In the interval of her journey from Jamaica, Flores had been deposed, and the new president would have none of Manuela:

To Señora Manuela Sáenz:
    The President understands that the Señora has returned from Jamaica to Guayaquil and is taking the road for cities of the interior. He also understands that she is spreading seditious talk in favor of her late brother General Sáenz, who died in 1834 fighting against this Government. I am disturbed about the effect on public tranquillity — therefore you are ordered to return to Guayaquil and leave this country as soon as possible.

Manuela was held under house arrest, and she was making her last stand. With fury she flung about, but once again, as in the dungeons of Cartagena, she could only listen to the echoes of her frenzy. The soldiers gave the small woman wide berth as she walked up and down the mud floor, striking her boots with a silver-headed riding crop. She made a last attempt to resist, writing her old friend General Flores:

> *Guaranda, October 10, 1835*
>
> Yesterday I left for Cusuiche and today, following the orders of the government, I must return to the coast. You know, from a copy of the orders for my exile that accompanies this letter, that the orders must have been dictated by a drunk and written by an imbecile. What reason is there for this canard, based on the argument of my former political activities? Sir, because of my brothers I have suffered much. But enough . . . When arrested I gave them the passport which you had the kindness to give me, which was an expression of my innocence. *Sir, I do not countermarch except with the use of force*
>
> Nothing will convince me. My resolution is formed Only if you command me . . . then I will obey, but with great anguish. I shall be docile toward you, and toward you alone. Now I bid you good-by.

The eternal recurrence of the sun, of gray dust, of a nirvanalike monotony, had brought to Manuela, in Payta-town, tranquillity. This metamorphosis was, like all fundamental variations in character, a slow, an almost imperceptible change. Poverty attended her, and she met it with a restrained courage. Many of her things were still in Bogotá, she had sold the last of her jewels and her clothes — they would not be needed in Payta-town — and with what she had left she rented for a pittance the leaning wickerwork house, and there opened a small store. Of all her retinue of slaves and servants, only three elected exile with her. Jonotás, the irrepressible Jonotás, was swallowed up by the dark stream of life, as was Natan. One by one the other slaves were sold, regained their freedom, left, died. There now remained only Juana Rosa, who had a capacious heart and an almost motherly regard for her mistress, and two dark-skinned waifs, Dominga and Mendoza, *criadas* whom the full heart of Manuela could not leave behind in Colombia.

News and rumors filtered in, but under the gray dust of the environment Manuela's reactions were detached. She, who before never could distinguish between a personality and an argument, now took the events of life as if they were a cruel malady through which one had to pass. In 1837 she learned that her old friend, de Lacroix, he who had sent the fateful letter about Simón Bolívar's death, was gone. Exiled and penniless, he had sunk into poverty and disgrace, and finally blew out his brains in a Parisian garret. Next, Pepé Paris. An injured arm . . . gangrene . . . amputation . . . then lovable Pepé was gathered into Mother Earth.

Through it all Manuela kept up her interminable crocheting, and sold her coarse black cigars.

Word drifted up from Lima, too, from her former friend and chronicler, Cayetano Freyre. Back in the graces of the government, he was now an advocate; he knew all the latest gossip in and about Lima. Some of it concerned Manuela's husband — she was after all still legally married to James Thorne. Don Jaime had first become executor of the estate of his late friend, General Domingo Orué; soon he somehow got control of the great sugar hacienda; now he was extremely wealthy. He was very close to the General's widow; and the children whom Señora Orué now had about her were definitely Don Jaime's. Now if Manuela — since she did after all have a legal position . . . No! Manuela had no interest in her husband's affairs.

She was done with all that.

After 1837, Manuela needed no longer to write in her letters, "Nothing ever happens in this miserable port"; for the half-moon bay was filled much of the time with whaling ships from New Bedford. Paita was the last port of call before these vessels, following the path of the whale, made their way into the limitless Pacific seas. Water brought on mule back from the inland moun-

tains, some fresh vegetables, an occasional steer, and tobacco were
to be had in Paita; and all the whalemen stopped here. There
were, naturally, desertions, brawls, heavy drinking; the Payta-
town jail was enlarged, still it could not contain the avalanche.
All this, plus the shipowners' protests to the government in Washington about the exorbitant costs of victualing ships at Paita,
brought an official representative of the United States. On July 1,
1839, Alexander Ruden, Jr. of Cincinnati, brushing the gray dust
off his tall beaver hat, moved into a small termite-infested building and hung out his sign — *American Consul.*

Alexander Ruden — the townspeople called him Don Alejandro
— had entered the South American scene early, coming down by
sea to Chile, and moving north in search of something worthy of
his labors. He learned some Spanish, and acquired a working
knowledge of the abracadabra of ships and whale oil. Then at the
age of twenty-nine he was named American Consul at Paita; he
was to remain there for sixteen years, until the whaling industry
began to fail. He was, as consuls go, fairly diligent, even though
there was an undated complaint, sent to the President of the
United States by the master of an American whaler, stating that
"Mr. Ruden is so deeply engaged in commercial transactions that
he does not attend to the business of the Consulate." Paita, for
him, was made less difficult because of the presence of Manuela
Sáenz. They spoke English together, she helped him with the local
authorities, and did translations when the Spanish was beyond
him Ruden in turn was able to ease her poverty.

She was invaluable when he had trouble over the *Acushnet*, a
358-ton whaler out of New Bedford. It dropped anchor in Paita
in the middle of November, 1841, and even before the sails were
reefed most of the twenty-six-man crew were storming ashore
seeking out the consul. It was the ship's master — a hard-bitten
martinet who treated them as criminals. To all complaints and
remonstrances, to mutterings of revolt, he replied with the mar-
linespike, convincingly administered.

It was an acrimonious three days; there were fights in the streets

which the night watch had difficulty in silencing. The second mate
deserted, and the captain roared in to demand legal protection for
the ship's articles. Manuela Sáenz, with experience in jails and
jailings, was called in to aid in the preparation of legal documents
for the local authorities. In the flickering of a burning candle,
with winged termites flying in erratic circles about the flame, her
scratching quill teased the salty English of the *Acushnet's* sailors
into Spanish.

One of the last to give testimony was a quiet, gray-eyed young
man of twenty-two. His name, when he affixed it to the document,
meant no more to Manuela than it did to his shipmates: Herman
Melville. But later, much later, when fame attended him, then
deserted him, he remembered Manuela. "Humanity, thou strong
thing, I worship thee not in the laurelled victor but in the van-
quished one." And he thought of the opaque grayness of Paita,
and Manuela mounted on the hindquarters of a burro: ". . . She
was passing into Payta town riding upon a small gray ass, and
before her on the ass's shoulders she eyed the jointed workings of
the beast's armorial cross . . ."

"If time could only stand still . . ." Manuela had said that once,
when in a burst of emotion she wanted to hold onto one delicious
moment. "If time could only stand still." Yet time did stand still
in Paita. Or was it that the dreadful monotony of the place preempted time? Manuela was made aware of it only when the news,
belated as it was, came from the outside. One by one her friends
and her enemies were carried off. General Rafael Urdaneta, main-
taining his conventions to the end, expired with the grace of a
gentleman, apologizing to the Archbishop who attended his soul
for dying in his presence. "Pray do! Do!" said the prince of the
Church, with a wave of his jeweled left hand. Santander of the
scrivener's soul had long since departed; he was immortalized in
Manuela's memory only by his name, which she gave to one of
her cats. In 1846 it became the turn of General La Mar, he who
had fought at the Battle of Ayacucho, the last of the famous gen-

erals who were in exile. What remained of La Mar touched briefly
at Paita, and Manuela reported on it: "There is a war vessel here
bringing back the remains of General La Mar which Señor Otoya
has brought from Costa Rica."

The passing years assaulted Manuela in vain; she seemed ageless, like ageless Paita. Her lithe and sinuous body, made hard and
firm from her active life, kept time's frontal attacks at arm's
length. Her skin still retained its alabaster white, the flesh remained firm, and the eyes dark and lustrous. Only here and there,
in the obsidian blackness of her hair, a wisp of gray appeared. But
it was the gray winter of poverty that assailed her most. She was
barely able to keep her establishment together. She could come
to no terms with the government in Bogotá to release her things,
and with Quito it was even worse. The part of her mother's estate
for which she had fought so tenaciously was in a legal tangle.
Even with her good friends there, she could not extricate the
money that should have come to her, and did not come. Lima had
nothing for her. For, although she was entitled to a pension
as one who held the Order of the Sun, her name was still
anathema to the government. Still she had not yielded to time,
she sold her cloves of garlic, measured out her grains of rice,
dispensed tobacco and cigars, became the counselor of young
and old in Payta-town — somehow retaining her eternal youthfulness.

When disaster came, it welled up from an unexpected and
almost trivial source. She had braved the horrors of jungles and
of Andes; she had lived through war and revolution for more than
half of her life; she had survived dungeons and exile. None of these
had left a physical mark upon her. Her life was approaching a half
century when, coming down the tilted stairs of her infested house,
a termite-eaten step gave way, and she was flung down the entire
length of the stairway. In agony she was carried upstairs until a
doctor, secured with difficulty from Piura, miles away, could
attend her. The active days of Manuela were over. She had dis-

located her hip. She would never ride or walk again. She would be forever confined to her hammock.

The pain of her fall was still upon her when other news came. In the middle of a letter to a friend she suddenly could write no more:

August 11, 1847

. . . I write no more. I am very upset with the notice, which has just come to me, of the horrible assassination of my husband, while it is true that I did not live with him, I cannot take indifferently his lamentable demise . . .

It was true. On June 19, 1847, a masked gang surprised the aged James Thorne walking with his mistress, fell upon them, and horribly mutilated the bodies. No one knew who killed the Englishman and Ventura Concha, or why. It may have been jealousy, for he had lived for some years with General Orué's widow, from whom he had acquired vast lands. Or it might have been assassins hired to avenge his assumption of the holdings, which more immediately relatives regarded as their own. It remains a mystery. All that *was* known was that James Thorne was dead, and that he had left a huge estate. Cayetano Freyre was alerted at once on behalf of Manuela. He waited until the testament was filed, obtained a copy of it. Thorne, certainly a man of probity, had indeed mentioned Manuela. He had left her precisely the eight thousand pesos which her father had given him as her dowry, plus the accrued interest of the years. And that was all.

Still, such a sum of money would have been manna to Manuela. She was now destitute, crippled by her fall, and confined perpetually to a hammock from which she could not walk unless assisted by two others. The money would have given her something to ease the pain of living. But she had not counted upon the malevolence of her enemies. The executor of her husband's estate was Captain Manuel Escobar, in whom in the past she had implanted an implacable hatred. Through Cayetano Freyre, she asked for her eight thousand pesos — and was given legal denial. The matter was pressed. Everyone in Paita who knew of Manuela's extreme poverty signed documents attesting to her need. But these, presented to the court in Lima, only seemed to arouse greater opposition. Her enemies raked over the dry dead leaves of her past. "All the world knows that Manuela Sáenz was a public woman, that her defects in this regard are so patent, so well known, that they cannot be denied . . ." Thus spoke the legal papers in interminable delay, while she was slowly engulfed by penury.

Manuela Sáenz had suddenly grown old.

18

"TIME WILL JUSTIFY ME"

IT CAME AS A SOLACE to her poverty, softening the harsh winter
winds of her soul, it came as a symbol of the plenitude of her life,
and a vindication of all she had lived and said. It came in a way
not at all strange in a world guided by no natural law, only natural
consequences — a world where the ironical twist is so often the
summation of things. Simón Bolívar found his glory.

A decade had ground slowly past since he was buried in the
Cathedral at Santa Marta, with a borrowed nightshirt for a shroud.
No honors were allowed him, and the Governor of Maracaibo
seemed to speak for all when he thundered out his anathema, "The
spirit of evil, the author of all our misfortunes, the oppressor
of the nation, is dead." And the name of Simón Bolívar was ordered
expunged from human memory. There were only a few friends left
who openly espoused his past glory, only a few who, like Manuela,
dared to defy the authorities. Manuela, and only Manuela, whose
love for him was a faith, had the courage to protest against the
public degradation of so great a man:

> He will never die. . . . Everyone would choose the Liberator
> as his saint. Even I, if I were to be so remiss as to survive him,
> even I would make him my saint.

Now from the pathos of distance she watched the transfiguration of her Simón, saw his deification from afar. For twelve years
following his death, his sisters in Caracas begged that they be

allowed to bring the Liberator's body to his boyhood home; it was denied. In 1842 the government relented; the request was granted. And overnight, in all the lands that had known him, the people spontaneously gave vent to an orgy of sentiment. His funeral was an international event. Warships from many lands boomed him a salute as his remains were placed aboard a man-of-war to be brought back to his native land. The streets of Caracas witnessed the most impressive cortege in their history. Those who had calumniated him in life now honored him in death, carrying his catafalque on their own shoulders along the cobblestone pavements.

Then, the idealization. Those who wrote him encomiums forgot that only a short time before he had been a living man, and, like a vast landscape of varying climes, a man of immense contradictions. Now everything about his life became romanticized, idealized; the force of mythogenesis was already at work. All over the Bolivarian lands the process of sanctification was developing. In the great plaza at Bogotá, where in 1830 Manuela had torn down a hideous caricature of the Liberator, the Colombians erected a monument to him by the famous Italian sculptor Tenerani. Memorials to him mushroomed in all the lands that had once been the crucible of his defeats and his glory.

At first a bittersweet emotion swept over Manuela's heart, when she heard how Bolívar was being raised to the position which she always knew would one day be his. Even as the news of each event seeped into Paita, she became aware of what Simón Bolívar's transfiguration would mean to her. She had become, to the idealizers, the great blot on his life; she was being immolated, sacrificed to the muse of distorted history. They did not know how to treat that amazing love affair, and being unable to understand it or to know its force, they found it easier to pass over those eight years altogether. ("The scandalous history of this woman is well known, as is her arrogant character, unquiet and daring.") She stained the memory of this great man. So Manuela had to go.

As Bolívar's star rose, Manuela's fell away; and in the course of the years she was blotted from the record of his life, passed over in studied silence. She who had sustained him through his years of travail, she who had saved his life, she who had loved him with a complete surrender of soul and body, without reservations, without conditions, she whose love for him had become a faith, who had fought to preserve his memory and had been exiled for her persistence — she, this Manuela, had to go, go to satisfy the distorted portrait which the apologists were painting of the Liberator.

There was, however, one old friend who would not subscribe to this campaign of silence. He knew what Manuela had meant to Simón Bolívar, and he for one had no intention of expunging her from his life story. It was General Daniel O'Leary. In the year 1847 he was back in Bogotá, as Consul General of Great Britain, and was in the process of preparing the life of Simón Bolívar through his public letters. This was to be the literary font of his glory; and as Manuela had many documents which were not in O'Leary's own collections, he sought her out in Paita. She wrote for his memoirs her personal recollections of what had happened on that stirring night of the 25th of September. And then, in response to O'Leary's plea, she revealed to him the hiding places of her papers in Bogotá, and allowed him to examine the coffer that contained all those letters of the eight years of their love:

> In respect to your inquiry for an autograph of Bolívar [O'Leary wrote to a friend], which I now send you, you have undoubtedly heard me speak of Doña Manuela Sáenz, the extravagant dear friend of General Bolívar. In the last few days there was delivered into my hands in Bogotá a leather-bound coffer containing many hundreds of letters sent to her by her illustrious lover, and many in his own hand. I had but a short time to go through them quickly. As revealed in his letters there never was a more ardent lover, nor one more passionate — and yet there shines through these letters a profound attachment for her, and a disturbance, too, over their illicit relationship . . .

Then, having taken from the coffer what was needed, O'Leary sent all the letters by special courier to Manuela Sáenz in Paita.

Now after all these years she had her letters. And this is the way she was found, half sitting, half lying in her hammock, when an old friend crawled painfully up the termite-bound stairway.

"Does the Liberatress live here?"

And from the interior came a commanding voice:

"Enter. Who wishes to speak with the Liberatress?"

In shuffled Simón Rodríguez. In the eventide of life he had found his way to be with Manuela. He was now eighty; he had the same pink cheeks, snow-white hair haloed his face. Only his clothes told of the thousand little hells that had been his life. When his illustrious pupil had died, he had published at his own expense a *Defense of Simón Bolívar,* in which like Manuela he vehemently defended the public life of the Liberator. After which, Rodríguez was pointedly asked to leave Peru. He moved on to Quito, where the government engaged him to teach his new educational system; but they forgot to pay him his twenty pesos a month Then he went north to Ibarra to start a candle factory, but, waxing more enthusiastic over the ladies than over the candles, he lost the plant to his creditors. He then thought of a plan to colonize the upper Amazon; but fortunately for him, the grandiose scheme evaporated before he could place his brittle-boned aging body on a mule. Finally at Latacunga he began a powder factory, since this was a commodity all could use; but he had hardly turned out his first contract than one night the place blew up. That marked the active end of his fabulous passage through the world; he would have no more of it. So on an outsized mule he packed the few things he had salvaged from his extravagant life, and left for Paita. He found a small hovel close by in the desert village of Amotaje. There he earned his food by writing letters; and when he could, he mounted a mule and rode over to see Manuela.

*   *   *

A matriarchal dignity settled over Manuela. The flesh gathered on her body, her hair was streaked with gray, yet her face, despite age and poverty, kept its youthfulness. When she could be moved, she sat "in a rocking chair like a queen on a throne." She accepted the gifts of the townspeople with proud dignity, for on them alone she lived; she existed on the pity of the people of Paita, that pity which is the most pleasant of feelings to those who have not much pride or any prospects of great conquest. But she did not allow herself to be overwhelmed by this pity. Her speech remained facile, correct, devoid of pretense, and dominated by an irony which went over the heads of her simple-minded benefactors. It was old gray December, and Simón Rodríguez shared it. Together these two who had loved Simón Bolívar spent their winter years, together reading those letters which told of other days.

Thus they were one day in 1851, when a gentleman mounted the angled stairway and asked for the Liberatress.

"Enter, who wishes to speak to the Liberatress."

He was a distinguished-looking man, with small blue eyes, a long nose, sunlit hair and a tawny full beard. He spoke Spanish well, as he introduced himself, but with the precise accents of a foreigner. His name was Giuseppe Garibaldi. Fever raged within him, and Manuela had a large leather-upholstered couch cleared of letters and insisted that he lie down. His name was not completely strange to her. She knew that he had fought for liberty in Uruguay, then headed the Italian Legion before Rome until, being overwhelmed, he sought exile first in Tangier, then in Liverpool, and finally — "although no one wanted me" — in Staten Island, where he made candles. He was now bound for Chile, but suffered from fever contracted in Panama. When the ship dropped anchor at Paita, he learned that Manuela was there, and he wanted to hear from her own lips the intimate details of Bolívar's life. Garibaldi, in his later greatness, remembered the day:

> We landed at Paita and spent the day. I was graciously received in the house of a benevolent lady who had been confined to her bed by a paralytic stroke, which deprived her of the use of her

limbs — I passed the greater part of the day on a sofa beside the lady's couch . . .

Donna Manuelita de Sáenz was the most graceful and courteous matron I have ever seen. Having enjoyed the friendship of Bolívar, she was acquainted with the most minute details of the great Liberator. . . .

After that day, spent with Manuelita, which by contrast with so many others passed in pain and weakness I may well call delicious — because spent in the interesting society of this invalid — I parted from her deeply touched. Both of us had tears in our eyes knowing no doubt that it was to us both our last farewell on this earth.

The year 1854 was a bad one for Manuela. She had kept up a correspondence with General O'Leary, filling her days with writing to him of the remembrances of the past, adding her own accounts of those eventful years. And that Irishman who venerated Bolívar had finished his memoirs, in twenty-nine volumes: twelve, he explained to Manuela, were to be of Bolívar's correspondence, fourteen of documents, two of narration; while the final volume, the appendix, would be one in which she would appear. But when the officials of Venezuela, who were to print the whole of it, found those passages on Manuela detailing her love for the Liberator, they gave one horrified look and suppressed it. In Bogotá a large folio of papers, entitled *Correspondence and Documents Relating to Señora Manuela Sáenz, Which Demonstrate the Esteem in Which She Was Held by Various People of Importance,* mysteriously disappeared from the shelves of the national archives. The elimination of Manuela from the life of the man she loved was almost complete.

But she was now beyond the reach of malice. She sat in her airy house, confined eternally to bed or chair, gazing for hours on the sea, the variegated, tender, tremulous skin of the Pacific. She was utterly at peace with herself and the world that had been hers. Yet 1854 was a bad year for her. General O'Leary died. Then Simón Rodríguez. She had missed his weekly visits, for he was now in the flood tide of misery and want, and was too weak to mount his burro. In a small dark room he was quietly expiring. Word came to Manuela of this, but she could not leave her room; all she could do was to commend his epicurean soul to the gods. And at last, with the village priest as his only attendant in death, Simón Rodríguez finished his life in classical style, in the language of his spiritual forefathers. Quoting *Comœdia finita est,* he departed, leaving Manuela to face the final scene of the human comedy alone.

It was not long in coming. In the middle of November 1856, a sailor was brought ashore in a fever. The local authorities tried to stem the course of the disease, but the ailment was beyond their knowledge; the sailor died gasping for air, strangling on his own phlegm. And before he was even buried two townspeople developed the same disease, burned with fever, and strangled to death. Within days it was epidemic, felling person after person; there was not an hour in which some silent funeral cortege did not shuffle down the street, raising a thick cloud of gray dust. All those who could fled the *bobbio,* the diphtheria; the ships refused them for fear of contagion, so they left by foot, by mule, by cart, over the desert to the towns that lay in the interior. By the end of November the plague was out of control. There was no longer time for individual burials. The masked committee of removal merely came to the houses, loaded the dead on a cart, and pulled them all to a common grave. Behind the committee came an elderly wrinkled man, so dried out as to harbor no micro-organisms, who acted as the sanitary corps of San Francisco de Paita. He gathered the effects of the plague victims, tossed them into the street, and burned them.

Manuela was doomed. She told this to her old friend General Antonio de la Guerrera, who had been caught in plague-bound Paita. She could not flee. She could take no precautions; for what precautions could one take when the whole air was filled with the miasma of the disease? Two of her servants died, and were pulled away in the death cart. Then her old slave-companion Juana Rosa succumbed, and the General, acting for Manuela, personally buried the ancient retainer.

Four days later, Manuela died.

Paita, December 5, 1856

MY DARLING PEPA,

   On the 23rd of the past month — in November — at six in the afternoon, our old friend Doña Manuela Sáenz ceased to exist. Three days before, we buried her old Negro servant Juana Rosa; they both died from that infernal illness of the throat, the *bobbio.*

Thus Antonio de la Guerrera to his wife. He had tried, when the deathwatch came along, to prevent them from treating Manuela as they did the others. But death knows no favorites; they carried her down the termite-infested stairway in her hammock and put her in the open two-wheeled death cart. Outside the town the survivors had hollowed a communal pit, under the gray cliffs of Paita; and into it all that was left of Manuela Sáenz was lowered to the anonymity of death.

When the old General returned from the mass funeral, he was horrified to find that the deathwatch had performed his duties well, all too well. As soon as Manuela's body had been removed, the desiccated old man had climbed the stairs and thrown out all of her personal possessions. In front of her leaning house on the dusty street he heaped clothes, pictures, medals, mementos of the battles and the peace; and, on top of all, the brown-leather coffer that held the hundreds of letters from her lover. Then he burned them. The destruction was complete. But, as the General sadly pushed his toe among the ashes of a love which had once stirred all South America, he found a single charred sheet whose message could still be read:

   The memory of your enchantments dissolves the frost of my years . . . your love revives a life that is expiring. I cannot live without you. I can see you always even though I am far away from you. Come. Come to me. Come now.

CHRONOLOGY

1783   Simón Bolívar born in Caracas, Venezuela

1789   French Revolution

1792   France a republic

1793   Reign of Terror

1797   Manuela Sáenz born in Quito, Ecuador

1799   Death of Washington
       Coup d'état of 18 Brumaire: Napoleon First Consul

1800   Revolutionary outbreaks in Venezuela

1801   Bolívar goes to Spain

1802   Bolívar marries María Teresa de Toro; she dies eight
       months later

1803   Louisiana Purchase

1808   Napoleon wars with Spain; Ferdinand VII deposed, Joseph
       Bonaparte crowned King of Spain, unrest in colonies

1809   James Madison President
       Revolt in Quito, "Men of August"

1811–1814   Bolívar fighting in Venezuela

1814   Napoleon exiled to Elba

1815   Battle of New Orleans
       Bolívar in exile in Jamaica
       Battle of Waterloo
       Ferdinand VII returned to Spanish throne
       Manuela Sáenz expelled from Convent of Santa Catalina;
       goes to Panama

1817   Manuela Sáenz married in Lima to James Thorne

1819   Battle of Boyacá
       Republic of Gran Colombia created

1821   Lima falls to patriot troops of General José de San Martín

1822   Manuela Sáenz decorated with the Order of the Sun
Battle of Pichincha for Quito
Manuela Sáenz becomes mistress of Simón Bolívar

1823   Bolívar enters Lima

1824   Battle of Ayacucho
Death of Lord Byron

1827   Revolt in Lima. Manuela Saénz exiled, joins Bolívar in
Bogotá

1828   Manuela saves Bolívar from assassination

1830   Bolívar exiled from Colombia, dies
July Revolution in France

1834   Manuela Sáenz exiled to Jamaica

1835   Manuela Sáenz living in Paita, Peru

1841   William H. Harrison President
Herman Melville sees Manuela Sáenz in Paita

1846–1848   United States at war with Mexico

1847   James Thorne murdered

1848   Revolution throughout Europe

1851   Garibaldi visits Manuela Sáenz in Paita

1854–1856   Crimean War

1856   Death of Manuela Sáenz

BIBLIOGRAPHY

In which the author tells how Manuela came to be

The life of Manuela — no matter how much it may at times read like some baroque romance — is biography, biography in the Stracheyan sense. Nothing here is inserted — not a word, not a quotation, not a date, not a conversation — that exhaustive research has not fully warranted. The book has purposely been written without footnotes; the precise detailed proof exists in the author's files, and published separately but simultaneously with this biography of Manuela is a volume in Spanish entitled "Documentary History of Manuela Sáenz." Those who wish to examine sources will find all the documents detailed in a special issue of the Bulletin of the Colombian Academy of History at Bogotá. So rich, so varied is this newly discovered material on the life of Manuela, and therefore of Simón Bolívar, that no biography can again be written on the Liberator without using it; it dispels the legends without making new ones, it shows a Bolívar shorn of the chiton of an immortal and makes of him, as he was, a passionate human being striving after an ideal, a man of complex attitudes and, like a vast country, of vast climates and vast contradictions. Fully to appreciate what we know now of this "lovable fool" of Bolívar's one need turn only to the inadequacies of past biographies of Simón Bolívar, which too often repeat all the idiocies and the legends about Manuela — her "faithful husband Dr. Thorne" begging her to return; she declining; he sending money which she refuses; "the doctor" dying in 1840 and willing her most of his fortunes; she again refusing. Manuela without myth is thus: Thorne was not a doctor, but a shipping merchant. After 1827 he lost touch with Manuela. He did not die in Lima in 1840 but was murdered in 1847 in Patívilca while walking with one of his mistresses. He had two mistresses, and sired four illegitimate children, all of whom he mentions in his will. He willed Manuela no more than the

8000 pesos which had been her dowry, and though she never recovered it, she instituted suit for it.

How then did all the early records escape biographers? Why in this century following Bolívar's death had not someone found them? The answer — and it is an answer — lies in the personality of Manuela. When Simón Bolívar was metamorphosed into a demigod by the very people who ten years before had execrated him, Manuela Sáenz, it was willed by the historians, had to go to make way for the myth. All details of her life were officially suppressed, documents which mentioned her disappeared, and her own last twenty years were lived in obscurity in Paita. And then, to complete the immolation, almost all the stirring love letters she exchanged with Bolívar were destroyed after her death during the diphtheria epidemic. For more than half a century the historians kept their gentleman's agreement — Manuela was never mentioned Yet the force of her extravagant personality kept her memory vivid and it lingered — and still does — at every point in South America where she set foot. Then in 1897 the agreement was abrogated by the publication of the memoirs of the French scientist, Jean-Baptiste Boussingault. Here was a man who had actually known Manuela, knew her and the runes of her fame; and he had been no ordinary traveler. He was one of a French mission who came to Colombia in 1822 and he remained there for ten years. He had carried a letter of introduction from Humboldt to Bolívar. He was a great scientist, a renowned author, a professor at the Sorbonne, a member of the French Academy of Sciences — and yet more: he had no historical ax to grind. *Manuela Sáenz now could no longer be ignored.*

But by this time the trail had grown cold. Almost all the revealing letters which Manuela must have exchanged with her lover had been destroyed at her death, the volume of the *Memorias* of General O'Leary which spoke of the love affair between Manuela and Simón Bolívar was suppressed; and the volume marked "56," the *Correspondence and Documents Relating to Señora Manuela Sáenz, Which Demonstrated the Esteem in Which Various People of Note Held Her and the Part She Played in Political Affairs*, disappeared from the archives in Bogotá. There remained only legends, traditions and attitudes to draw upon to sketch the portrait of the woman Simón Bolívar loved. Who or what was this disquieting woman who aroused a storm of protest wherever she went? Every biography of Bolívar fictionalized her, drawing her vignette in distorted lines, pyramiding myth upon myth until the real Manuela was left without reality. There were articles about "the true Manuela," she appeared in the *Secret Life of Simón Bolívar*, she was recalled in *The Loves of Bolívar*, but all this was based on extraneous legendary material; Manuela Sáenz had escaped history. Yet the legends of this strange and disturbing woman would not be quieted; scholars looking in the vast reservoirs of never-consulted documents began to unearth fragments, authentic fragments, of Manuela's existence.

My active interest in this strange and delectable life began in 1944; then the actual factual material gleaned from her known letters would not have covered two sheets of foolscap. Through the years when I was engaged in writing other books on Latin America, I read the whole of the literature on Bolívar and his times, and through an elaborate system of notes managed to get the feeling of the milieu in which La Sáenz lived. By 1947 the actual search for Manuela had begun — the libraries of Bogotá, public and private, were scoured for material, the archives were subjected to minute searching, every place where Manuela had lived was visited, her travels were duplicated as she took them, by mule and horse. In Ecuador, where previous long residence had given me a thorough knowledge of the country, I found numerous unknown documents, pertaining to Manuela, buried in the uncatalogued registers of the public archives; and here again Manuela's extravagant life was relived. But it was in Lima that the puzzlements of Manuela's marriage were made clear; the secret archives of the Archbishop of Lima yielded her banns, and the details of her marriage to James Thorne. Here in the archives the mysterious James Thorne, the much maligned cuckold of the triangle which became a *chronique scandaleuse*, took on at last flesh and blood as one of the principals in this drama.

Then, the National Archives of Peru — these became the font and source of the goings and comings of Manuela Sáenz. And for simple reasons. Under the colonial system of Spain, every commercial act, the buying and selling of a slave, the purchase of a carriage, the act of departure, all had to be set down by a public scrivener on *papel sellado*. These stamped papers (which furnished a good revenue to the Crown) were a progress sheet of one's commercial transactions. They began in this fashion: "I, Manuela Sáenz, who attest to the truth of the following by making the sign of the cross, declare that I am twenty-four years of age, married to Don James Thorne and reside at La Magdalena, outside of the walls of Lima, depose . . . and say . . ." and then followed the transaction. The original document was always given to the petitioner (in the case of Manuela they were destroyed) but the copy was kept by the scrivener, who, in time, bound all his notarial papers together and eventually deposited them to swell the many millions of documents (dating from 1539) which form the collections of the National Archives of Peru. There is no index and the only way to make one's way through this labyrinth of paper, foxed and yellowed, is to select the years of Manuela's known residence in Lima and subject the whole of those numberless volumes to a page-by-page search. This was done — over a period of a year — and the result was an almost month-by-month knowledge of what Manuela was doing in the environs of Lima.

The trail of Manuela was followed everywhere — over the hard rock-land of the Andes to the lake of Junín, where a battle was fought above the clouds, and then to Ayacucho, and to Trujillo, once walled like Lima, where Manuela watched General Bolívar build the army that would defeat the Spanish legions, and on to the desert-bound seaport of Paita to search for the nothingness that became Manuela there — and then on to the town of Piura, where for many hot days I stood knee-deep in moldering notarial records, trying to unearth some biographical fact from those dusty pages. So it went on. Every nook and cranny of history was searched out, everything that could yield a detail to give this biography the romance of reality was sought — almanacs for the condition of climate, museums for precise descriptions of dress, houses for the study of interiors, letters in private collections for the breath of scandal; and through that preparation the whole life of Manuela was re-created. Nothing here, then, is inserted which research cannot prove. For beyond the presence of dates and of history, Manuela's story is a timeless story, and the most fertile of novelists would have been hard put to find a plot that would tell her life better than by following what actually occurred. One could change the names of the dramatis personae, rearrange the battles, or replace the locale of South America at the time of its revolution; one could even give it a different milieu, adding glint and glitter at the expense of reality. It would change nothing The story is the thing, and this is Manuela's story.

Acknowledgments

This biography of Manuela Sáenz was first initiated and much of the research, under my direction, was done by my former wife, now Christine Powell; under this "talking out" the pattern of Manuela's personality took form and was further fleshed by the revealing research. All of the research material, in the form of documents, letters and books, came out of South America over a period of ten years. In Venezuela, Dr. Vicente Lecuna, the eminent editor of the collected letters of Simón Bolívar, gave over a period of years much aid. In Bogotá, which a century ago had been Bolívar's capital of Gran Colombia, there came consistent help from Dr Luis Augusto Cuervo, who allowed his collections to be photographed, great aid came from Dr. Enrique Ortega Ricaurte, Director of the National Archives; and editorial assistance from Dr. Enrique Otero D'Costa, and from J. R. de la Torre Bueno, affectionately "Bill."

In Quito "under the equatorial line," where Manuela was born and where time has given her a saintly nimbus, I had the assistance of General Angel Issac Chiriboga, whose family a century ago was intimate with La Sáenz; from the library of the late Señor Don Jacinto Jijon y Caamaño, the correspondence of his ancestor, General Flores, with Manuela; and from Dr. Enrique Arroyo, former Undersecretary of Foreign Affairs, much help and direction. In Lima, where Manuela made her history and her scandal, the historical letter telling of Manuela's death came from the collections of Señor Don Aurelio Miro Quesada, Director of *El Comercio*. Señor Don Francisco Moreira y Paz Soldan opened up his private library, in which the records of his ancestors, the Counts of San Isidro, provided the finest of colonial material. But it was in the National Archives of Peru in Lima that the richest material was discovered. My good genie, in the person of Señor Don Felipe Marquez, searched through countless thousands of documents to find the details of Manuela's life. These archives contain one of the richest collections of manuscripts pertaining to the private life of Simón Bolívar that has been found within the century.

Bibliographical Note

The listings that follow are not intended to be a formal bibliography, which can be found in the author's detailed study, "The Documentary History of Manuela Sáenz" (*Boletin de Historia y Antiguedades*, Academia Colombiana de Historia, Bogotá, February 1952). The books and articles are placed, as in any dramatis personae, in order of their appearance:

1827 Manuel de Vidaurre, *Suplemento a las cartas americanas, etc.: Correspondencia con los generales Bolívar, Santander y La Mar.* Lima, 1827.

(Manuel de Vidaurre [1773–1841] was Minister of Foreign Affairs in 1827, during the time that Manuela Sáenz tried to bring about a counterrevolution in Lima. He ordered her expulsion from Lima, and the letter of expulsion is here published.)

1830–1845 *Correspondencia y documentos relacionadas con la Señora Manuela Sáenz que demuestran la estimación que en ella hacion varios jefes y particulares, y la parte que tomaba en los asuntos de la política.*

(Marked as "Volume 56" in the old Library of Bogotá, this volume is irretrievably lost. It was seen as late as 1875, when its contents were commented on by the authors Leonidas Scarpeta and Saturnino Vergara.)

1840 Augusto Le Moyne, *Viajes y estancias por la America del Sur.* Bogotá, 1945. Reprint.

(Lemoyne was one of the mission from the King of France which came to offer Bolívar a crown under the protection of His Most Christian Majesty. Le Moyne describes Manuela at Bolívar's Quinta, or villa.)

1858 P. Prouvonena, *Memorias y documentos para la historia de la independencia del Peru y causas del mal éxito que ha tenido esta.* 2 vols. Paris, 1858.

(Prouvonena is the pseudonym of José de la Riva Aguero, who set up a rival republic while Bolívar was in Peru. He was sent into exile by General Bolívar. This is a vitriolic attack on Bolívar, as well as on Manuela Sáenz.)

1879–1888 Daniel Florencio O'Leary, *Memorias* 32 vols Caracas, 1879–1888.

(This is the famous compilation of letters, documents and memoirs made by General O'Leary, the friend of Bolívar and Manuela. In the appendix of Volume 3 of this collection O'Leary wrote of Manuela. That volume was suppressed, and the copies burned, only three survived. The volume was reprinted in Bogotá in 1914.)

1887 Venancio Ortiz, "Recuerdos de un pobre viejo." *Papel Periodico Ilustrado*, April 1887, Bogotá.

(Ortiz, who was more than eighty when he wrote his "Recuerdos," writes of Manuela Sáenz in Bogotá as he remembered her.)

1887 Manuel J. Calle, *Leyendas del tiempo heroico.* Quito, 1887.

(Publishes for the first time the tradition of the famous episode in Manuela's history — the throwing of the wreath at Bolívar's head at his triumphant entrance into Quito in 1822)

1889–1903 J.-B. Boussingault, *Mémoirs* 5 vols. Paris, 1889–1903.

(The very rare *Mémoirs* of Jean-Baptiste J D. Boussingault [1802–1887], with only one set known in the United States, at the Harvard College Library. He was the French scientist who was one of the mission invited by Simón Bolívar to come to Gran Colombia in 1822 to aid in the reformation of the schools of scientific instruction. He remained in America until 1832. A famous chemist, the "father of chemical agronomy," a professor at the Sorbonne and a member of the French Academy, he was the author of numerous books and numerous scholarly monographs. In his old age he dictated his memoirs to his daughter, Madame Holzer. An engaging raconteur, who always gave a droll and ironical twist to things, Boussingault seemed to remember everything. Almost everyone who played a part in the drama of the wars of independence in South America comes under his notice — Bolívar, Santander, Córdoba, General Harrison and, most of all, Manuela Sáenz. Volume 4 gives a good part to her — she has the most detailed *feuilleton* of all who parade themselves in front of Boussingault's memory. (Latin American historians, generally, do not much like these memoirs since Boussingault writes of Bolívar without sentimentality.) But all that he says of Manuela — and he was the only literary figure of note who knew her intimately — is so borne out by the records that I have used his account of the *amable loca* fully and unreservedly, since his is the only fulsome contemporary portrait of this delightful and dangerous Manuelita).

1890 Arístides Rojas, *Leyendas historicas*. 2 vols Caracas, 1890.
(Precisely what the title says: they are "historical legends," especially the part entitled "El Libertador y la Libertadora del Libertador." These legends possess no value)

1892 *Vida de Rufino Cuervo*. 2 vols. Paris, 1892.
(The life of one of the great literary figures of nineteenth-century Bogotá, who remembered something of Manuela Sáenz)

1892 Guiseppe Garibaldi, *Memorie autobiografiche*. 9th edition. Rome, 1892.
(A short personal reminiscence of Manuela by the great Garibaldi, himself in exile from Italy, who met and was treated kindly by Manuela Sáenz in Paita in the year 1856)

1893 José María Cordovez Moure, *Reminiscencias*. 6 vols. Bogotá, 1946
(Cordovez Moure [1835–1918] did not know Manuela Sáenz, but he knew almost all the performers who took part in the drama of her life, and he remembered what those who knew her said of her. Manuela appears in Volume 4, pages 111–118.)

1895 Ricardo Palma, "La Protectora (Rosita Campusano) y La Libertadora (Manuela Sáenz)," in *Tradiciones peruanas*. 6 vols. Madrid, 1935.
(The great Limean raconteur, Ricardo Palma [1833–1919], who did not like a good story spoiled by the interposition of a sordid fact, is in this story the font and source of some of the legends of Manuela. Palma says that he saw Manuela Sáenz in the port of Paita in 1856, the year of her death, when he was a paymaster on a coastal sailing vessel called the *Loa* I shall not dispute him. However, a good half of the *"tradiciones"* given in this short piece proved untrue when the actual records were discovered.)

1896 Prospero Pereira Gamba, *Memorias*. Madrid, 1912.

(Contains a personal recollection of the appearance of Manuela during the years 1830–1835)

1908 Edurado Posada, "La Libertadora." *Trofeos,* Bogotá, Diciembre, 1908.

1908 Jacinto Jijon y Caamaño, "Doña Manuela la Libertadora" *Boletín de la Academia Nacional de Historia,* Quito, Julio–Diciembre, 1908.
(An attempt by the late Jipon y Caamaño, known for his work on the prehistory of Ecuador, to give Manuela the gossamer of national heroine.)

1911 A. Arcos, *Historias, leyendas y tradiciones.* 4 vols. Cartagena, 1911–1914.
(Of the *"Tradición"* school of Ricardo Palma. There are, however, some personal recollections of Manuela Sáenz while she was on her way to exile.)

1925 Luis Augusto Cuervo, *Apuntes historiales.* Bogotá, 1925.
(The gently erudite Dr. Cuervo, member of the Academy of History of Bogotá, gives in the chapter entitled "Amores de Bolívar" [pp. 174–222] many of the legends about Manuela Sáenz.)

1927 Jorge Bailey Lembcke, "La verdadera Manuelita Sáenz" *El Universal,* September 9, 1927, Caracas.
(A literal translation of J-B. Boussingault's *feuilleton* on Manuela with an emphasis on her waywardness, which is an attempt on the part of the Caracas school to discredit Manuela so as to keep intact the demigod aspect of Simón Bolívar.)

1934 Hugo Moncayo, "Evocación de San Francisco de Quito y elogio a Doña Manuela Sáenz." *Boletín del Instituto Nacional Mejía,* Quito, 1934, Nov./Dec 1934
(The Quito school, in direct opposition to the Caracas school which would paint Manuela as a Messalina; here an attempt to make her stainless and play down her peccadilloes.)

1936 Camilo Destrugge, "Doña Manuela Sáenz." *El Ejercito Nacional,* pp. 337–386, Quito, 1936.
(More of the Quito school on Manuela.)

1936 Cornelio Hispano, *Historia secreta de Bolívar.* Ediciones Literarias, Paris–Madrid, 1936.
("Manuelita La Bella" occupies a whole chapter in this "secret

life" of Bolívar by Hispano [Ismael Lopez]; as he is a literary man he treats the subject well, presenting all the facts as they were known when he wrote, in 1936)

1938   Augusto Arias, *Manuela Sáenz en Paita.* Caracas, 1938.
(A glimpse of Manuela as she was in Paita during her years of exile.)

1939   Alberto Miramon, *Los septembrinos.* Bogotá, 1939.
(The night of the 25th of September and the attempt on Bolívar's life, and Manuela's part in the drama, by one of Colombia's well-known historians.)

1940   Ramón Nunez del Arco, "Los hombres de Agosto." *Boletín de la Academia Nacional de Historia, Quito,* Vol. 20, July–December, 1940.
(In which the Aispurus, Manuela's maternal parents, are mentioned as patriots and there is described the part they played in the uprising against royalist rule.)

1941   Joaquín Tamayo, *Nuestro Siglo XIX: La Gran Colombia.* Bogotá, 1941.
(One of the finest and most judicious of histories of the South American revolution and in particular Colombia's part. Manuela appears in true historical perspective in the chapter "Cesar o nada," pp. 241–301)

1942   Fernando Bolívar, "Recuerdos de Fernando Bolívar," an essay written only for the edification of his sons by Fernando Bolívar. *Boletín de la Academia Nacional de la Historia,* Caracas, Volume 25, October–December 1942.
(The favorite nephew of Simon Bolívar, whom the general sent to the Germantown Academy in Philadelphia, and later to the University of Virginia. He arrived in Bogotá just before the attempt on Bolívar's life Fernando Bolívar's observations on Manuela, short as they are, are invaluable as a contemporary account.)

1942   General A. I. Chiriboga, "Los Sáenz en el Ecuador." *Boletín de la Academia Nacional de Historia de Quito,* Vol. 22, July–December 1942.
(In which General Chiriboga, whose ancestor was a correspondent of Manuela Sáenz, gives the ancestral background of the Sáenz family of Quito.)

1944   Jorge Pérez Concha, "Manuela Sáenz, Libertadora del Libertador." *America*, Quito, January–March 1944
(More of the Quito school.)

1944   Alfonso Rumazo Gonzales, *Manuela Sáenz: La Libertadora del Libertador*. Buenos Aires, 1944.
(This is the first full-length book attempted on Manuela Sáenz)

1944   Concha Pena, *La Libertadora. El ultimo amor de Simón Bolívar*. Panama, 1944.

1944   E. Naranjo Martínez, "Bolívar y la Belle norteamericana Jeanctte Hart." *Boletín de Historia y Antiguedades*, Vol. 31, November–December 1944, Bogotá.
(An account from original source material of the affair of Bolívar and Jeanette Hart and Manuela's part in its break-up.)

1945   Vicente Lecuna, "Papeles de Manuela Sáenz." *Boletín de la Academia Nacional de la Historia*, Caracas, Vol. 28, October–December 1945.
(The first publication of some of the missing papers of Manuela Sáenz — important for the beginning of the breakdown of the legends.)

1946   Luis F. Borja, "Epistolario de Manuela Sáenz." *Boletín de la Academia Nacional de Historia*, Vol. 26, July–December 1946, Quito.
(More original source material: Manuela's letters to her old friends in Quito while she was in exile in Paita.)

1946   Alberto Miramon, *La vida ardiente de Manuelita Sáenz*. Bogotá, 1946.

1948   Gerhard Masur, *Simón Bolívar*. University of New Mexico, Albuquerque, 1948.
(This is the finest and most judicious book yet to be published on the life of Simón Bolívar. Written by a German historian long resident in Colombia, the material that bears on the Republic of Colombia and of Venezuela is most complete. Manuela Sáenz is fully treated in Chapter 26, "Interlude," and although Dr. Masur has relied on Rumazo Gonzales, he has carefully avoided giving Manuela either the "discrediting" of the Caracas school or the "saintly nimbus of the Quito school." This is a brilliant work.

1949   Dimitri Aguilera-Malta, "La Caballeresa del Sol." *El Norte,* June 1949
       (Purported to be an extract of a book on Manuela Sáenz, based on original material.)
1951   Waldo Frank, *Birth of a New World.* Boston, 1951.

The original material on which this biography is based was found in the following places:

LIMA (Peru)
   Archives of the Archbishop
   Archives of the Church of San Sebastián
   National Archives of Peru
   Archives of the Ministry of Finance and Commerce
   The private library of Francisco Moreira y Paz Soldan, San Isidro, Lima
   The private library of Luis Ortiz de Cevallos, Miraflores, Lima
   The collections of Señor Don Aurelio Miro Quesada
PIURA (Peru)
   The Notarial Archives of Señor Sanchez Condemarin
PANAMA
   The National Archives of Panama
QUITO (Ecuador)
   The Archives of the Municipality of Quito
   National Archives of Quito
   Archives of the Archbishop of Quito
   Private library of Jacinto Jijon y Caamaño
BOGOTÁ (Colombia)
   National Archives of Bogotá
   Private library of Señor Don Luis Augusto Cuervo

Unpublished manuscripts:

   Diario en la Jornada de Ayacucho (1834), by "F. C."
   (300 manuscript pages by an eyewitness and participant in the Battle of Ayacucho.)
   The Battle of Ayacucho, by Dr. Justo Sahuaranra Inca.
   (Fragment of a larger heretofore unknown and unused manuscript on the events leading up to the last battle for independence.)

Index

INDEX

CPSIA information can be obtained at www.ICGtesting.com
Printed in the USA
LVOW05s0337241013

358381LV00003B/21/P